THE EDIBLE CITY

TORONTO's food from farm to fork

Edited by Christina Palassio & Alana Wilcox

Coach House Books | Toronto

Published with the generous assistance of the Canada Council for the Arts and
the Ontario Arts Council. Coach House Books also acknowledges the support of
the Government of Ontario through the Ontario Book Publishing Tax Credit and
the Government of Canada through the Book Publishing Industry Development
Program.

The Edible City is in no way associated with Edible Communities Inc. or its family
of magazines, including *edible Toronto*.

We have deliberately included a diversity of perspectives for this collection
in prder to reflect a multifaceted Toronto. The opinions expressed in these essays
do not necessarily represent the opinions of the editors or Coach House Books.

Library and Archives Canada Cataloguing in Publication

The edible city : Toronto's food from farm to fork / edited by Christina
Palassio and Alana Wilcox.

Includes bibliographical references.
ISBN 978-1-55245-219-6

1. Food--Ontario--Toronto. 2. Food industry and trade--Ontario--Toronto.
3. Restaurants--Ontario--Toronto. I. Palassio, Christina II. Wilcox, Alana

TX360.C33T67 2009   641.309713'541   C2009-906531-2

Secondo

Contorno

Dolce

Introduction Writing about food is no picnic. Our talk around the subject
has long been characterized by banal clichés, wince-worthy
puns and a dearth of complexity. The most important element
of our survival, after oxygen and water, food has been the thing
we are least able to discuss with any sophistication; we have
food or we don't, we like it or we don't, and this seems to be
the sum of the public discourse on the subject. Recipe swaps,
sure, and restaurant recommendations and gardening tips,
but most of us don't get beyond that.

But now our spinach has made us sick, and our bacon too,
and we've heard that if all the bees die we'll starve, and the
price of bread has skyrocketed, and Susur Lee has closed his
restaurant, and the word 'locavore' has emerged, and many of
us – people for whom the extent of the conversation had been
what to have for dinner – have begun to think more about our
sustenance: where it comes from, how it gets to us and how it
affects and is affected by the people along the way.

And so, in the fall of 2008, as pages from *H$_T$O: Toronto's
Water from Lake Iroquois to Lost Rivers to Low-flow Toilets*
were flying off the Coach House presses, when the question
inevitably arose – what would be the theme of the next
Toronto book? – the answer, from all corners, without
exception, was clear: food. It made sense: from the Stop
Community Food Centre's year-round greenhouse in the

Artscape Wychwood Barns and Not Far from the Tree's amazing feats of fruit-gleaning to the publication of the City's 2008 'Cost of the Nutritious Food Basket' report and its approval of the Local and Sustainable Food Procurement Campaign, momentum was building in the city's foodscape.

You'll note that the above examples are all set in Toronto. We have allowed our food to be globalized, which means we can eat pineapples in Ontario in February, but it also means our strawberries – even in July, when our Golden Horseshoe is flush with berries – might have been trucked in from California, which isn't so great for their taste, their carbon footprint or struggling Ontario farmers. Food-security worries and the locavore movement have reminded us of the importance of de-globalizing – re-localizing, if you will – our food supply. And that's why we think it's crucial to root our talk of food in our own city. We feel the momentum of our fellow Torontonians; as we browse the stalls at the Evergreen Brick Works farmers' market, pick up some Local Food Plus–certified produce at Fiesta Farms or go out for Ethiopian food with friends, it's hard not to feel that the discussion has been taking on an increasingly participatory tone – less 'What are other people doing?' and more 'What can I do?'

Toronto has a long history of food production and activism, from the eighteenth- and nineteenth-century family-estate

gardens of settlers like Alexander Macdonell to Harry Webb's world-famous wedding cakes and the Victory Gardens of World War II. In his essay, 'How Toronto found its food groove,' Toronto Food Policy Council manager Wayne Roberts enumerates Toronto's many food advantages, from its proximity to large tracts of Class 1 farmland, vast water resources and populated U.S. cities to its commitment to nurturing a vibrant food community through progressive policies and funding of community-relevant organizations like FoodShare and the TFPC.

In selecting essays for this book, we strove to showcase what Torontonians across the 'mobile food web' – to use Roberts' term – are accomplishing as a result of these food advantages. As it turns out, they're doing a lot – from Afri-Can Food Basket's Urban Farm Project, the Centre for Food Security at Ryerson University and Second Harvest's Harvest Kitchens program to Mammalian Diving Reflex's *Eat the Street* project, the Toronto Vegetarian Association's Vegetarian Food Fair and the revival of St. Andrew's Market, Torontonians at all levels of organization are getting involved in the way the city eats. And while they're advocating on behalf of migrant farm workers, growing kale on balconies and dishing out heirloom beets and Prince Edward County goat's cheese hors d'oeuvres at dinner parties, they're talking about where to get the best empanadas, which VQA wines actually use Ontario grapes and who has

access to the cuts of meat on offer at the city's excellent organic butchers.

The great joy of food activism – beyond that warm fuzzy feeling that comes from doing the right thing – is that it's one of those rare arenas where politics and pleasure can intersect; the Ontario strawberry betters the California one not only in ethics but also in taste. And so we bring you Chris Nuttall-Smith writing about not-quite-legal but stratospherically tastier eggs, Jamie Bradburn on the Wonder-ful history of Toronto bread and Liz Clayton on how our neighbourhoods are the real winners in the coffee wars. Wayne Reeves dives into the history of local craft beer, Katarina Gligorijevic taste-tests a quietly seductive cocktail and Erik Rutherford asks French chefs around town if the sophistication of our palate measures up.

Whether or not our palate does, our enthusiasm certainly measures up. We're well on the road to re-localizing our food supply, and to thinking about food in more responsible and tastier ways – let's try to keep talking about it that way too.

Christina Palassio
Alana Wilcox

Antipasto

Sarah B.
Hood

Pickerel, pork and President's Choice:
A historical food map of Toronto

Toronto is a fertile place. British writer George Henry remarked in his 1832 book *The Emigrant's Guide, or Canada As It Is* that '[m]any fruits and vegetables are raised in Upper Canada which will not come to perfection at home, or at least not in the open air.'[1] Shaped by the scraping glaciers that gouged rivers out of rock, the first settlement was defined by the lake, the Humber and the Don. Not only were these bodies of water plentiful with fish and game, they also served as transportation corridors linking Niagara and the St. Lawrence with Lake Simcoe and the west.

The coming of a railroad that mirrored water routes intensified the possibilities of food production and enlarged the market for that food. The railroads nurtured the growth of food-manufacturing businesses, some to international proportions. Over time, many activities associated with the procurement, preparation and distribution of food shaped the city, from the first furrows dug by early settlers to the growth of public markets and the conglomeration of abattoirs in the Junction. Here's a map of that evolution.

The hunter-gatherers

It all begins with fish. In fact, it seems that the word 'Toronto,' popularly defined as meaning 'gathering place,' may actually derive from a Wendat word for 'a fishing weir constructed of standing sticks in the water'; in other words, a place for gathering fish.[2] In the 1790s, Elizabeth Simcoe, wife of John Graves Simcoe, the first lieutenant-governor of Upper Canada, was intrigued to watch native locals spearing fish through holes in the frozen lake ice in winter; in summer they would spear-fish by boat at night, using torchlight to attract the catch. This skill was evidently passed on to the Europeans, because it was still the standard method used to catch fish in Lake Ontario in the 1830s.

In the first half of the nineteenth century, lake fishing yielded salmon, whitefish, herring, pickerel, perch, muskellunge, bass and sometimes sturgeon. Salmon was caught in the now-buried Garrison Creek and possibly in Taddle Creek, which lies today beneath Philosopher's Walk at the University of Toronto. Furthermore, 'the Don, which we know today as a sluggish, sewage-laden stream, was once a magnificent river … famous,

1 George Henry, *The Emigrant's Guide, or Canada As It Is* (Quebec: William Gray, 1832), 101–117, in *The Town of York 1815–1834*, ed. Edith G. Firth (Toronto: University of Toronto Press, 1966), pp. 325–333.

2 Heather A. Howard-Bobiwash, 'Toronto's Native History.' First Nations House (2008–2009. fnhmagazine.com/issue1 /nativehistory.html [accessed March 1, 2009]).

like the Credit and the Humber, for its salmon.'[3] The last salmon known to have been caught in the Don was speared near Pottery Road in about 1874.

Hunting and foraging were once also dependable ways to acquire food. Torontonians used to enjoy shooting ducks and other edible birds on Gibraltar Point. Dr. Walter Henry tells how, in 1834, he not only prescribed snipe for the terminally ill Chief Justice Sir William Campbell, but himself bagged a supply of 'these delectable little birds' on the Point. 'On this delicate food the poor old gentleman was supported for a couple of months; but the frost set in – the snipes flew away, and Sir W— died.'[4]

The local landscape also offered wild berries, honey, maple sugar and syrup, mushrooms and many edible roots, herbs and greens. In the 1830s, one could pick 'quite relishable' sorrel in a field near St. James Cathedral at King and Church streets. These practices persisted for decades. In the same period, it was also normal to see First Nations hunters 'driving in a load of frozen deer to market.'[5] But although the uncleared forest was close at hand, the difficulties and dangers of hunting were formidable. Susanna Moodie, who lived near Peterborough in this period, describes the challenges of travelling any distance through the bush, or over the bone-jolting 'corduroy' roads made of logs. Hunters were also at peril not only from bears, but lynxes and wolverines, 'as they often

3 Eric Arthur, *Toronto, No Mean City*. (Toronto: University of Toronto Press, 1964), p. 4.

4 Walter Henry, *Trifles from my Port-folio*. (Quebec, 1839), vol. II, 112 in Arthur, p. 41.

5 Henry, *The Emigrant's Guide*, p. 326

In the early nineteenth century, York residents could buy fresh fish caught in the harbour at an informal beachfront market near what would now be Berkeley and Front streets.

FISH MARKET 1880.

spring from trees upon their prey, fastening upon the throat with their sharp teeth and claws, from which a person in the dark could scarcely free himself without first receiving a dangerous wound.'[6]

6 Susanna Moodie, *Roughing it in the Bush* (Toronto: McClelland & Stewart Inc., New Canadian Library edition, 11989). p. 285.

In 1848, Thornton and Lucie Blackburn, escaped slaves from Louisville, Kentucky, who founded the city's first taxicab company, bought a home on Eastern Avenue, near Sackville Street; the archaeologists who dug up the site in 1985 found that wild game and fish had supplied a good portion of the family's meals. As late as 1884, the St. Lawrence Market carried deer, 'black bear ... all manner of birds of the air, the huge wild turkey, sometimes the rare wild swan, the prairie chicken, grouse and partridge.'[7] And in 1952, naturalist Charles Sauriol named raspberries, blackberries, strawberries, elderberries, currants, blueberries, gooseberries, grapes and cherries among the fruits growing wild in the Don Valley. For some of us, the will to forage has never abated; current city dwellers pluck grapes from the vines behind Campbell House, munch berries in ravines and public parks and jealously guard the location of the precious morel mushrooms that spring up in certain secluded spots.

7 Charles Pelham Mulvany, *Toronto: Past and Present* (Toronto, 1884) in *A Toronto Album, Glimpses of the City That Was* by Michael Filey. (Toronto: University of Toronto Press, 1970), plate 22.

Urban agriculture

It would be difficult to identify a city block in downtown Toronto that has never been used to grow food. In the early 1800s, most homes had gardens; the largest were full family estates that were all but self-sustaining. Alexander Macdonell (1762–1805, Sheriff of the Home District and later Member of the Assembly for Glengarry) built a house in 1818 on land now bounded by John, Simcoe, Adelaide and Richmond streets whose 'grounds were devoted to gardening purposes, and also farming'; they 'included an orchard of 60 or 80 apple, pear, plum, cherry, peach and quince trees, as well as grape vines, all of which, including the peach and quince, bore abundantly; and many a boy of the era ... relished the flavour of its stolen fruit.'[8]

8 John Ross Robertson, *Landmarks of Toronto; A Collection of Historical Sketches of the Old Town of York from 1792 until 1833, and of Toronto from 1834 to 1893* (Toronto: J. Ross Robertson, 1894), pp. 470–1.

The Jarvis family had an orchard on their land, between Queen, Shuter, Jarvis and George streets; small boys apparently liked to steal the apples there. George Taylor Denison's Bellevue estate orchard lay between Bellevue and Leonard avenues, north of Wales, on the banks of the now-buried Russell Creek. An inkling of the agricultural activities on these larger estates can be gleaned at Spadina House, whose gardens give a sense of the kind of self-sufficiency described

by York resident James Laidlaw in a letter of 1819: 'we have a good Garden that we Can Live upon, and has Sold a great dale out of it a 100 Duson of Cowcombres and therty Bushels of potatoes. We had peas 10 foot High, and Beans 12 foot Some Hundreds after one.'[9] Although some residents, like Laidlaw, sold their produce, most Toronto households grew food primarily for their own use.

In the 1830s, the suburban area north of Queen, west of Peter and east of Parliament was 'remarkable for the rich appearance of its numerous gardens.' Crops included apples, currants, plums, cabbages, celery, cauliflowers, pea, melons, cucumbers, onions, carrots, parsnips and asparagus.[10] In 1832 James Worts, co-owner of the Gooderham and Worts distillery, cultivated asparagus, cauliflowers and cabbages on King near the Don River. But with growing industrialization, urban vegetable gardening began to be viewed as faintly suspect, and there is more than a whiff of class prejudice in the legendary naming of Cabbagetown after the cabbages that were said to be grown in front yards by the very poor – a fact that failed to deter later Toronto residents from harvesting untold hundreds of bushels of tomatoes and twining innumerable backyards with grapevines.

In about 1914, locals were forbidden to gather mushrooms in Willowvale Park (now Christie Pits) to protect the turf.

9 Firth, *The Town of York*, p. 30.

10 Henry, *The Emigrant's Guide*, p. 329.

To market

Of course not all foods could be supplied by hunting, fishing and farming alone. From the beginning, goods like sugar and salt were imported. Richard Feltoe, curator and corporate archivist at the Redpath Sugar Museum, explains that early York received shipments of cone-shaped 'loaf' sugar, which was processed from sugar cane in Britain. Over time, Ontario began to supply some of its own sugar by extracting it from beets; the local beet-sugar industry grew from about 1900 to 1950, then fell off as cane-sugar prices dropped. In 1854, Redpath started processing cane sugar in Montreal, and Toronto's supply was shipped from there by water; it was not until 1959 that the company opened its factory on Queen's Quay East.

Salt, another essential commodity for preserving and disinfecting as well as cooking, was a costly product, and came in the early days from the Onandaga Salt Springs near Syracuse, New York, where it was extracted from brine by solar evaporation. Knowing the importance of ensuring an afford-able local supply, and no doubt wishing to curtail the existing salt-smuggling business, John Graves Simcoe spearheaded a viable local salt industry in Niagara. He had already given orders that salt wells should be explored before he arrived in Upper Canada in 1792. The Merritt operation near St. Catharines became one of the most successful of these.

Until 1845, Cooper's Wharf, located at the foot of Church Street, was Toronto's primary shipping and receiving area, and food bound for the market and the largest businesses arrived there. In the late 1850s, the buildings still standing at 81–85 Front Street East were warehouses that 'backed out onto the piers, where horse-drawn wagons loaded with products would enter through the rear, ascend the grade and come out onto Front Street. These tunnels have long since been bricked up, except for the one used by The Performing Arts Lodge as a passageway out onto Market Street.'[11]

The first St. Lawrence Market was built shortly after 1803, more or less on the present site, while other vendors of fresh produce lined Front Street. Even early on, it was 'uncommonly well supplied daily with fresh meat, poultry, vegetables, butter, cheese, &c, both in summer and winter.'[12] It was not until the Ontario Food Terminal opened in 1954 that the St. Lawrence Market was displaced as Toronto's primary food distribution centre. With the building of the railways in the late part of the

11 Bruce Bell, 'History of Old Town Toronto' (2009, http://oldtown-toronto1793.com/index.php?option=com_content&view=article&id=41&Itemid=147&showall=1 [accessed March 1, 2009]).

12 Henry, *The Emigrant's Guide*, p. 326.

nineteenth century, Front Street only intensified as a shipping area. The shoreline was gradually extended into the bay, Union Station became an import/export hub and growing numbers of local food manufacturers would send and receive shipments via private sidings on local rail lines.

Meanwhile, in the early 1900s, Kensington Market was evolving from a patchwork of front-door vendors and wagons. 'It was called the Jewish Market, and open mostly on Thursday and Friday, for shopping before the Sabbath. Far from being a tourist attraction, it was shunned by most of Toronto's citizenry.'[13] It took a while for Toronto to warm up to Kensington. In the late 1950s, Toronto would choose to bulldoze a thriving Chinatown to make way for its new city hall, driving the Chinese markets west to Spadina and east to Broadview and Gerrard.

13 Joan Cochrane, *Kensington* (Erin: The Boston Mills Press, 2000), p. 35.

The manufacturers

Toronto has spawned many food businesses that have, like the fish that once fed the town, grown bigger by eating one another up. By the 1790s, mills were already springing up on the rivers, among them Old Mill, York Mills, Don Mills and Todmorden Mills. Wheat, rye and barley used in food and alcohol production were ground by windmill at the Gooderham and Worts site. Just after 1800, on King, east of Princess, 'there long stood a solid circular structure of brick of considerable height and diameter, dome-shaped without and vaulted within. This was the public oven of Paul Marian,' who baked loaves for families who supplied their own flour.[14] Commercial bakers soon multiplied, and a baking district developed along the rail line at Dupont around Bathurst. By the 1920s, it included Western Canada Flour Mills (287 MacPherson), Maple Leaf Milling (388 Dupont) and Harry Webb Co. (southwest corner of Davenport and Kendal).

14 Henry Scadding, *Toronto of Old*, ed. F. H. Armstrong (Toronto: Oxford University Press, 1966).

Soon, all kinds of food-production facilities began to cluster around rail lines. William Davies started his pork business – the company that put the 'hog' in Hogtown – in the early 1860s at 145 Front Street East (still known as the William Davies Building). In 1879 he moved to Front at the Don, just across the river from a massive cattle-feeding operation run by Gooderham and Worts. In 1927, Davies merged with Gunn's Limited and the Harris Abattoir Company to form Canada Packers. The new company operated in the meat-packing district around the Junction, along with Swift and Union Stock Yards.

15 Charles Sauriol, 'Boyhood Memories' [unpublished ms.] (Toronto Archives, Fonds 4, Series 107, File 26), ch. 6, p. 2.

16 Adam Graeme Mercer and Charles Pelham Mulvany, *History of Toronto and County of York, Ontario* (Toronto: Blackett Robinson, 1885), pp. 376–7.

17 George Weston Limited, 'About Us: Company History,' George Weston Limited, (2008–2009. www.neilsondairy.com/en/about_history.htm [accessed March 1, 2009]).

Additional Sources

Beacock Fryer, Mary. *Elizabeth Postuma Simcoe 1762–1850: A Biography* (Toronto: Dundurn Press, 1989).
Bird, Malcolm G. 'Unintended Outcome: The Ontario Food Terminal Board as a Case Study in Post-War Ontario Agricultural Policy' (PhD diss., Department of Public Policy and Administration, Carleton University, 2005, www.cpsa-acsp.ca/papers-2005/Bird.pdf [accessed March 1, 2009]).
Funding Universe, 'George Weston Limited.' Funding Universe. (n.d. www.fundinguniverse.com/company-histories/George-Weston-Limited-Company-History.html [accessed March 1, 2009]).

By the 1920s, E. W. Gillett (baking supplies), Cowan (chocolate), Joe Lowe (popsicles), McCormick (biscuits), T. A. Lytle (condiments) and Telfer Biscuits were all located on Sterling Road, north of Dundas and west of Lansdowne; Charles E. Hires (root beer) and Lawlors Bread Co. were both on Davies Avenue north of Queen at the Don Valley; and Imperial Extract Co., makers of Shirriff jams and jelly powders, were just around the corner at 18 Matilda Street. All were served by private rail sidings.

In the late nineteenth and early twentieth centuries, family-founded food manufacturing businesses had a profound impact on their neighbourhoods. Charles Sauriol worked as a boy at Shirriff's around the time of World War I. In an unpublished manuscript titled 'Boyhood Memories,' he described his strong loyalty to the company, the kindness of the owners and the feeling 'that I was beginning to earn my way.' Like the Sauriols, no doubt many Toronto families were grateful for the perks of factory jobs. 'We ate a lot of jelly at home in those days,' Sauriol wrote. 'Each Friday the employees were given an opportunity to buy five pound damaged tins of marmalade for bargain prices ... and many the can I brought home.'[15]

Several of these brands grew to national importance. William Christie started his company in 1858 after winning a biscuit competition at the Toronto Exhibition. In 1868, he joined Alexander Brown 'on a rather more extensive scale ... under the name of Christie Brown & Co. at 626 Yonge Street.'[16] By 1874, the company filled a huge new building that is now the 200 King Street East campus of George Brown College. By the time Christie died in 1900, the company was valued at $500,000 and, in 1929, Christie's heirs sold it to Nabisco.

George Weston, on the other hand, got his start operating humble bread wagons. In 1892, he took over Bowen's Bakery on Sullivan Street, and from 1896 to 1913 he ran the Model Bakery at 18 Beverley Street. In 1910, his bakeries merged with others to become Canada Bread Company and, in 1928, his son Garfield Weston launched George Weston Limited, which today also runs Loblaws.

In 1897, Walter Massey bought a farm located north of Danforth between Main Street and Victoria Park. He named it Dentonia Park and started a dairy herd there that would be the foundation of his City Dairy, whose imposing 1908 factory and stable buildings still stand at 563 Spadina Crescent. Founded upon the principle of sanitary, pasteurized milk, the company

was also loved for its ice cream. However, it was surpassed by the success of William Neilson, who built his home and ice-cream factory on Gladstone Avenue in 1904, soon adding chocolate production equipment to bolster sales in the slow winter months.

'By 1915, when William Neilson died at the age of 71, the Neilson company was producing a million pounds of ice cream every year and 500,000 pounds of chocolate.'[17] Neilson's eventually acquired other dairies and the Canadian arm of Cadbury. Perhaps it was inevitable that Neilson and Weston would finally merge late in the twentieth century when the heyday of the independent family-run factory had given way to an era of globalization.

Toronto's food map continues to change. Many neighbourhoods are still permeated by wafting food-factory smells – from Campbell's Soup near Lakeshore and Royal York and Christie's near Humber Bay to the Dempster's bakery in Liberty Village, the old Neilson factory on Gladstone and the Peek Frean bakery on Bermondsey in Leaside. But much of the city's food manufacturing has moved to more inexpensive locales, and in its place are the condo lofts that have altered downtown demographics: the Candy Factory and the Chocolate Factory on Queen West; the Pop Factory on Manning; Ideal Bread on Dovercourt; the Peanut Factory on Sackville; the Wrigley lofts at Carlaw and Dundas.

Is this evolution or atavism? As food factories disappear, community gardens, farmers' markets and bread ovens are springing up – with City Hall's approval – in parks and public spaces. People still comb the urban landscape for edible herbs and bait worms; the fanciest eateries make a selling point of farm-raised meats; poultry activists raise chickens in secret and urban beekeepers nurture hives inside city limits. We won't be seeing orchards in the Entertainment District again, and it's unlikely we'll be uncovering our buried streams anytime soon, but it's clear that the map of twenty-first-century Toronto has plenty of space for local food.

Gibson, Sally. *Toronto's Distillery District, History by the Lake* (Toronto: Cityscape Holdings Inc. and Dundee Distillery District [GP] Commercial Inc., 2008).

Hayes, Derek. *Historical Atlas of Toronto* (Toronto: Douglas & McIntyre, 2008).

Kennedy, R.L. (n.d.). 'History of Private Sidings.' *Old Time Trains* (2001, trainweb.org/ oldtimetrains/industrial/ history/train_sidings. html [accessed March 1, 2009]).

Maple Leaf Foods Inc. and/or Canada Bread Company Limited, 'Our History' (2005, www.mapleleaf.com/Ab outUs/OurHistory.aspx [accessed March 1, 2009])

Sauriol, Charles. *Remembering the Don* (Toronto: Amethyst Communications Inc., 1981).

Shuttleworth, E. B. *The Windmill and its Times* (Toronto: Edward D. Apted, 1924).

Smardz Frost, Karolyn. *I've Got a Home in Glory Land* (Toronto: Thomas Allen Publishers, 2007).

Wilson, W. R. 'Simcoe and Salt' (2007, www.upper-canadahistory.ca/simcoe /simcoe4.html [accessed April 24, 2009]).

Andrew
Braithwaite

Toronto, je t'aime!

Paris is the greatest food city in the world – the Rolls Royce, the Château d'Yquem, the Brigitte Bardot of gastronomic capitals. There's no need to argue about it. Everybody agrees.

Okay, sure, there was a bit of a fuss a couple years ago when Tokyo eclipsed the French capital as the city with the most Michelin-starred restaurants. But everybody knows it was all part of an elaborate conspiracy masterminded by Parisian foodies, who work hard to guard their secrets – a trick of misdirection to cut back on the sheer volume of tourists crowding out locals at the city's greatest bistros. I mean, isn't it a little suspicious that they're called Michelin stars – that nobody cares how many 'Yokohama stars' your restaurant has?

Yeah, it smelled fishy to me, too.

So last year, when my wife scored a job transfer to Paris and asked me to quit my job on Richmond Street and relocate with her, the decision was a no-brainer. I don't just mean that figuratively: my brain had no say in the matter. Before I could even think it through, my stomach had already signed us up, rumbling its consent.

To be fair, none of this optimism for the wonderful and amazing gastronomic discoveries awaiting us in Paris would have existed without Toronto. In the five years I called the city home, I cut my teeth as both an inventive home cook and a fine diner. Many young Canadians move to Toronto and discover the music scene, the activism scene or the guys-wearing-hilarious-trucker-hats scene. I discovered food.

A hobby begat a passion begat an obsession. My wife and I, young professionals who were also slaves to student-debt payments, saved money by hunting for produce deals directly from farmers at St. Lawrence Market, by combing outlying neighbourhoods for the cheapest ethnic cantinas and by buying whole chickens on sale, butchering them ourselves and making stock from the carcasses weekly. I cooked so often on the common-use outdoor grills at our Mount Pleasant and Eglinton condo building that our Pakistani concierge, Kaleem, who had to unlock the propane for me each time, nicknamed me 'the Lord of the Barbecue.'

Of course, we didn't pay off our loans any faster with the money we managed to save. Instead, we splurged on once-a-quarter meals at Mistura, Canoe and Auberge du Pommier, making our first forays into the haute-cuisine world of seared foie gras and porcini foams. We cooked lobsters at home, rationalizing the expense with the knowledge that we were

getting two meals out of the crimson beasts – lobster on Saturday night, and lobster bisque, made from the shells, on Sunday. Anytime I received a raise at work (or a well-timed GST rebate cheque), I would arrive home triumphantly bearing a new Henckels knife or a top-of-the-line stovetop toy from the Calphalon store on King West.

In sum: I learned to eat well in Toronto, but in my mind the place was still just one above-average city in a country not exactly renowned for its cuisine – one well-fed big fish in a small pond. I knew in my gut that there must be something more out there. Then Paris came calling, and just like that I was headed up to the big leagues.

Paris lived up to my wildest expectations. It was a veritable food riot, and I was the guerrilla gourmet pillaging the city's *boulangeries*, *pâtisseries* and *charcuteries* of their Gallic treasures.

My wife and I arrived in February, which is prime oyster season (the rule is 'months with R's in them,' of which February, or *février*, has two), and quickly became addicted to Normandy's finest. I learned to shuck them myself at home, where we would suck them back by the dozen with glorious French shallots and Maille sherry vinegar. We became good friends with our local *caviste* Nicole, a stocky old Parisian woman with hexagonal glasses who runs a tiny wine shop – one of half a dozen within four blocks of our apartment – where she stocks scores of amazing French wines under fifteen dollars from small producers in Bordeaux, Alsace, the Loire and the Languedoc, filling our hearts with little more than pity for our friends who still shopped at the LCBO.

We didn't ignore the city's upmarket treasures, either. At the Hôtel Costes, a see-and-be-seen spot for fashion-industry bigwigs on rue Saint-Honoré, I devoured the restaurant's signature *tigre qui pleure* ('tiger who cries'), a sixty-dollar beef dish served with little more than a couple green beans on the side. At Christmas, Nicole sent us up to Montmartre to visit Arnaud Larher, the man she described as Paris's best chocolatier, so we could try his traditional yule dessert, a chestnut-cream *bûche de Noël*. One fine summer afternoon, we uncovered a store near Place de la République that deals almost exclusively in saffron and saffron-based products – threads and powders, sure, but also rock candy and saffron-flavoured ice cream. The shop's glass front door is locked at all hours – you have to ring a doorbell to summon the shopkeeper, who greets customers clad in a black double-breasted chef's jacket.

Over the course of our first year in Paris, my wife and I cracked more and more secret codes, and earned the trust and word-of-mouth recommendations of more and more Parisians. Our culinary roots quickly became a distant memory, an ocean away.

But then, exactly one year after our big move to the City of Light-and-Flaky, we returned to Toronto to update some emigration-related paperwork. In the lead-up to our departure, memories of great meals past sprouted up like a long-forgotten planting of onions. I could no longer deny that there were things I had missed. But it was only once seated on the plane, 30,000 feet above the Atlantic and surrounded by speakers of a hauntingly familiar dialect of English, that reality set in: we were heading home, with a chance to give our old city a fresh appraisal.

If I may repurpose a Michael Ignatieff maxim: sometimes you only see your local cuisine clearly from far away.

My wife and I are riding the streetcar along King Street on a cold morning in February, debating what our first flashback meal will be. 'Mmmm, what do you think of the Peter Street Deli for lunch?' she suggests. I haven't once thought of this place in the year we've been away, a little Chinese greasy spoon halfway between our old offices where we used to meet for chicken chow mein or beef with black bean and rice noodles.

Toronto, I'm pleased to be reminded, still does cheap and fast exceedingly well, and the best of it is peasant food prepared by immigrants from around the world. Paris has a pretty diverse population of its own, but comparing the two only reinforces the breadth of Toronto's exotic range. Most of what stands out in Paris comes from prominent post-colonial diasporic communities: the couscous and tagines of North Africa, Lebanese mezze platters, Cameroonian goat ndolé and the chicken yassa of Senegal. I've often enjoyed the latter at a hole-in-the-wall spot on boulevard de la Villette first introduced to me by an Associated Press technology fixer originally from Toronto. He lives around the corner from this place, which is convenient because you have to drop by in the afternoon to order your dinner for that evening.

Toronto is a true Renaissance man of ethnic cuisine: it does a great many things very, very well. Greek souvlaki on the Danforth. Korean bulgogi on Bloor West (where, a few days after our Peter Street Deli lunch, I meet up with my younger brother, a varsity rower at U of T, for some great feats of eating). Jamaican patties, Trinidadian doubles, Mexican burritos. North Indian

gravies, South Indian dosas and Sri Lankan hoppers. Bubble tea. So many nations to visit vicariously through food.

Toronto even trumps Paris on what should be safe post-colonial turf: Vietnamese. Several times, I've been to the spot that Parisians tout as the best soup-and-noodle joint in town, a Left Bank institution called Le Bambou, and all I can think when I'm eating there is how much I miss Pho Hung. Le Bambou's soup stock is just a little less fragrant, the beef a little less tender, the mix of greenery in the bo bun just a little off and the jackfruit milkshake nowhere to be found. In fact, I miss Pho Hung so much that I eat there two days in a row in Toronto – once at the Bloor-and-Avenue location, across from Libeskind's ROM Crystal, and again the next day at its cuter sister location on Spadina. We order the exact same meal – same entrees, same soups, same noodles, same drinks – both times.

Of course, there's plenty of exotic cuisine in Paris, courtesy of 'immigrants' from other parts of France – from Lyon, where they've mastered every part of the pig from snout to foot; or Provençe, with its stuffed tomatoes and peppers; or Brittany, land of galettes and oysters. Quiche lorraine and boeuf bour-guignon didn't originate in Paris (the former is from Lorraine and the latter from Burgundy, to risk stating the obvious), but they thrive here. The regional specialties of Saskatchewan or the Yukon are fewer and further between in Toronto, to be sure.

But, then again, in Paris, and especially in the haute dining scene, everything is coloured by French expectations for what food should taste like – food is 'Frenchified.' Normally this involves adding butter. In Toronto, I'm pleased to rediscover the counter-approach of articulating what sort of influences the vernacular North American style has taken on. It's modern Canadian food, but with a Spanish, pan-Asian or Polish twist.

However, the circumstances of our visit conspire to push us directly into the arms of the atypical practice of the 'Canadi-anification' of foreign dishes. We have a gift certificate to use while we're in Toronto and, in scanning the list of restaurants to choose from – Canoe, Jump, Biff's Bistro – we realize they're all places that put a Canadian spin on French food, typically by incorporating caribou, bacon or maple syrup. Biff's turns out to be the best choice because we can stretch our wine budget a little further there, and their frites measure up to the best we've had in Paris.

I take great pleasure in a more novel twist on this theme later in the week at Nota Bene, a new Franco-Canadian spot at Queen and Simcoe, whose cocktail list includes an ingenious ice-wine martini. And when your magazine editor is footing

the bill, what writer can refuse one or two or four? If eating out in Paris teaches you anything, it's that a drink or two at lunch makes the afternoon breeze by in a serene haze.

We've all heard the expression that Toronto is New York run by the Swiss. But based on the tales of a Torontonian friend who moved to New York to run a restaurant, and subsequently bemoaned the drop in quality of the produce there, you could also say Toronto is New York supplied with Parisian-quality ingredients.

It's true that winter in Toronto can be grim for a home cook. Anyone who's ever had the misfortune of having to buy rock-hard, flavourless tomatoes from Metro in January because the thought of trudging across town in the snow to Kensington or Whole Foods is just too grim knows what I'm talking about. I've faced this dilemma more times than I'd like to recall, so Paris's proximity to such places as Morocco, Spain, Tunisia and Kenya, suppliers of great off-season lettuce, green beans, mangoes and avocadoes, at non-astronomical prices, is a dream come true. But being Canadian means you learn to accept, and even embrace, the valleys because they give so much more potency to the peaks. Come summertime, when corn and peaches and Leamington tomatoes start rolling in from southern Ontario, all is forgiven.

By the end of our return visit, I've confirmed my lingering suspicions of what I miss most about food in Toronto: shopping at the market. Which is weird, because Paris is a city of sublime markets. Our fridge there is tiny, so shopping, or *les courses*, is an everyday job best performed not at a grocery store – *sacrilège!* – but at a market, where small vendors assemble. Culinary commerce there requires a level of specificity: you buy your vegetables from the vegetable guy, your cheese from the cheese guy, your meat from the meat guy, your tripe from the tripe guy. (Full disclosure: I've never actually bought tripe from the tripe guy, but I've heard it makes a great hangover-curing soup.)

These markets can be found in Toronto, too, of course. Kensington and Chinatown are two of the most convenient and varied, but, for my money, nothing beats Saturday morning at the St. Lawrence Market.

The weekend hits in Toronto, and it just feels natural to head down to Front Street. Following an epic Friday night of dancing on Queen West, we require immediate sustenance, and the St. Lawrence is happy to oblige. I wait in the long queue at Carousel Bakery for my peameal bacon sandwich, and sacrifice some of my prize in exchange for a couple bites of my wife's

Portuguese roasted chicken. Then we wander, gawking at the butchers' abnormally massive chicken breasts, huge racks of pork ribs and well-aged steaks, which are sadly illegal in France (it's a hygiene trade-off that allows you to order your hamburger cooked raw pretty much anywhere). We recall all sorts of dishes that have fallen out of our repertoire in Paris: 'Oh, man, let's get some Chinese Forbidden Rice from Rube's!'

The vegetable stands, too, are a far cry from what we're used to in France, where it's considered uncivilized to paw at someone's precious produce. There, you tell the woman what you want and she selects it for you. Every Parisian expat has a story about being at the market, stupidly grabbing for something and having their paw slapped by an old lady with worn, dirt-stained hands. My particular version is set at the Marché rue Monge, in the Latin Quarter, and the offending overreach involved a grapefruit. *'Ah, ta-ta-ta-ta-ta-ta! Ne touchez pas aux pamplemousses, monsieur. On ne fait pas ça içi!'*

At the St. Lawrence I'm handling melons with gusto, juggling limes to identify the heaviest ones for juicing and picking out the precise quantity of rapini I need, instead of asking for '*assez pour deux personnes*' and getting enough to serve a 100-strong cell of *la Résistance*. Still, an excess of rapini wouldn't bother me now. It was always one of my favourite go-to greens in Toronto, and it doesn't seem to exist in Paris. I've searched and searched and asked at my Italian deli and I still haven't had any luck.

So I buy up several bunches of that bitter green and commandeer a friend's kitchen on Camden Street for a dinner party, just to have an excuse to cook sautéed garlic rapini and drink Steam Whistle pilsner. And for one night, at least, I no longer feel like a food tourist in Toronto, my old city.

Parisians are always curious to hear about life in Canada. They respond to Montreal, but Toronto's a mostly unknown quantity. 'What's it like there?'

'Well, for starters, it's a city with fantastic food …'

When they hear me say this, they invariably look at me like I'm a crazy person. I haven't quite pinned that look down. It either means something's been lost in translation, like maybe I've accidentally asked them if I can fondle their grapefruits, or else they're thinking, 'Great food? In Toronto? Silly Canadian, don't you realize you're speaking to a Parisian? *Ce n'est pas possible!*'

I never really press the point. Don't worry, Toronto. Your secrets are safe with me.

Jessica
Duffin Wolfe

City of snacks

'A day when you can eat for two dollars is a good day,' a friend
once said to me while munching on a Jamaican double, a kind
of curried-chickpea-filled pancake, sold for $1.25 at a small
Kensington Market shop. And it's true: on some days, freedom
tastes a lot like being able to eat for two dollars while walking
around admiring the colours of your city. Mobility has become
the urbanist's clarion call – from cellphones to bicycle and
public-transit advocacy, people who are passionate about
realizing the full potential of urban life are focused on breaking down barriers to free and easy movement through the city.
Food mobility, realized as a cornucopia of readily available
snacks in the streets, seems poised to be the next evolution of
this movement in Toronto. Dietary requirements can keep
people within a tether-length of home, but if you can eat wherever you are, affordably, and without compromising whatever
ethical or nutritional food habits you prefer to maintain, your
freedom will be instantly enhanced, and you can wander
farther and farther afield.

Celebrated for the vast diversity of its restaurants, Toronto
is less known for its incredible array of delicious snacks, which
wanderers can discover all over the city in unlikely shops, tiny
delis and unexpected bakeries. From Japanese mochi balls –
gluey rice dough filled with red-bean paste and floured with
coconut shavings – sold three for a dollar in a small Chinese
bakery on Spadina, to walnut-filled Korean mini-waffles on
Bloor, from savoury Polish pastries on Roncesvalles and
kimchi empanadas in Kensington Market to the secret samosa
dealers that dot the entire city, Toronto is a delectable wilder-
ness of snacks. If you know the city, that is – if you know which
back kitchens to sneak into, and which corners hide the tastiest morsels. But the walking gourmet needs to know a few
things about the neighbourhood she's strayed into, about
the culture that dominates those particular blocks, and what
fist-sized bit of food that community munches on at four in
the afternoon.

This connoisseurship among Toronto's mobile snackers
has developed precisely because the city lacks good outdoor
street food – perhaps, in part, because of our cold winters, but
also because of legislation that until recently restricted street
food to 'cooked meats,' which is to say, the ubiquitous hot dog.
British food historian Alan Davidson has observed that a city's
street food isn't defined by its dominant national culture, but

by the particular tone and flavour of its own everyday life. Since restaurant space adds expense both for chefs and diners, cities with less developed economies frequently have greater spreads of street food, as do warmer places, where nibbling outside is convenient. Yet street food also flourishes in places with a distinctive culinary tradition, or with many immigrants. Despite our inhibiting winter, the great diversity of Toronto's people would probably, under other circumstances, have grown a thick and variegated weave of outdoor food stands around the city. Instead, sluggish policy mechanisms have kept us all chewing on the same tired old hot dog.

Agitation for change began in the spring of 2007. The urban-innovation group Multistory Complex sparked conversations about the issue in Toronto blogs and newspapers by launching the Street Food Vending Project, a competition and exhibit of better designs for hot dog carts that could also carry more interesting foods. By July, the Ontario government had announced its intention to loosen the health regulations that restricted street food to precooked meats, but, with the change scheduled to take effect only on August 1, the streets weren't likely to see their new snacks until the next summer.

An eight-month lead before the start of the new outdoor snacking season should have given policy-makers time to accommodate the new order; by late January 2008, however, while City Council had approved the plan to open Toronto to a great spread of snacks, the project had ballooned in proportion and complexity. Unwilling to let small business owners design their own carts, under the scrutiny of health inspectors, the City went searching for charities (yes, charities) to fund a fifteen-cart pilot project under the leadership of Toronto Board of Health chair John Filion. This strange plot was in fact the next evolution of a plan for the City to borrow $700,000 to buy carts it would then lease to vendors in a complicated and expensive administration program. Critics of the plot pointed out that too many policy objectives were being pinned to the street-food project: they included rebranding the city, promoting healthy diets in poor neighbourhoods, improving the general economy and even combating diabetes. At a January 29 meeting, councillor Denzil Minnan-Wong moved to scrap the accumulation of proposed policy in favour of going back to basics with a simple gate-opening regulation amendment to ease licencing for would-be vendors eager to sell new kinds of street food. His motion was soundly defeated, and Toronto spent the summer of 2008 still famished for decent snacks.

Spinning itself into a street-food quandary, City bureaucracy let an almost puritan embargo fall on outdoor deliciousness.

After recruiting and selecting potential vendors through the winter of 2008–09, 'Toronto a la Cart,' the final version of the city's street-food project, released eight 'ethnically diverse and nutritious' food stations around the city in late spring 2009. Summer visitors could munch on Greek and Persian food in Nathan Philips Square, Thai delectables in Mel Lastman Square, Afghani morsels at Metro Hall, Eritrean delights at Roundhouse Park, Middle Eastern wraps and kebabs in Queen's Park, and Caribbean and Korean cuisine on Yonge – and the rest of the city got to keep their hot dogs.

In its focus on the street-food 'cart,' the final name of Toronto's street-food program belies all the political hand-wringing that went into its genesis. For two years policy-makers sat at the boardroom table, befuddled into silence by their inability to imagine the ideal food cart. Whether the city will eventually allow individuals to create their own little outdoor cooking pods – whether it can stomach the idea that safe and sanitary street kitchens could be eclectic and odd-looking – reveals what kind of city Toronto officials think they're catering to. That the city wants its street-food carts to be homogeneous suggests it would like to think our kitchens are homogeneous, which they most certainly are not. The mechanisms that regulate life in this city tripped over the thought of bringing kitchens outdoors – and suddenly we realize that the scene of our most complicated, political, personal yet culturally inflected expressions of individual urban life has always been the kitchen.

While it's strange that this political quandary has persisted for so long – two and a half years, at the time of writing – it's stranger still that Torontonians haven't revolted in any way. There have been no stories of renegade pastry dealers setting up on the sidewalks, or falafel carts trolling the parks, or spring-roll pushers beckoning from the alleyways. Maybe this is because food-industry people rarely have cash to spare, let alone to spend on projects that risk hefty fines. But would-be street-food munchers could have made more of a fuss. Toron-tonians can be very good at watching bureaucrats and whin-ing, but rarely do we grab freedoms to which we feel entitled. If, as everyone seems to concur, Toronto *should* have deli-cious and diverse street food on every corner – an idea that poses no ethical or sanitary threat – why have we not simply exercised our right to reasonable and good pursuits?

Why have no street-food activists taken the fight to the street, doled out samosas to a crowd of ravenous snackers until the entire lot was dragged away and incarcerated by police, so the media could shame the government into finally relaxing regulations? This kind of rebellion hasn't happened because the people of this city are serious and law-abiding to a T for Toronto. Quite pleased to let policy-makers curb our habits, we allow them to deny our snacks with only the melodramatic snivel of an obedient child told to wait until dinnertime.

Of course, snacks seem like a minor cause, not worthy of political action. Yet food is one of the most charged political symbols: if we are what we eat, and we eat to remind ourselves of who we are, then our ability to eat what we like, and the ability of vendors to cook what they please, should be taken as a cherished right. The word 'diversity' is thrown about Toronto so much that we lose what it really means: encountering new things, not being blind to the experiences and cares of others, discovering precisely what you did not know you were looking for as you wander down the street. By opening up the streets to foods of all kinds, we could be working towards making our city a space where the experience of genuine diversity simply happens, a space that rewards every visitor and local wanderer with something new, strange and delicious. Being hard-nosed about snacks may seem whimsical, but we have every reason to take a political stand for our right to experience Toronto as a walkable palate of the most wild, motley and colourful flavours.

Steven
Biggs

High off the hog: Hogtown as food-processing hub

You're not alone if you assume Toronto's nickname, Hogtown, refers to our corporate excesses or Bay Street high-fliers, or maybe even a Torontocentric media that hogs the national spotlight. But corporate shenanigans and tunnel vision have nothing to do with it; this unshakable alias was sired by some-thing far less glamorous: Toronto's long-standing – and often overlooked – food-processing industry. We can thank the humble pork-packing business for the 'hog' in Hogtown.

While Toronto's wide array of food merchants and restau-rants is pretty visible, most Torontonians never see the bustling hub of food-processing companies behind the scenes that make chocolate, bread, muffin mix, condiments, crackers, gum, confectionaries, canned soup, meats, cheese and count-less specialty foods. In fact, Toronto is the second-largest food-processing hub in North America, after Chicago.

Michael Wolfson, food and beverage sector specialist with the City of Toronto, believes the city has, over the years, become a hub by accident, not through any coordinated municipal plan. Historically, protectionist trade policies encouraged foreign companies to establish Canadian subsidiaries; Toronto's central location in both North America and Canada, along with an ample supply of labour, made it an obvious location for these subsidiaries. A good example is the Campbell Soup Company, which set up its first foreign subsidiary in New Toronto (now Etobicoke) in the 1930s; the smell of soup cooking still wafts across Etobicoke from the soup plant.

The hub today

A full half of the food-processing jobs in Ontario are in Toronto. In 2008, the food-processing industry employed approximately 52,500 people in the Toronto Census Metro-politan Area (which includes some neighbouring munici-palities). Within the City of Toronto, the industry employs 12 percent of the industrial workforce, making it the second-largest manufacturing employer in the city, with assembly-line workers, food-safety technicians and skilled workers who operate and maintain high-tech equipment.

Toronto is now nestled in the midst of a regional market of six million people, and within a one-day drive of 150 million consumers. Along with this nearby consumer base, it is a North American hub for trucking, rail and air transport, allowing for easy transport to more distant markets.

The city is home to about 500 food processors; when the surrounding region is included, this figure jumps to 1,600. Bakeries make up the largest group of plants, followed by meat processing and beverages. Approximately two-thirds of the plants in the region are small (one to ten employees), while fewer than 10 percent of plants have 100 or more employees. But the economic spinoff extends beyond direct employment, as the industry also fuels a need for packaging, warehousing and distribution.

The Cadbury Adams plant, 277 Gladstone Ave.

While there are processing plants throughout the city, Wolfson points out a large concentration of processors in south Etobicoke, home to plants such as Kraft's Christie Brown & Co. bakery and Future Bakery; and an additional cluster near highways 400 and 401 in North York, where Fiera Foods, a large maker of baked goods, can be seen from the highway. Scarborough, too, has its own cluster. In older parts of the city, industry is sometimes interwoven into residential areas, like the Cadbury Adams plant near Dundas and Dufferin streets, nestled in a tree-lined neighbourhood opposite residential houses. It is here that chocolate bars, including Caramilk, Mr. Big and Wunderbar, are made. And beyond the city borders, there are sizeable clusters in Brampton, Vaughan, Woodbridge and Mississauga.

Toronto is a major decision-making centre in Canada's food-processing industry: half of Canada's top-ranked food and beverage manufacturers are headquartered in the city, including well-known companies such as Cadbury Schweppes, Fiera Foods Company, Kraft Canada Inc., Maple Leaf Foods Inc., Nestlé Canada Inc., Unilever Canada Limited and Weston Bakeries Limited.

The allure of Toronto today

'Companies like Toronto, all things being equal,' says Wolfson, talking about the advantage of a large labour force, twenty-four-hour transit and nearby markets. But some things aren't always equal – like the cost of land and taxes. Wolfson acknowledges the costs of doing business in Toronto may seem high, but notes that some companies have recently returned to Toronto following a stint in the suburbs. Lower suburban tax rates, he says, aren't always worth the savings when the cost of finding labour is considered. And Toronto offers a large workforce that is mobile days, nights and week-ends because of a good public transit system.

ShaSha Navazesh, founder of ShaSha Bread Co., says his bakery is situated in Toronto for one main reason: labour. Here he can find employees for both management and production positions. But while he likes having his company in his home city, he believes it comes with a heavy cost when taxes, expenses and land prices are considered.

While the costs of operating in Toronto concern Navazesh, Elena Quistini, president of Toronto-based Pasta Quistini Inc., recently moved her company back to Toronto from a neighbouring suburb after leaving the city for the promise of lower suburban taxes. But Quistini says the suburban move came with a heavy price: not having a Toronto address. She explains that food buyers know and recognize Toronto. When Pasta Quistini was located in the suburbs, she often found herself having to explain to foreign buyers that her company was 'close to Toronto.'

Despite its prominence, Toronto faces jurisdictional competitiveness. Navazesh has been courted by Canadian and American mayors hoping he'll move his bakery to their cities. He says when the business grows enough to allow him to pay employees extra money to commute to a suburban plant, he'll consider relocating.

Helping the industry grow

The City is eager to keep plants such as ShaSha Bread Co., so it recently launched a pilot project for processors building new facilities. Under the scheme, newly constructed plants are taxed on the pre-construction value of the land. Taxes are gradually increased until, after ten years, the company is paying tax on the full value of the land and the plant. Wolfson explains the logic, noting it's far from corporate favouritism: the city's tax base grows, too, and companies have a ten-year window of tax savings to invest in being industry leaders.

'The food-processing industry is a high-tech industry,' explains Jane Graham, executive director of the Alliance of Ontario Food Processors, noting that skilled workers are the foundation of any high-tech industry. But, she explains, there aren't enough skilled workers – people trained to work with automated equipment and processes – for Ontario food processors. Her organization found that the food-processing industry isn't even on the radar screen as a career opportunity for secondary school students. To change this, AOFP is helping develop college-level training focused on food-processing technology, along with

an awareness campaign for students. While this initiative is not specific to Toronto, it will benefit the city.

Meanwhile, the City of Toronto has collaborated with the Toronto District School Board to organize specialized language training for workers in the industry. This training goes beyond food-industry jargon to cover basic English-language skills – something critical in an industry where a high proportion of employees are new to Canada. Coupled with a City initiative to help employers develop good human-resources policies and practices, this should decrease employee turnover and increase chances for employee advancement.

The city can help food processors in other ways, too. Quistini applauds the recent City of Toronto pilot program to buy locally produced food: 'If cities don't protect local growers and suppliers, who will?' she asks.

Along with measures to help existing businesses, there's an opportunity to grow new ones. The proposed Toronto International Food Processing and Innovation Centre will house up to thirty small, medium and start-up companies. Wolfson explains that money saved by pooling infrastructure costs such as waste removal, facility maintenance, energy and security can be channelled towards innovation and equipment – two essential competitive advantages in this industry. The City also works with the Toronto Food Business Incubator, a non-profit organization that provides start-up facilities and training for food entrepreneurs, teaching regulatory requirements and offering industry insight and contacts.

Any municipality the size of Toronto is bound to have bureaucracy, and Hogtown is no exception. Wolfson notes a recent push to improve cross-divisional communication within the bureaucracy: his department partners with food companies setting up shop in the city, and a dedicated person helps pilot the myriad applications through red tape or

References

City of Toronto website. The History of Toronto. www.toronto.ca/culture/history/history-1901-50.htm

International Food Processing and Innovation Centre: An Opportunity for Growth and Economic Development, Giffels Associate Limited, January 2006. (A report to City of Toronto, TEDCO and Government of Ontario) www.toronto.ca/business_publications/pdf/IFPIC-report-nov-06.pdf

Campbell Company website: www.campbellsoupcompany.com/atw_canada.asp

New Toronto Historical Society website: www.newtorontohistorical.com/Campbells Soup.htm

Workforce Ahead Summary: A Labour Study of Ontario's Food Processing Industry. Alliance of Ontario Food Processors, 2005. www.aofp.ca/Publications/Reports.aspx.

Food Industry Outlook: A Study of Food Industry Growth Trends in Toronto. WCM Consulting for the Ontario Ministry of Agriculture and Food and the City of Toronto, Martin Bohn, Manager, Investment Development Unit, OMAF. www.toronto.ca/business_publications/pdf/omaftor_finalreport.pdf

City of Toronto website. www.toronto.ca/invest-in-toronto/tor_overview.htm

City of Toronto website. www.toronto.ca/invest-in-toronto/food.htm

Cadbury website; www.canada.en.cadbury.com/ourcompany/local_story/Pages/default.aspx

communication breakdowns. Quistini, who benefited from this service in moving her operation back to the city, describes it as a goldmine: 'They've been a tremendous help guiding us to the right people to get things done quickly.'

The City has started to toot its own horn, and now actively promotes its business community. The City's food and beverage team arranges for out-of-country food buyers to visit Toronto, coordinating meetings at which processors can display their products. It also takes part in shows such as the Ethnic and Specialty Food Expo, held in Toronto, where it sponsors a booth for new Toronto companies to display goods.

External factors

While free-trade agreements make it possible for foreign companies to close subsidiaries, Wolfson downplays the idea that free trade will harm the sector. As a former broker in the food industry, his experience is that Canadian companies are well-regarded in the U.S., known as being more innovative and flexible when it comes to meeting customer requests. This reputation, he feels, makes free trade an opportunity, not a threat. He cites the example of the President's Choice brand, a successful line of products spearheaded by the Canadian grocery chain Loblaws, and says President's Choice had an edge: innovative and willing Canadian processors. He notes that the brand is now exported to the U.S., where many retailers sell the entire line of inventive, well-packaged products.

While Wolfson thinks trade is an answer, not a problem, trade hinges on transportation. Toronto's notorious traffic gridlock hurts food processors promising just-in-time shipments. It isn't specific to Toronto – it affects the whole of the Golden Horseshoe region stretching from Niagara Falls to Oshawa. And it's not just road capacity: border delays, too, can slow shipments. One thing the City has been able to do is facilitate changes at the border, where Agriculture and Agri-Food Canada has responded to requests for more border capacity, allowing trucks to clear the border more quickly.

Getting recognition

Wolfson shakes his head as he talks about the success of the automotive sector at lobbying and promoting itself. He wishes the same could be said for the food-processing sector. 'Small to medium processors have absolutely no representation

whatsoever,' he says. This leave these processors – who comprise two-thirds of the food-processing companies in the city – with no effective industry association and no voice in government. Navazesh agrees. The problem as he sees it is that while there are associations for many foods at the farm level, there's no association for small food processors.

Along with a strong industry voice to articulate the needs of the sector to government, Wolfson points out another challenge. The food industry falls under the auspices of the Ontario Ministry of Agriculture, Food and Rural Affairs. This ministry is, by nature, rurally focused. He wonders if the city's proposed International Food Processing and Innovation Centre – which would house new food businesses and serve as an incubator – would already have secured provincial funding if it had been proposed for a rural area.

Toronto Labour Force Readiness Plan: The Food Processing Industry in the Toronto Region, Toronto Economic Development, 2004. www.toronto.ca/business_publications/tlfrp/labour_force_food_screen.pdf

International Food Processing & Innovation Centre, Toronto Economic Development. www.toronto.ca/business_publications/pdf/IFPICbro-lowres.pdf

Toronto CMA 2008 Industry Profiles, City of Toronto Economic Development based on Statistics Canada Labour Force survey data.

Looking ahead

Sales in the sector have had an approximate annual growth rate of 5 percent. The City expects this trend to continue, but foresees faster growth in the sub-sector of smaller, specialty food processors, where it projects 12 percent annual growth. As of 2008, the five-year employment growth in the food manufacturing sector for the Toronto Census Metropolitan area was 22 percent – and the fifteen-year growth was 35 percent.

For Toronto to remain a food-processing hub, a Toronto address must be seen by food-processing companies as a good business decision. To help make the numbers for the business decision attractive, the City has initiated the pilot tax-phase-in program for new food-processing businesses, and it's trying to be a better business partner for processors by assigning dedicated go-to people to guide companies through the bureaucracy. In collaboration with the Toronto District School Board, it is helping to boost the availability of workers. And through the local procurement policy, it will support companies situated within its boundaries.

While all these initiatives will help make a Toronto address a good business decision, an increased public and governmental awareness of the industry – like that achieved by the automotive industry – would be invaluable. Graham, talking about the Ontario food-processing industry as a whole, is optimistic about the future, saying, 'We can become an epicentre for food processing in North America.' If Ontario becomes an epicentre, Hogtown might just hog a bit of that spotlight.

Bronwyn
Underhill

A tale of three peaches

My grandmother Glenna's peach chutney
Yields 20–25 cups of chutney

12 lb ripe and flavourful peaches, skinned
1 lb green peppers
½ lb fresh ginger, finely chopped
1 lb unsalted whole cashews
3 lb raisins
2 cloves garlic
2 qt white vinegar
4 lb brown sugar
6 oz mustard seed
1 tbsp salt

Chop everything except the cashews. Put all the ingredients in a large, heavy-bottomed pot and cook for two to three hours on medium-low heat, stirring frequently. Preserve in jars or freeze.

Growing up in southern Ontario meant there was always a wealth of peaches come late summer. While I mainly ate peaches fresh, my grandmother and other family members often prepared chutney with the fruit, which I would savour once the peach season had passed. Four years ago, I spent a summer picking fruit and teaching ESL in the Niagara region; through 'peach rash'[1] and access to more peaches than I could ever have imagined, I began to better understand this sumptuous fruit. In honour of my time on the farm, and seeking to produce a batch of chutney to see me through the winter months, I decided to examine just what it is I value about this recipe and about the peaches that bring it flavour.

I have three options for preparing my chutney. If I go to my local grocery store, I can pick up California peaches at ninety-nine cents a pound, or sweet Niagara peaches at $1.29. I can also buy Niagara peaches from the Dufferin Grove or Artscape Wychwood Barns farmers' markets at a similar price. Or I can help strip the peach tree at Spadina House with Not Far from the Tree (NFFTT), an urban food picking and gleaning group that picked over 7,000 pounds of fruit in Toronto in 2009. My three choices engender many questions: how can the California peaches be so cheap if they travelled so far? Is it better to buy a Niagara peach from the supermarket or a farmers' market? Will the peaches from Spadina House be buggy, or over- or under-ripe? I decide to investigate my options by following the voyages of these three peaches.

1 A lot of time spent in contact with ripening peaches (and their peach fuzz) yields an itchy, burning, red rash on any exposed skin.

I begin with the California peach, which, like many peaches, started its life in the sap of a heavily pruned tree. As it blossomed and grew beside its siblings and cousins, some of the more than three million undocumented labourers working in that state thinned out the peach ranks and applied a significant volume of pesticides, like endosulfan or carbaryl, to prevent blight and pest invasion and to provide it with the space and energy to fatten up.[2,3] These workers risked their health, family disruption and deportation to prepare the peach for export to Toronto, a voyage of 4,500 kilometres for which it had to be picked green.

The California peach looks great when it arrives to Toronto, but it's tired from its voyage, and sun deprivation has robbed it of much of its potential sweetness. Even at a bargain-basement ninety-nine cents a pound, I can't bring myself to bring it home because I know it won't have the flavour I'm seeking.

In search of that flavour, I travel to the Niagara region. Due to the protection offered by the Niagara Escarpment and the climate-moderating effects of the Great Lakes, peaches grow well here even though they are not native to the region. The ancestors of these trees likely arrived in North America from China via Europe in the early days of colonization.

The Niagara peach has had a similar developmental process to that of the California peach, but the workers who bring this one to market are part of a long-standing legal migrant work program operating between Canada and Mexico and the Caribbean. Annually, more than 16,000 Mexican and Caribbean agricultural workers come to Ontario, staying anywhere from a few weeks to eight months, during which time they are paid at least minimum wage. Their migrant status is facilitated by the Seasonal Agricultural Workers Program, a forty-year-old federally sponsored initiative. While touted

2 pewhispanic.org/files/reports/7.pdf; www.ppic.org/content/pubs/jtf/JTF_IllegalImmigrantsJTF.pdf; www.ppic.org/content/pubs/cep/EP_707AGEP.pdf

3 These are both substances that have been banned or heavily controlled by a number of countries due to health and environmental hazards.

A peach sorting and packing facility in Virgil, Ontario.

internationally as a positive example of migrant work programs – workers receive accommodation, tax benefits, private insurance and OHIP from the day of their arrival – this program is also heavily criticized for not adequately protecting the health and the occupational and human rights of its participants, and for prioritizing farmers' interests over those of employees.[4] During the four months I spent working on a Niagara farm, I witnessed occupational-related injuries, treated and untreated illness and gross violations of the rights afforded to migrant workers by the UN, including the right to peaceful assembly and freedom of movement.[5] Of course, the program is also the source of many positive interactions, offering workers an opportunity for gainful employment and a standard of living often unattainable in their countries of origin.

Working on a farm is inherently risky, but, for migrant workers, this risk is compounded by challenges such as migrant status, language barriers and discrimination. One morning, after a series of twelve-hour shifts during a heat wave, a co-worker became sick with heat exhaustion, but our employer refused to take her into a clinic because he was 'too busy.' (A co-worker and I took her into the regional hospital – the only health facility open on a Sunday.) Her options for transport and access to medical care were limited by her condition, her rural location, her poor English skills and her lack of knowledge about her rights as a migrant worker. After two days' rest, she was back to work, although she was sent home not long afterwards, and I later found out she was never accepted back into the migrant worker program.

The Niagara peach's time on the tree is far from tranquil, its short life filled with regular pesticide sprayings, dry spells, irrigation visits and assaults by hail, crows and falling branches and peaches. Once the Niagara peach is almost heavy enough to fall from the tree, male workers return to pick it and take it to the packing plant, where female hands and eyes examine it for imperfections such as split pits, bruises, hail scabs and bird pecks. Many of its cousins end up in 'seconds' bins, relegated to the corner of the barn and sold at a discount or composted. At the height of peach season, my co-workers and I would pile up peaches that were too ripe to pack, and therefore perfect to eat. Our kitchen counters and refrigerator overflowed, even when each of us was eating upwards of five peaches a day. Making chutney with the surplus was not an attractive option, however, given the hot weather, the tin-can trailer we lived in and our long work days.

4 For further information, see *Migrant Workers in Canada: A Review of the Canadian Seasonal Agricultural Workers Program* (Ottawa: The North-South Institute, 2006) and www.justicia4 migrantworkers.org/

5 For more information on these rights, see the International Convention on the Protection of the Rights of All Migrant Workers and Their Families, www.unhchr.ch/ html/menu3/b/ m_mwctoc.htm

Picked when it's large, rosy and just slightly ripe, the Niagara peach travels just over 100 kilometres to the Ontario Food Terminal in Toronto, where it is likely auctioned off to a buyer for a chain grocery store and is soon basking under fluorescent lights. Once, during my time in Niagara, I found peaches from the farm I worked on being sold in a local chain grocery store. The peaches had travelled to Toronto and back, as this particular store relied on shipments from the OFT rather than from area farmers. It was only because I was familiar with the names of Niagara-area peach farms and packing plants that I recognized these peaches in their well-labelled basket.

Given that the names of farms and farmers aren't marked on the fruit itself, it's often difficult to know when peaches are logging double food miles. This concern disappeared once I started picking fruit at Spadina House with NFFTT.

Spadina House's verdant gardens and small orchard are all that remain of the farm that once stood on those lands, and they are intentionally planted with heirloom crops that would have been common in kitchen gardens from the 1800 and 1900s. The Spadina House peach tree may be close to 100 years old. Two years ago, Laura Reinsborough took on the task of gleaning fruit from these trees, and some of this fruit was sold at the Stop Community Food Centre's Saturday farmers' market. In only a few years, NFFTT has expanded to become a city-wide movement that brings volunteers into private backyards to harvest fruit that might otherwise go to waste. This fruit is donated to local charities and enjoyed by volunteers and residents alike. Ever-expanding lists of fruit-tree owners and eager volunteers are matched up through email messages; novice and experienced pickers come together in yards across the city to fill bike baskets, knapsacks, cloth bags, etc., with what they can reach from the ground, from ladders provided by residents and even from garage roofs. At the time of writing, more than 320 volunteers and 160 fruit-tree owners were registered with the program.

The Spadina House peach is accompanied through its development by numerous siblings, since its tree is not regularly thinned. Although it received a quick chemical bath early in the season, its life is spent mainly pesticide-free; as a result, moths and other insects take up residence in its flesh. The peaches' proximity to one another in these un-thinned trees causes rot spots in fruits that have lured wasps with their heady scent. Looking for sweet peaches for my grandmother's chutney, I grab a fruit, only to be dismayed that insects have

Peaches ripe for the picking during the 2009 Niagara-on-the-Lake Peach Festival.

Peach 'seconds' awaiting sale or compost.

already spoken for it. I drop it on a growing pile of fallen fruit and select a different peach for a trip to my kitchen.

The Spadina House peach is smaller than both the Niagara peach and the California peach, and it's a little rough around the edges, with scabs and a slightly misshapen appearance. It is sweet, though likely not as flavourful as its wasp-eaten cousins. Fruit-picking with NFFTT is a virtually no-cost way to get peaches for my chutney, though the recipe calls for considerably more peaches than I could access through a Spadina House fruit pick.

Torontonians from a multitude of backgrounds and of varying ages pick fruit with NFFTT, united in their desire to connect with their food system in ways we have lost. NFFTT and Growing for Green's new community orchard initiative at Ben Nobleman Park – across the street from Eglinton West subway station – further increases the opportunities for food connections and local food production in the city. At the time of writing, nine fruit trees had been planted, with five more planned.

Though the voluntary urban gleaning activities organized by NFFTT have garnered considerable interest from the media and the public, this interest in agricultural activity does not reflect current agricultural employment trends. Legally, Canadian growers are required to give employment priority to Canadians before migrant workers, but a long history of Canadian labour shortages in rural agriculture, due mainly to relatively low wages, low population density in rural areas and the seasonal nature of the work, stands in contrast to the eagerness of urbanites to pick fruit.[6] Many farmers find it

6 In her book *Tortillas and Tomatoes: Transmigrant Mexican Harvesters in Canada* (McGill-Queen's, 2003), Tanya Basok shows how Ontario farmers have been in need of a stable labour force since at least World War II.

difficult to staff their farms with Canadians over an entire harvest, which is why programs like the Seasonal Agricultural Workers Program have been adopted.

As peaches, California, Niagara and Spadina House all fit the main prerequisites for inclusion in my chutney pot, yet they are very different. Should I prioritize price over locality? Convenience over a lack of chemical inputs? Labour practices over appearance? I make my choice, and leave all three behind. Witnessing the vast amount of peach waste that results from a typical harvest has made me aware of how artificial our notion of a 'perfect' peach really is. Luckily, my personal connection with farms and labourers in Niagara – and my access to a car – makes it relatively easy for me to access seconds for my chutney recipe. The Niagara peach's neglected cousins will fill my kitchen.

I pick up my seconds while visiting the annual peach festival in Niagara-on-the-Lake, where it is obvious that the landscape of peach production in Niagara is shifting, and that finding peaches there may soon become increasingly difficult. In 2008, CanGro, the last factory that canned peaches in the area, closed, leaving many farmers without a buyer for their crops and forcing them to rip up their orchards to make way for more profitable crops like grapes. According to an April 23, 2008, article in the *Kitchener-Waterloo Record*, 365 hectares of peaches may be lost as a result of the plant's closing.

With peaches pouring in from large-scale operations in California and elsewhere, small-scale farmers in Ontario are pressured to keep prices low to stay competitive, while facing increasing costs of inputs, limited infrastructural and institutional supports and pressure to bring a 'perfect' crop to a fickle market. In the face of larger food-system issues, using local peaches for my chutney recipe feels like a drop in the ocean, but en masse, chutney and jam preservers can act alongside the fresh-peach-eaters to protect this crop we have claimed as part of our heritage and our cuisine.

Sweeter than most peaches I could find in a store, but with rot spots, split pits or scabs inhibiting sale, 'seconds' fit my needs perfectly, since I will chop up the chutney ingredients anyways. In this way I can preserve local peach flavour and the taste of late summer all year long.

Peaches coming in from the orchard to be packed and sorted.

Darren O'Donnell

Eat, Meet and other tactics to chew my way to Sesame Street

'... being in the network implies sharing a new idea or compatible ideas for society. Initially, small and isolated groups hold these ideas, but as those groups begin to talk to each other, quite suddenly, the entire society can shift paradigms. I see this as an alternate explanation of how revolutions occur, as opposed to the "great man" idea still beloved in many history books. I also find it offers a strategic idea – perhaps the path to social change is to initiate dialogue and seek connections between groups that are superficially disparate in their ideas.'

– Todd Parsons, mathematician and dinner guest

Growing up in the late 1960s and early 1970s, I watched *Sesame Street* like it was real life, and it anchored itself in my imagination as an ideal for neighbourhood engagement: you know everybody on the block (even the green-furred asshole who lives in the garbage can), you learn together, you hang out together and you even *work* together – the show's enthusiastic championing of the various jobs and vocations that contribute to civic health lent all workers credibility. This image of the city as a productive, supportive and creative place has never been so clearly and thoroughly imagined and illustrated. Even now – perhaps especially now – Sesame Street remains an inspiration for many of my social and professional activities.

As an ideal, however, Sesame Street is bound to be elusive, and my search for the mythic neighbourhood hasn't been easy. My first impression of Toronto was that I had found a place with similar promise; the mixed-use neighbourhoods and civic culture felt much more vibrant than the Edmonton suburbs where I grew up, and its cultural diversity offered the possibility of mind-expanding encounters. But Toronto is not Sesame Street – there are no talking frogs at Trinity-Bellwoods Park and the birds are small. It didn't take long before I found myself in social circles defined strictly by vocation, with mind-sets too often in agreement, and engulfed by an escalating sense of alienation, boredom, loneliness and an intense antipathy towards dinner parties, where I could expect to meet only like-minded people – a dull sameness that made me feel very alone. Parties are hard work for me. My favourite manoeuvre is to slide out the back door without saying good-bye, head out into a beautiful night and climb on my bike to coast away alone, ecstatic to have answered to no one – and this at parties where I'm having fun. I rolled through years, experiencing feelings of intense isolation oscillating with

varying degrees of community; Sesame Street remained a boulevard upon whose sidewalks I had yet to skip.

In spring 2002, my life stalled with a bout of fatigue and an injured back, sending me into an intense and protracted agony comprised of an annoying stew of pain and exhaustion. My condition was so challenging that my chiropractor brought out the big guns and revealed that she's a shaman, studying with the Institute for Contemporary Shamanic Studies, and offered to bring her peers in on my situation. I was desperate, ready to try anything, even a healing circle with a bunch of naked strangers.

Not knowing how the Incorporeal Entities who participated in my ceremony feel about confidentiality, I'll play it safe and keep the details quiet, except to say that it was wacky and not at all sexy, involved giving me a spirit name, which, if you ask me nicely, I'll whisper in your ear, and, ultimately, boiled down to three resolutions, one of which was to have dinner parties. This particular resolution was intended to open my heart and make me love everyone; my physical problems, it turns out, were a result of the litres of vitriol I was always choking back in response to my utter disappointment at still not having found my Sesame Street.

I undertook the Incorporeal Entities' assignment nervously, worried that no one would want to hang around with me; to keep it safe, I invited plenty of people who didn't know me all that well. My dinner parties, then, included a fail-safe: if they happened to blow as a relaxed social time, I was off the hook, because I was simply meeting new people and enlarging my social circles. This meant that the dinners – particularly during the first few moments – were kind of tense. I would roll through these moments by keeping myself busy: I really enjoyed washing dishes with my back to the party.

Still, not content to produce the kind of party I was loath to attend, I needed to introduce some device, a way to lay the foundations of Sesame Street. Turning to participatory food-making to lubricate the social gears, I forced everyone to make their own wafflusa,[1] a dish of my own invention, a hybrid of the waffle and the pupusa. I provided a bunch of ingredients and left the construction of the dinner up to the guests . This not only drew some of the attention away from me and my cooking, it also provided a way for my guests to occupy themselves if they were feeling as overwhelmed as I was by the social pressure.

[1] **Wafflusas**
A bunch of corn masa
Some oil. This is very important; don't forget the oil or you'll end up with crackers.
An array of things to stick inside: beans, cheese, meat, olives, sun-dried tomatoes.
And some stuff to put on top, such as salsa, guacamole, etc.

Make the dough by mixing the corn masa with water and oil. You can put an egg or two in the dough to make it fluffier, but it's still good without. Invite your guests to make a ball of dough around their choice of stuff and then stick it in the waffle iron.

As I began to ease into my role as host, developing culinary skills to accommodate about twenty people at a time, I shifted gears, raising the stakes and asking more from my guests, starting off with a dinner entitled Salads and Salvia. *Salvia divinorum* is a legally available form of sage used by indigenous shamans in Oaxaca, Mexico.[2] Smoking salvia produces a very strange but short-lived experience (six minutes or so) and offers the possibility of states of being well beyond the familiar touchstones of space, time, corporeality and the individual. It had, for me, already created an experience that felt a lot like being trapped at an eternal dinner party, where the improper thoughts I was always suppressing were manifest in the very architecture of the unreality that engulfed me for what felt like a few hundred thousand years. If that sounds slightly idiotic and confusing, it was. But it was a horror I felt compelled to offer my dinner guests. It's a disaster for the ego and, thus, perfect for developing friendships, building connections with new people and filling my bile-soaked arteries with love.

2 www.sagewisdom.org

It was the hottest night of the summer, and my fifth-floor apartment was unbearable. We sat around, drenched in sweat, and enjoyed the array of salads,[3] and then, one at a time, gave the herb a try. One guest suffered uncontrollable laughter; another experienced reality being apportioned into pie-like slices of space-time. One visited a tiny city hovering somewhere above us, peopled by small Doozer-like beings, and the last person insisted in a hallucinatory panic that no one else in the room should smoke the evil shit – we regretted to inform her that we all already had.

Like other survivable and contained disasters, the trauma induced by salvia creates a moment where habitual social habits just won't cut it – a room full of people who don't know each other all that well are not going to sit around chatting awkwardly about the weather while one by one they're blowing their minds apart. The conversations that follow are marked by open admissions of confusion, fear and awe, generating an alien intimacy between strangers. It could be argued that inhaling hallucinogens, regardless of legal status, is not very Sesame Street, but that would leave you ill-equipped to discuss the source of those mysterious lyrics in 'Mahna Mahna' or the debatable existence of Snuffleupagus: that bird must have been smoking *something*.

Sesame Street as hallucination for the livable city is perhaps at its best when it explores the people whose labour animates

3 **Sini Sambol potato salad**
A bunch of potatoes
Some spring onions
Some mayonnaise or olive oil and lemon juice.
And some Sini Sambol, a Sri Lankan condiment that features an array of spices including chilies, cloves, cardamom, cinnamon, tamarind and dried Maldive fish – a very tasty item, similar to Japanese katsuobushi. You can pick it up at a couple of stores on Bloor between Dufferin & Lansdowne.

Cook the potatoes, mix in everything else, cool and serve. Or don't cool, just eat it.

and facilitates healthy civic functioning. This, in my preschool, pre-class-conscious mind, seemed a self-evident no-brainer: of course the garbage worker was a noble figure, as was Mr. Hooper the grocer and everybody else who fuelled the day-to-day. Forged in the optimism of the late 1960s, *Sesame Street* was permeated with the notion that work should be life, life should be work, and all of it should be art. I began to focus my dinners, naming the series *Eat, Meet*, each night featuring two people talking casually about their work. Here, I began looking for vocations beyond the insular clique of mostly artists that I usually hung out with. We met Lenine Bourke and learned about her work with young people in Australia. We encountered Cara Eastcott and her film work, and I coerced Jordan Tannahill to research German theatre company Rimini Protokoll for us – he has since gone on to create a bunch of work inspired by his research. And we heard from architect Rohan Walters, whose very odd home, perched on stilts over an impossible tract of land, can be spotted from the window of my apartment at College and Lansdowne.[4]

At one *Eat, Meet*, mathematician Todd Parsons demonstrated how a bifurcation – or sudden change of state[5] – occurs in a social network. Through names drawn from a hat, we connected up people (nodes) with lengths of string (edges). At first, small networks between the participants occurred: Richard DiSanto was connected to Jon Sasaki, Elaine Gaito was connected to Ernie Bolton, Misha Glouberman was connected to Sameer Farooq who was connected to Natalie De Vito. Morgan Yew was connected to Anh-thi Tang, Emmanuelle Dauplay was connected to Michelle Jacques, I was connected to Souvankham Thammavongsa who was connected to Heather Haynes who was connected to Danielle Allen who was connected to Margaux Williamson. Suddenly, when the number of edges was near to the number of nodes, the entire group was connected. Todd explained that the more complex the network – the more nodes, the more connections per node – the more abrupt the change from a group that wasn't particularly well-connected to one where everybody is part of the network.

Around this time I got an email from Gregory Nixon from Toronto's Live with Culture office – he had always been invited to the dinner parties but had yet to attend. He suggested moving the dinners into neighbourhood restaurants, shifting the focus to a more public forum. The increased exposure demanded an increased rigour when programming the guest

4 Rohan says his use of conventionally useless plots of land to build unusual but highly functioning structures 'represents the ability to craft necessary, artistic, economically appropriate solutions in a positive and unexpected way.' www.spacesby rohan.com/

5 For example, water remains unchanged as it becomes warmer, each degree from 1 to 99 not making any noticeable difference, but with the addition of a single degree of heat at 100, a bifurcation occurs and it suddenly transforms into steam, or to ice when one degree is subtracted from one to take it to zero.

speakers – if the City was getting involved, the utopian lessons of Sesame Street had to be deployed with more integrity and intensity, so I proposed we showcase speakers who had jobs that fortify the civic sphere but are not considered artistic, and ask them to discuss the beautiful and creative aspects of their work.

The Beautiful Hungry City was held under the auspices of my performance company, Mammalian Diving Reflex, with artistic producer Natalie De Vito joining me in producing them. Firefighter Stacey Hannah spoke about the colours and choreography of the flames of different materials as they burn; paramedic Shiraz Vally outlined his experiments with adopting different characters from Coen Brothers films in order to deal with young drunks, finding that Lebowski is too weak, Chigurh too strong, but the pregnant cop in Fargo, Marge Olmstead-Gunderson, provides the perfect balance, combining a folksy likeability with a passive determination that young drunks find impossible to resist. Tagalog court interpreter and Elvis impersonator Steve Comilang sang 'Love Me Tender,' and the owner of the Common café, Ed Lau, explained the rationale behind the name of his establishment: common tables induce a communal experience.

Of course, the problem with utopias is that they are dislodged and separated from historical development; a trench must be dug around the utopian to distinguish it from the non-utopian, the world of history as opposed to the post-historical utopian.[6] Not that one would expect dinner parties – or, for that matter, children's television – to engage with history in any meaningful way. For the most part, dinner parties are properly apolitical affairs, but if Todd Parsons' hopes have any weight, we could expect that all these dinners would eventually yield some confluence of socializing that would have some political import, however minimal.

In the summer of 2008, I received an email from Dan Young asking if I would throw a dinner party for Kanishka Goonewardena's friend Manoranjan, a Sri Lankan journalist who had a project he was looking for some support on. Dinner, we decided, would be at eight and Dan would bring all the materials necessary to make pasta from scratch. Dan came late, well after the guests had started to show up, and he conscripted us all into a two-hour session of pasta preparation, the forced labour creating a lively, if famished, conviviality.[7]

6 Fredric Jameson, Archaeologies of the Future (London: Verso, 2005).

Dinner done, Kanishka introduced Manoranjan with a long, impressive bio that positioned the journalist of Tamil origins in the middle of the Sri Lankan conflict, hated by both the Sinhalese government and the freedom-fighting Tamil Tigers, and now a refugee in Canada. Manoranjan insisted that the only thing most Sri Lankans want is peace. He itemized a long list of artifacts he possessed: hundreds of raw digital images, hours of video and piles of facts he wanted to share with the world. He had rented the lobby of Roy Thomson Hall for August 23 to present this material. It was the highest profile venue he could think of in which to grab the mainstream and spotlight the problem. I did the math: thirty-five days. Mano concluded, 'I need your help. Can anybody help me put together this show? Please help me.'

It was an incredible request, and the guests were alarmed, the desperateness of Manoranjan's situation triggering a realistic, if not particularly optimistic, response. There was a struggle of wills as people tried to escape the corner Manoranjan had trapped us in, offering weak suggestions and trying to avoid the material considerations by discussing politics. Some guests were annoyed with me for letting things drift for so long and so far from the task at hand, so I quietly slunk over to my computer and turned on some music, trying to signal that it was time to party. The vibe didn't take. The evening dissipated, leaving Manoranjan, Kanishka, Dan and me alone to chat about Sri Lanka into the night.

The next day, determined to prove that a project coordinator could be found, I, with the help of Natalie De Vito, drafted a job description, posted it to the Instant Coffee listserv[8] and did my best to convince myself that I'd done all I could.

A month later, I attended the event and, strolling through the crowds that filled the lobby of Roy Thomson Hall, I spotted Dan, who beamed at me, gesturing towards Andrew Reyes, who had taken the gig. I looked around the show: printed photos, information and stats on big vinyl sheets were hung around the space, and monitors showing videos that Manoranjan had produced dotted the lobby, attracting clusters of people. Manoranjan moved through the crowd, looking sharp in his suit and in relaxed control. Months later, in the spring of 2009, the Tamil community took to the streets, and I couldn't help but fantasize that Manorjan's show had been part of the buildup that galvanized the community.

So, finally, the dinners offered the possibility – actualized or not – of attaching themselves (at least in my febrile

7 Dan's pasta
adapted from *Made in Italy*, by Giorgio Locatelli, (Fourth Estate, Ltd. London, 2006)

The sauce
2 tbsp capers
4 tbsp black olives
5 anchovy fillets (rinsed)
2 tomatoes (super-ripe heirloom are best)
2 tbsp tomato paste
Bunch of basil
5 tbsp olive oil
Salt and pepper

The fresh pasta
1 c soft white flour
1 egg
1 pinch of salt
(multiply to make as much as you need)

Mix all the pasta ingredients together until they're doughy. Cover and refrigerate for one hour. Take out and cut into ten or so pieces. Roll out each one with your pasta machine to be as thick as a loonie, then put through the spaghetti attachment. (If, at any point, your pasta is sticking together, add flour.)

For the sauce, chop tomatoes into small pieces. Chop up olives. Heat olive oil in pan (reserve 2 tbsp for later), then add everything but basil. Cook for 5 to15 min. Add salt and pepper to taste.

Cook the pasta in well-salted water. It should take about 90 seconds. Drain, saving about 1 cup of pasta water. Add pasta water and pasta to the sauce. Add basil. Toss and keep on tossing, and add the reserved olive oil. The pasta should suck up the watery part of the sauce.

8 www.instantcoffee.org

imagination) to the actual streets of Toronto. The Tamil protests – particularly their occupation of the Gardiner Expressway, a site filled with spectacular potential[9] – offered a great example of how to secure the attention of the rest of the city, a terrific reminder that infrastructural attributes can be used for multiple functions.

To whatever extent I can tell myself that Mano's dinner had anything to do with anything, there still remained one central aspect of Sesame Street that was glaringly absent from the dinners: children. No matter how developed, nuanced and complex one's social networks are, if they lack children, they not only don't register on the utopian Sesameter but they hardly qualify as properly civic.[10] But I'm a single middle-aged male, so these connections are rare and can occur only in strictly regulated circumstances. Since 2005, Mammalian Diving Reflex has worked intensively with the students of Parkdale Public School on more than a dozen projects that showcased the kids and invited them in on all the fun that Toronto's art community was up to.[11] They cut hair, DJed dance parties at Nuit Blanche, were featured onstage at Buddies in Bad Times Theatre, played music with bands from Blocks Recordings Club at the Gladstone Hotel and designed menus for Coca Tapas Bar. But with all of this activity, there remained a fissure between my kid friends and my adult friends; the dinner parties were completely homogeneous. And this lack of young people thwarted the Sesame Streetification of my life.

Eat the Street was an event that made the students at Parkdale Public School into a jury of preteen food critics as they sampled the fare at a dozen Queen West restaurants. We worked with about forty students from the school, including a few we had already extensively collaborated with and a bunch of new ones, focusing on students who were new to the country and working on their English-language skills. In groups of ten, the kids checked out the restaurants in their neighbourhood over the course of six weeks. It was a healthy cross-section of establishments ranging from family-run spots like Shangrila, Mother India and Addis Ababa to places more geared towards nightlife like Cadillac Lounge, Mitzi's Sister and the Beaver, from restaurants focused on the experience of dining, like Oddfellows, Czehoski and the Drake, to the Skyline, Parkdale's classic diner.

Positioning kids as food critics worked well within popular culture's turn towards an interest in children's subjectivities, as

9 Marney Isaac and Darren O'Donnell, 'The Gardiner Garden of the Multitude: Visions of Provision,' *GreenTOpia: Towards a Sustainable Toronto* (Toronto: Coach House Books, 2007).

10 Darren O'Donnell, 'Toronto the teenager: Why we need a Children's Council,' *uTOpia: Towards a New Toronto* (Toronto: Coach House Books, 2005).

11 Carl Wilson, 'The party line: Toronto's turn towards a participatory aesthetics,' *The State of the Arts: Living with Culture in Toronto* (Toronto: Coach House Books, 2006).

evidenced in recent documentary films focusing on kids (*Spellbound, Mad Hot Ballroom*), television shows (*Kid Nation, Are You Smarter Than a 5th Grader?*), academic fields (Children's Geographies) and the success of programs such as Dave Eggers' 826 Valencia project.

But for Mammalian Diving Reflex, this was merely the sideshow to our main goal, which was to bring the Parkdale kids together with adults in the community to build a social network that spanned these segregated communities. The public was invited to be an 'audience,' to join the jury, eat with them, get to know them, listen to their pronouncements and get in on the fun. This was our stated, public objective but it remained a distant second to our desire to create an atypical social time for everyone – a goal we couldn't really publicize. Simply inviting the public to eat with and meet the kids of Parkdale without draping the event with at least a whiff of artistic intent would have generated confusion and anxiety, which, as it stood, we still encountered to some degree.[12]

The dinners went off without a hitch; the forty kids on the jury managed to meet about 300 adults who live in and around Parkdale, thus generating a whole new bunch of edges in the network, and bringing us a little closer to Sesame Street.

Currently, my energy levels are high, my back is much, much better and my spirit name – which I do promise to whisper in your ear – serves as a reminder that an individual's social circles are potentially a community's social circles, worth cultivating and guarding. To revisit Todd Parsons on the issue: 'as ... groups begin to talk to each other, quite suddenly, the entire society can shift paradigms.' Obviously this paradigmatic shift is nowhere in sight, but that would be one of the main characteristics of a bifurcation of this nature: it's always nowhere in sight until the moment that it's everywhere in sight, not unlike the Snuffleupagus, condemned to remain a compete enigma, his very large existence regarded as a figment of Big Bird's imagination by all but us kids, watching, waiting and longing for a neighbourhood where we can all be together, united by a conviviality fostered by the simple fact that we happen to share this place – nothing more.

12 'O'Donnell-land' by Chandler Levack ran in the April 8, 2009, issue of *Eye Weekly* and was a sensational survey of my career, complete with some heavy factual errors. Among other things, it strung a flimsy but titillating thread between an isolated psychotic episode I experienced for a few days in 1993 and my current work with children. Psychosis and kids is not a mix that tends to relax people.

Primo

Pamela
Cuthbert

A pressure cooker simmers on the back burner

Go to your fridge. Open it wide. Make a list of all that's inside.
Repeat this process with your freezer, your kitchen cupboards
and wherever else you store food. Examine the inventory. Now
answer the following questions: If there is no more food to add
to your stockpile, can you and the members of your household
survive on this collection of comestibles? If so, for how long?
What happens if you're unable to prepare or safely store the
foods you possess? And what about your neighbours: will they
help or hinder the situation? Finally, if you're in a panic, is
there someone in charge who can access immediate supplies?

This is the stuff of food security: ensuring access to our
nutritional needs in the case of an obstruction. The obstacle
can come from many sources, from a sudden closing of borders
to the most widespread and quotidian cause, poverty. The UN's
Food and Agriculture Organization, the world's leading authority on these issues, defines food security as this: 'when all
people, at all times, have physical and economic access to sufficient, safe and nutritious food to meet their dietary needs and
food preferences for an active and healthy life.'

At first glance, Toronto appears to have all it takes to
be food-secure. A thriving metropolis rich in government-
supported social services, it is surrounded by fertile farmland
and abundant in food choices, from restaurants to supermarkets, cafeterias to farmers markets. But the city is much like
any other in North America: if the transport of foods were
suddenly brought to a standstill, the food supply would be
eaten up in three short days.

'We have a food system that is totally dependent on open
borders and is married to the wholesale philosophy of just-in-
time delivery,' says Wayne Roberts, manager of the Toronto
Food Policy Council (TFPC). 'From the point of view of public
health, these two things together are an accident waiting to
happen.' In the meantime, there is the daily, grinding reality:
the city is awash in food banks and other subsidized programs
that were intended as intermediary but are now entrenched in
an effort to keep citizens from going hungry.

Although food security logically demands to be a top priority for any healthy society, Roberts says it's 'always the brides-
maid, never the bride.' It's overwhelmingly ignored on a
government level until it becomes impossible *not* to deal with.
A Canadian relief worker with the United Nations puts it
another way: 'Food security is everybody's problem and
nobody's business.'

That's where Toronto stands out as a leader: in 1991, the TFPC was created through the World Health Organization's Healthy Cities program, which supports communities around the world in search of means to make food supplies secure, especially for low-income and at-risk citizens. It was the first municipal organization of its kind anywhere. Its goal is to develop 'a food system which is just and environmentally sustainable.' It operates under the jurisdiction of the Toronto Board of Health. With a staff of one – Roberts, a journalist, activist and self-proclaimed 'green economist' who has headed up the TFPC since 2000 – plus support staff shared with the government department, it runs as a membership-based operation of volunteers, city councillors, farmers, anti-hunger advocates, educators and others interested in the issues at hand who gather to develop policy. 'We're an amalgam of public accountability and NGOs, but we're more open than most government organizations and more bureaucratic than most NGOs,' explains Roberts.

Yet the TFPC is not a policy writer, and it cannot change laws. It might seem an ineffective tool without the power, but the organization's record shows otherwise. 'We're a link tank: we bring people and solutions together,' says Roberts. In 1991, the TFPC wrote the City of Toronto Declaration on Food and Nutrition and developed the Field to Table program, a not-for-profit model created to bring healthy food to low-income citizens. The next year, the program was assumed by FoodShare, an organization that offers self-help models such as collective kitchens and community gardens. In the early 1990s, the TFPC helped community organizations secure $3.5 million for projects that increased access to food. Its other accomplishments include writing Canada's first Food Access Grants Program, which provided $2.4 million for setting up kitchens in 180 schools and social agencies; assisting in creating the FoodLink Hotline, an emergency service for people in need; and working on City Council's Food and Hunger Action Committee.

'I call us an opportunist organization,' says Roberts, emphasizing that they take a glass-half-full approach. 'I try to deliberately keep it on a positive agenda. We have new possibilities that we can do easily and joyfully. But it's also true that if we're not careful, we're going to be in trouble.'

He admits it's an ongoing battle to get the writers of public policy engaged in issues beyond their immediate realm of concern – primarily because there is no one to make accountable. 'Whose business is it to know about this?' Roberts asks. 'There isn't a person to advocate to. You can go to the

supermarkets but that won't work.' We have the Canadian Food Inspection Agency, which regulates food safety and controversially represents public and private interests, and many urban, provincial and national departments, each dedicated to areas directly connected to food security, from energy to water, agriculture to trade. 'But not a single go-to source,' says Roberts.

Rod MacRae, author, professor and founder of the TFPC, points out that Canada had a Ministry of Food only during WWII, in a time of crisis. Since then, there's been no one in charge. 'Take the discussion on obesity,' he says. 'The only real discussion back in 1996 was about taking individual action to control your weight. Nobody wanted to talk about how the food system contributes to obesity, they only wanted to talk about diets. And ten years later we have an obesogenic environment. This doesn't need to happen.'

Liberal MP Carolyn Bennett is on a mission to change all that with a national food policy. It would be a first the world over – although Scotland, England and Wales are well into developing similar strategies. Bennett has posted a draft resolution on her website that includes this description of a national comprehensive food policy: '[it] includes mechanisms to ensure that the production, distribution and consumption of food in Canada, including the protection of traditionally harvested food by First Nations peoples, and is based in the principles of food sovereignty, environmental sustainability, accessibility, public health and safety.'

Bennett, who was appointed as Canada's first state minister for public health in 2003 and is the MP for Toronto's St. Paul riding, decided to host a series of roundtable talks to generate interest in the development of a food policy. She started in Toronto in spring 2009, turning to Roberts, Stop Community Food Centre executive director Nick Saul and a handful of colleagues. She summed up a food policy as 'a good social policy, good economic policy, good environmental and responsible foreign policy.' What it wouldn't be is an independent ministry – 'not another silo among silos,' she says – but, instead, an interdepartmental crossroads.

Roberts is all in favour. In the meantime, he's offering a few basic solutions for Torontonians, and the first line of defence is something most people can do at home: 'We have to widen the spectrum of people who have basic food skills, which includes cooking from scratch and, if necessary, cooking with the very minimum in aids. Like not having to use the microwave.' If your ability to cook is limited to, say, taking a frozen pizza and heating it up, you're less independent than the guy who can

take seeds and make sprouts. 'That person is gonna have their greens without much problem, and almost within a day or two,' says Roberts.

Next on the list is ensuring that every neighbourhood has a good place to buy food within walking distance. 'For city planners, you gotta have street lights, sometimes sidewalks, always parking spaces, but not a food store,' marvels Roberts. And he'd like to see a community centre like the Stop in every ward. 'I would argue that in the same way we have a fire station and a health centre, we need a food community centre.'

Last, but not least, is an issue that is inspiring local green thumbs and turning some Torontonians into illegal chicken-keepers: urban agriculture. 'Growing our own food is pleasurable but it's also an insurance policy,' says Roberts. 'We should encourage everyone to grow food in their own backyard.'

Utopia, in Roberts' eyes, looks like this: we have some food-production capacity in our home, we have somebody in our family that knows how to cook from scratch, a community centre with solar-powered cooking facilities and we get our major staples from the Greenbelt. 'It's a good demand, but it's not going to happen,' he says. 'It's not relevant, so we need to find another strategy. We're trying to unpack what this means: to say we've gotta provide food security for people on low income. We're working on it.'

To keep the council progressive and relevant, Roberts has shifted the focus of his job: 'I've identified my role as moving beyond policy and research and developing programs that you can implement.' He cites, as an example, a plan to create ready access to nutritious food for at-risk youth. 'I'm trying to figure out how to design street-vendor opportunities for non-profit organizations serving underserved communities,' he says. The concept makes good sense: 'How could the Stop or FoodShare or an organization like that set up vending carts that would break even and provide healthy, affordable and multicultural foods for youth?' The first step is to get a grant to support the initiative – more than an irritant for Roberts. 'If the auto industry needs $7 billion, all it has to do is say, "We need $7 billion,"' he explains, 'but if public health needs a grant for street youth to have food, we gotta find some complex thing that will withstand peer scrutiny.'

It's the age-old problem: food security keeps getting put on the back burner, no matter how urgent the issue. 'C'mon,' sighs Roberts. 'We don't need to prove street youth need healthy food.'

Lorraine
Johnson

Revisiting Victory:
Gardens past, gardens future

'All over Toronto...[m]any a head is bowed over the weeds, many a back is bent over the hoe in backyards and on vacant lots these sunny evenings and weekends. Soon there will be homegrown vegetables on tables in many parts of town – and they will taste like the food of the gods.'[1]

1 *The Globe and Mail,* June 8, 1943.

It's June 1943, and one of those bent-over backs belongs to Mayor Fred Conboy. He's tending an onion patch behind his home at 1043 Bloor Street while speaking with a *Globe and Mail* reporter. The flowers in his border have been replaced with tomatoes and his lawn with potatoes. The mayor is encouraging his fellow Torontonians to join the growing brigade of home gardeners, to 'dig for victory' in the war effort by planting vegetables on every available bit of land.

Torontonians responded to the call. The police and firemen at the Forest Hill Village station cut four patches out of their 465-square-metre lawn. As the *Globe* described it, they used 'any off time they [could] spare from upholding the law and keeping firefighting equipment in tip-top condition' to grow tomatoes, radishes, Scotch kale, carrots, cabbages and

2 Ibid.

more.[2] The Ontario Hydro Horticultural Club's Victory Garden Committee cultivated 425 gardens in Toronto alone (750 throughout the province) on land donated by municipal commissions and private owners, and grew $26,000 worth of

3 *The Globe and Mail,* March 13, 1944.

food in 1943 ($331,000 in 2009 dollars).[3] The Community Gardens Association of Toronto tended plots on major streets such as Bayview Avenue, Queen Street, Keele Street and Cosborne Avenue, cultivating $30,940 ($385,741 in 2009 dollars) worth of vegetables. The Pine Crescent Joy Club, an east-end activity club for youngsters, turned the lawn where once they played badminton, horseshoes and lawn bowling into a thirty-five-foot-long Victory Garden in the shape of a V.

Along with all this concerted community work, organized mainly by clubs and societies, thousands of regular folks planted their backyards with 'fruits for freedom.' A Dr. G. A. De Jardine, of 283 Wright Avenue, in the west end, interspersed his showy flower beds with tomatoes and berry plants: 'His garden is really something, and has been filmed in color by Chinese fruiterer Jo Jen of Roncesvalles Avenue, for display in various Toronto churches in aid of Chinese War Relief,' noted the

4 *The Globe and Mail,* June 8, 1943.

author of a June 8 *Globe and Mail* article.[4] Seed companies did roaring business, too: one seller gave the following response to

a reporter's enquiry: 'We're so busy selling seeds for Victory Gardens that we have no time even to discuss them.'[5]

5 *The Globe and Mail*, May 1, 1943.

All this food-focused labour bore results, and not just in Toronto. According to the federal Department of Agriculture, a total of 52 million kilograms of vegetables were grown in Canadian cities in 1943 – more than 200,000 wartime gardens produced an average of 225 kilograms each.[6] Five out of every ten urban households surveyed that year planned to have a Victory Garden. (In small towns, it was six out of ten.)[7]

6 *The Globe and Mail*, April 29, 1944.

7 *The Toronto Daily Star*, May 8, 1943.

Patriotic duty in a time of national crisis explains part of the food-growing fervour. Appeals to help allies must have struck a deep chord – images of British gardeners growing food in craters left by bombs, or of the Tower of London's moat being used to grow cabbages, were surely potent motivation. And no doubt Victory Garden promoters at both government and civic levels were aware that success would spread more quickly if they tapped into the competitive gardening instinct to grow bigger, better, *more* than one's neighbour. At the 1943 Harvest Fair, held in the Hydro Commission's office building on University Avenue, and organized to showcase the Victory Garden produce grown by the nearly 800 members of Ontario Hydro's Horticultural Club, eager gardeners showcased potatoes weighing half a kilogram each and tomatoes the size of cabbages.[8]

8 *The Globe and Mail*, September 6, 1943.

But alongside these emotional appeals were the very practical realities of policy. The Torontonians of 1943 responded to the call to grow food, to become 'a city of community gardens,' not only because it was the right thing to do in a time of war, but because the City enacted policies that turned it into an

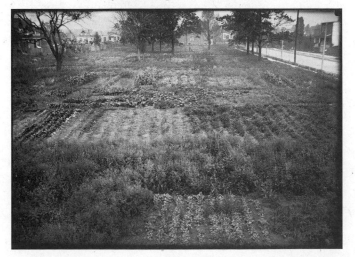

easily *possible* thing to do. For example, the City offered the use of municipally owned lots to individuals and groups for gardening purposes. Permits cost twenty-five cents (or $3.20 in 2009 dollars), a fee that even covered police protection for the gardens.[9]

9 *The Toronto Daily Star*, May 8, 1943.

Likewise, federal policies made the practice of food growing more urgent. In July 1943, for example, the Wartime Prices and Trade Board ordered canners and wholesalers to withhold stocks of canned fruits and vegetables from the retail market 'to assure supplies of canned fruits and vegetables for civilian and military requirements for the following winter.' According to the board's food coordinator, K. W. Taylor, 'In putting this plan into operation the board is merely doing on a national scale what thrifty housewives do in holding their home-canned products on the shelf or in the cellar while fresh products are in season.'[10]

10 *The Hamilton Spectator*, July 26, 1943.

Such policies were predicated on earlier practices that had eased the populace into committed and wholehearted food production. For example, in April 1934, with the city in the throes of the Great Depression, Toronto mayor William James Stewart turned the sod on a eighty-hectare plot of land on St. Clair Avenue just west of Keele, providing community garden space for approximately 5,000 unemployed families to raise food.[11] And prior to the harsh economic conditions of the 1930s, World War I also saw huge numbers of Torontonians growing food in creatively cultivated abandoned corners. In the early 1900s, for example, the Toronto Vacant Lots Cultivation Association was formed, and in May 1915 amalgamated

11 *The Evening Telegram*, April 23, 1934.

with a similar program, Vacant Lot Gardens, run by the Rotary Club of Toronto. By 1918, they had more than 2,000 gardens under cultivation and member-growers had realized $75,000 in profits (more than $980,000 in 2009 dollars).[12]

The Ontario Department of Agriculture was particularly active in promoting food production at that time, framing it in wartime language. Their full-page ad in the April 1918 edition of *The Canadian Horticulturist,* for example, urged 'a backyard garden for every home,' and asked, 'Have you enlisted in the greater production battalion?' One of the department's circulars, published in March 1918, had a similarly military message: 'Every backyard is fighting ground for the empire.' And, in one of the most explicit connections between battleground and growing ground, the Ward's Island Association turned a four-acre plot on the Ward's Estate into a Red Cross Garden, growing produce and selling it to island residents and handing the profits over to the Red Cross treasury. The *Toronto Star Weekly* noted that the garden was tended by fourteen-year-old George Boyce, whose father had been killed in action.[13]

The Department of Agriculture bolstered its patriotic appeal to Ontarians with a moral argument for resisting idleness. In a number of publications from the time of World War I, they variously promoted food gardening as good for those 'who suffer from tired minds and overworked nerves,' as a way to teach children 'industry and method' and as useful for directing energies 'into a healthy and normal channel.'

During both world wars, and in times of economic hardship such as the Depression, it seemed that everywhere in Toronto people came together, urged by governments and civic leaders to produce food for the common good. So how are we doing now, during *this* time of war and economic hardship? Are we coming together to produce food for the benefit of all?

The holstered guard who insisted on frisking me as I walked into a public meeting organized by Councillor Joe Mihevc to discuss a proposal for a community orchard in a midtown park should have alerted me to the fact that the evening was going to be less than convivial. As the guard rooted through my purse, holding up my metal water bottle with suspicion, I got steamed. And the emotional temperature *inside* the April 28, 2009, meeting was even steamier.

We were gathered to discuss a proposal, put forth by local resident Susan Poizner and sponsored by Growing for Green and Not Far from the Tree, to plant twenty-seven fruit trees in

12 George Baldwin, *Canadian Home Journal*, September 1919, p. 23.

13 John Duke, *The Star Weekly*, September 22, 1917, p. 11.

Ben Nobleman Park, just across from Eglinton West subway station. Poizner had organized a group of volunteers to carry out the project and, over the previous months, they'd offered ten workshops, held a community meeting to discuss their plan with locals and enlisted the volunteer labour of a landscape architectural designer to draw up a professional plan. On this warm, late April evening, as cherry buds were just starting to burst into blossom all over Toronto, Poizner and the team gathered to hear the community's response.

'Someone with a beautiful fantasy convinced a city councillor of this beautiful fantasy,' said one resident, with anger seeping through his irony. 'Our children's clothes will be stained with cherry juice,' said another. 'Coyotes and foxes will be drawn to the orchard and run into traffic!' 'We'll have roadkill!' 'Rats and mosquitoes will infest our neighbourhood.' 'Our taxes will be hiked to pay for water to keep the fruit trees alive.' 'Has a cost-benefit analysis been done?'

In the face of this opposition, Poizner's group called various experts up to the front of the room to address the residents' concerns. A health researcher talked about the safety of eating fruit from city trees. A playground designer talked about the need for children to engage with nature wherever they live. A horticultural supervisor from Toronto's Parks, Forestry and Recreation department talked about the maintenance work the City would do to look after the trees. A representative from Not Far from the Tree talked about the dozens of people willing to pick the orchard's fruit, keep the ground free of rotten plums and distribute excess produce to a food bank.

Even so, by the end of the meeting, when Councillor Mihevc asked if any of those opposed to the community orchard had been swayed by what they'd heard (and, in particular, by the pro-orchard team's willingness to reduce the number of fruit trees from the original forty to a compromise of twenty-seven), no hands went up. 'Everything has an element of controversy,' mused Mihevc. 'The question I need to answer at the end of the day is: Is this in the broad community interest?'

Four days later, Mihevc produced his answer. Ben Nobleman Park would get its community orchard, but not without a political sleight of hand engineered to appease: the city would plant fourteen fruit trees and nine flowering and shade trees. 'You may be asking what the difference is between fruit ... and flowering and shade trees,' Mihevc's announcement read. Well, just the name apparently. In the compromise plan for

the park, the pawpaw trees and serviceberries – tasty fruit trees both – were repurposed as non-food-related flowering and shade trees. The orchard would still be an orchard, but some of the fruit trees had to be demoted through a change in label. As Mihevc's announcement put it, 'They do have small fruits which usually are eaten by the birds before any human gets them.' The message? Those opposed to the community orchard would have nothing to fear, because this garden project would bear fruit and grow food … for the birds. In this one small battle, the fruits of victory tasted rather bitter.

What drove the community's fear and anger in response to the orchard? And why did the proposal to grow food in a public park meet with such reluctance? Sitting in that high-tension meeting, I had the distinct impression that two

cultures were colliding: it was as if convention were on a collision course with possibility – established ways versus new
thinking. Convention dictates that a park playground is made
up of swings and teeter-totters; possibility suggests that kids
can have just as much fun in a grove of fruit trees, finding
imaginative ways to play and, yes, maybe getting cherry-
stained in the process. Convention dictates that food growing
is a private, not public, act, something to be tucked away in
backyards; possibility suggests that placing food production
in the centre of our community's public places is nourishing –
symbolically and literally.

A vocal minority of stain-fearing, community-fruit-phobic
folks in midtown aside, more and more Torontonians are
embracing the food-production potential of our city, much
like citizens did during the world wars and the Depression.
They're tucking tomato plants into ornamental gardens, kale
and corn on boulevards. (Wander the streets of Toronto and
you're guaranteed to see more food plants in front yards than
at any other time in the past two decades; it's still not the
norm, but it's a trend that's growing.) They're sneaking hens
into backyard coops, sharing eggs with neighbours to keep
complaints – and visits from bylaw officers – at bay. (Witness
the current efforts by the City's Environment Office to investigate the possibility of changing the bylaw that disallows poultry in Toronto yards; urban chicken-keeping is now on the
political radar.) They're lining up for plots in community

gardens and even starting their own if necessary. (Toronto now has more community gardens than ever before.) They're organizing organic workshops at libraries and community halls. They're planting food gardens at neighbourhood schools. They're toting squash seeds to guerrilla plantings on abandoned lots. They're gleaning fruit from street trees and growing pawpaws in parks.

In short, more and more people are participating in a public ethic of production that, much like the gardening activity that was commonplace during the world wars and the Depression, has its roots in a response to need. The difference between then and now, though, is the definition of need. In the past, the need being met by wartime gardens was relatively straightforward – access to food was under threat and Victory Gardens were an immediately possible way to supplement the shaky supply. There's little doubt that now, too, many, many people have limited access to fresh, healthy food due to a whole host of economic and social conditions, but the hunger being met head-on by today's community food projects encompasses food access and, also, more. The orchard in Ben Nobleman Park, for example, is about more than fruit. It's about reimagining our city – and our place as citizens within it – as productive and generative.

Here's to growing our city one cabbage, chicken and cherry at a time. Each is a victory in a garden – and a Victory Garden in the much larger battle for a productive, possible place.

The author would like to thank Pleasance Crawford for sharing her extensive research into the history of gardening; Edwinna von Baeyer and Maria Nunes for suggesting many leads; and the archivists at the Canadian War Museum, the National Archives and the City of Toronto Archives for their assistance.

Mary F.
Williamson

For wedding *déjeuners* to *recherché* repasts:
The Webb family bakers, confectioners, caterers and restaurateurs, by appointment to Victorian Toronto

In the nineteenth century, the name of New York's Delmonico clan resonated with epicures around the world. Toronto's Webb family, highly respected bakers, caterers, confectioners and restaurant owners throughout much of Queen Victoria's reign, fancied themselves 'the Delmonico[s] of Canada.' And there is no doubt that, for fashionable Torontonians, the Webbs were the preferred choice for wedding *déjeuner*s, banquets, club dinners, late-night suppers or any kind of *recherché* repast when no expense was spared and the food, service, presentation and decorations had to be the best. It is a measure of the celebrity enjoyed by the Webbs that when a devastating fire gutted their restaurant at 66–68 Yonge Street on January 6, 1895, causing an estimated $1 million in damages, the news was reported in the *New York Times*, the *Chicago Tribune* and the *Los Angeles Times*.

    The Webb family's business began modestly enough in 1842 as a bakery and then confectionery store at the northwest corner of Yonge and Agnes (now Dundas) streets, with Tom Webb, a recent English immigrant, as proprietor. Still a colonial town – it wouldn't become the capital of the new province of the Canadas for another seven years – Toronto was moving through a depression into a period of industrial expansion and frantic immigration. The city's population ballooned from just over 14,000 residents in 1841 to more than 25,000 by 1850, resulting in an increase not only in the number of taverns, but also of bakeshops. These shops supplied the festive cakes, glacé fruits and jellies, trifles and creams, fancy baskets and pyramids, and brandies and liqueurs that were essential to professional middle-class entertaining. In spite of this rise in demand, Tom Webb still faced stiff competition from long-time confectioners Mary Dunlop, Robert Scott and Thomas McConkey.

    Tom Webb retired from the catering business in 1876. However, his son Harry, born in Toronto in 1843, nurtured grand ambitions for the family firm and had already moved the bakeshop/confectionery store into two-storey premises just north of Carlton Street. Here, under the banner 'The Ontario Wedding Cake Manufactory,' he advertised fancy ices, jellies, creams, soups, entrees and his much-ballyhooed wedding and Christmas cakes, plus an ice-cream parlour upstairs. His plum pudding, 'cooked, ready for heating and serving,' was based on

Thomas Webb's Dominion Wedding Cake House in 1842 and 1877.

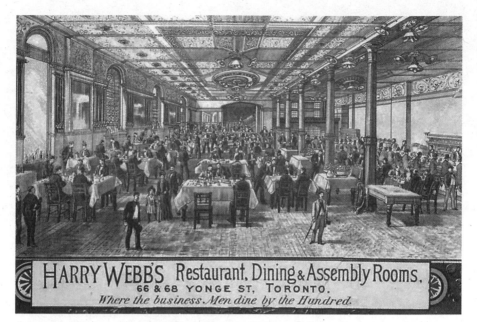

HARRY WEBB'S Restaurant, Dining & Assembly Rooms, 66 & 68 YONGE ST, TORONTO. *Where the business Men dine by the Hundred.*

the recipe – 'expensive, but probably unequalled' – used by Queen Victoria's chef, Charles Elme Francatelli.

Interior of the Webb Restaurant, Saturday Night, *Nov. 18, 1889.*

Soon, a society wedding reception in Ontario was unimaginable without Webb delivering the essential silver, china and glass, epergnes, candelabras and fine linens, the reception food and, inevitably, the company's specialty, a richly ornamented wedding cake. Beginning in 1879, newspaper advertisements informed the public that Harry Webb had been appointed Caterer to His Excellency the Governor-General, the Marquis of Lorne, and his wife, Her Royal Highness the Princess Louise, daughter of Queen Victoria. In 1877 and again in 1885, the Webbs were awarded gold medals in London for their wedding cakes, which they mailed all over the Dominion and even to the United States. Towards the end of the century, Webb's bakeshop invested several thousand dollars in an imported bake oven for Vienna bread and twenty other varieties, and mammoth refrigerators to chill creams, jellies and ices.

In 1889, the famous Harry Webb's Restaurant, a spacious two-storey dining emporium, had been launched at Yonge and Melinda streets. The ground-floor restaurant seated 300 diners, and upstairs, which could be reached by an elevator, private banqueting rooms awaited male guests, while women lunched and relaxed in retiring rooms. Dinners sponsored by fraternal and professional societies, politicians, university

graduating years and military regiments might have taken place in the upper rooms, in a public space such as the Horticultural Gardens, or catered by Webb's staff at their organization's own headquarters.

By the mid-1870s, when Harry Webb began handling the catering for a second generation of Ontario families, Toronto's heady banqueting years had already passed. While Tom Webb was in charge, however, dining *à la Française* or *à la Russe* were endlessly debated distinctions and, routinely, nine or more courses were presented, with several choices per course, each served on richly festooned dining tables. The customary excuse for such occasions was to celebrate a patriotic society's patron saint, to meet fellow members of a fraternal organization or to bring lawyers and politicians together to honour one of their own. But to outsiders – and wives – it must have seemed that the interminable series of toasts, which traditionally progressed until after midnight, and the resultant drunkenness, were the intended goal. It was in February 1856 that Tom Webb provided the dinner in the library of Osgoode Hall that honoured the retirement of Chief Justice James Buchanan Macaulay. Among the guests were 100 barristers, including the Hon. John A. Macdonald, still eleven years away from becoming Canada's first prime minister. The following was the bill of fare offered to guests at the dinner.

Bill of Fare

Soups

Oysters, Mock Turtle, and Ox Tail.

Fish

Codfish, Salmon Trout, Fillets of Whitefish.

Entrees

Oysters and Lobsters, Sweetbread, Vol-au-Vent,
Calf's Tongue and Brains, Veal, Lamb and Mutton Cutlets,
Oyster Patties, Curried Veal, Beef,
Olives, Preserved Tongue,
Fricassée of Chicken Kidneys.

Joints

Roast Beef, Saddle of Mutton, Saddle of Venison,
Fillet of Veal, Boiled Leg of Mutton,
Boiled Round and Brisket of Beef.

Poultry

Turkeys, Boiled and Roast; Chickens, Boiled and Roast.

Game

Prairie Chickens, Partridges and Quail.

Second Course

Custards; Plum and Cabinet Puddings; Gooseberry,
Apple, Cherry, Damson, Currant, and Raspberry Tarts;
Cheese Cakes, Jellies,
Charlotte Russe, Cream.

Dessert

Ratifia Basket, with fruit; Meringues; Rout Cake;
Preserved Ginger, Apricots, Prunes, Figs; Nuts,
Almonds and Raisins; Oranges;
Wine Sponge Cake, Pound Cake;
Vanilla, Lemon, and Water Ices, &c.

The dinner menu was memorable on a number of counts.
Listed are choice dishes of French as well as English origin that
would have been served at upper-class banquets in the old
country, and an Anglo-Indian curry favoured by old India
hands in Canada and England. Curry of veal was always a

popular entree, and the array of spices used in its preparation – among them ginger, allspice, nutmeg, turmeric, coriander and cumin – would have been freshly ground. Chicken, rabbit, duck, lobster, oysters and cod were often curried.

Baskets of ratafia biscuits, the macaroons based on the ratafia liqueur, had been banquet menu fixtures for years. Fruit tarts were likely prepared from preserves put up the previous summer. And Niagara fruit growers, who had perfected the technique of keeping fresh fruits in straw into the early winter months, were proud to delight guests at just these sorts of occasions.

It is sobering to note on the menu the several dishes based on species that would soon all but disappear. The oysters in the soup and patties came up the Erie Canal from New York Harbor, a source that evaporated by about 1910 as a result of the pollution of the oyster beds. The mock turtle soup was made from a calf's head, turtles having been replaced after overfishing decimated the large land turtles that had once swum in the lagoons of Toronto Islands. The prairie chickens that once thrived in the long grass of southwestern Ontario had vanished before the end of the 1800s and today can barely be found on Canada's prairies. Ontario's early settlers fished for salmon trout, whitefish and other freshwater fish such as maskinonge, sturgeon and bass – some of which could weigh nearly five kilograms! – in the rivers and creeks of southern Ontario. However, few species – these ones much lighter in weight – were swimming in the province's rivers at century's end. By the 1880s, salmon trout and whitefish had to be brought in from Georgian Bay, together with much smaller hauls of perch, pike and pickerel.

Another splendid occasion when Harry Webb's culinary skills were called into play occurred on December 28, 1897, when the Earl and Countess of Aberdeen welcomed 2,500 guests to a viceregal fancy dress ball celebrating Queen Victoria's Diamond Jubilee in the Armouries on University Avenue. To provide supper for Toronto's social elite 'in a dainty and comfortable fashion,' the Harry Webb Company was awarded the largest catering contract of its kind. Months of preparation had already prompted frenzied discussions in the newspapers about the elaborate costumes that had to be ordered from tailors and dressmakers, the music, the dance sets, theatrical ballroom decorations and, of course, the refreshments.

Following several rounds of dances, the guests trooped into the supper room to the accompaniment of the orchestra's patriotic airs, where they were greeted by a succession of hot and cold delicacies. Individual menus listed *petits salpicons de venaison* (small pastry cases filled with diced venison in a sauce), *galantine à l'impératrice* (cold chicken stewed and jelled in its own juices), *mayonnaise de volaille* (diced cooked chicken on shredded lettuce, covered with mayonnaise and garnished), roast turkey, tongue in aspic, quails roasted in tomatoes and desserts of Baba à la Parisienne (yeast cake steeped in rum syrup), Charlotte Russe, jellies, a selection of gâteaux, Neapolitan ice creams, petits fours and glacéd fruits and bonbons. The January 27, 1898, edition of *Leslie's Weekly* of New York declared it to be 'the largest and most brilliant function in the history of Canada.'

Despite this social triumph, in the final years of the century the Webb Company had begun to extend its clientele beyond the fashionable society that had been its bread and butter. Its spacious Dining Hall at the Industrial Fair (renamed the Canadian National Exhibition in 1904) was 'catering for the thousands' with 'a really first-class meal at as cheap a rate as anywhere in the city.' And when, on New Year's Eve of 1898, Timothy Eaton treated 2,500 of his employees to dinner on the second floor of his department store at Queen and Yonge streets, ordinary working men and women were able to experience a meal created by the veteran caterer. A lengthy business lunch menu from August 1904, while clearly drawing on locally produced fresh meats, vegetables, cheese and fruits, offered diners the kind of nourishing yet tasty fare they could as easily enjoy at the Walker House or McConkey's, including boiled salmon trout, corned beef and cabbage, prime ribs of beef and lamb's fries followed by fruit pies, ice cream, fancy cakes and fresh fruits with cream. The Webb catering business had evolved from meeting the requirements of the city's elite to becoming 'the favorite restaurant in the business section' and, finally, to serving the general public.

Webb's restaurant closed in 1906 and, after a long illness, Harry Webb died the same year. With Harry gone, the firm carried on selling bread until it was purchased by the Canada Bread Company in 1928. Harry Webb's remains lie in Toronto's Mount Pleasant Cemetery underneath a walnut tree. Each fall the tree casts off the kind of plump nuts that the Webb Company, in its heyday, would have put to good use in its prize-winning confections.

Katarina
Gligorijevic

A town so great they named a drink after it

My love affair with classic cocktails began with a battered old cocktail guide I found in a local thrift shop. The book, a 1962 paperback version of *The Art of Mixing Drinks*, is based on the 1956 *Esquire Drink Book*. The original, which I've since acquired a copy of, is a whimsically illustrated, witty how-to guide on the art of drinking that aims to teach the future consummate host not only how to mix a damn good old-fashioned but also features essays on how to revel in your excesses and, yes, pay for them the morning after.

Drinks in the *Esquire Drink Book* are listed by their main alcoholic ingredient, so it took a while for me and my guinea-pig friends to drink through the various sections before stumbling upon the Toronto in the 'Rye and Bourbon' chapter, nestled between the Thompson (a simple concoction of equal parts whisky and sweet vermouth) and the Virginia Julep (a minty bourbon cocktail that tests the patience by taking over an hour to mix).

Other Canadian cities aren't too well-represented in the *Esquire* guide. Vancouver gets no mentions, unless the Van cocktail (a mixture of gin, vermouth and Grand Marnier) is meant to refer to it, which I somehow doubt, and Montreal has only the Montreal Club Bouncer, a questionable mélange of equal parts gin and absinthe, mixed with cracked ice and sipped slowly. The recipe concludes with the warning that 'the legs are the first to go.'

The Toronto cocktail, unlike the Montreal Club Bouncer, gets no witty commentary, just a basic list of ingredients and simple instructions:

Toronto

> 1 oz simple syrup
>
> 2 oz Fernet Branca
>
> 6 oz rye whiskey
>
> 1 dash Angostura bitters
>
> Stir with large cubes of ice, strain into cocktail glasses.
> Decorate with orange slices.[1]

Essentially, the Toronto is a variation of the old-fashioned, perhaps the very first concoction ever to be called a 'cocktail.' An old-fashioned consists of rye or bourbon, mixed with a bit of sugar or simple syrup (a basic mixture of sugar and water) and topped with a dash or two of Angostura bitters. Add Fernet

1 A six-ounce cocktail might seem a tad stiff, so I should clarify that even though the book doesn't say this, you can get four Torontos of perfectly respectable size out of this recipe. For a single drink, use a quarter of the recommended quantities of rye, Fernet and simple syrup (but don't reduce the amount of Angostura).

Branca to this basic mix and you've got the Toronto – a unique version of the most classic cocktail of all.

So, what makes it a Toronto? The ingredients? I considered the possibility that the Toronto's Canadian connection might have something to do with rye – after all, 'rye' and 'Canadian whisky' are synonymous, or so I thought. As I soon discovered, spelling isn't the only difference between American rye whiskey and Canadian rye whisky. Both are blended, multi-grain liquors, but American rye must be distilled from at least 51 percent rye and has no aging requirements, while the Canadian stuff can legally be called 'rye' with a lower percentage of the grain, but it must be aged for at least three years in small new-oak barrels. I hoped to find some mention of Toronto's history as a distillery town in connection to the Toronto – which is, after all, a whisky cocktail. Alas, there is no reference to a single Gooderham and Worts or Hiram Walker & Sons product (or any brand, for that matter) in any of the guides, and my hopes of a relationship between the Toronto cocktail and the companies that once did business in our historic distillery district were dashed.

Angostura bitters, of course, are a common ingredient in many cocktails. Turns out the fragrant bitter drink was invented by a German doctor who went to Venezuela in the 1820s to fight with Simón Bolivar against the Spanish throne. No Toronto connection there.

This leaves us with the mystery ingredient – the one I had to look up when I first encountered the recipe. Fernet-Branca was invented in Italy in 1845, where it is distilled to this day, though it's most popular in two unlikely places: Argentinians drink over three million cases of Fernet each year (usually mixed with cola), and San Franciscans have the distinction of consuming more Fernet-Branca per capita than any other place in the world. The West Coast devotees drink it straight with a ginger-ale chaser. It's such a craze in San Francisco that a few years ago, Count Niccolo Branca, CEO of the distillery that makes the mysterious elixir, paid the city a visit to meet with some of his biggest buyers. Meanwhile, in Toronto, just trying to find a bar that stocks Fernet-Branca is a Herculean task.

Fernet-Branca is a type of bitter, a thick, dark-brown aromatic spirit usually served as a digestif after meals. It tastes a bit like Jägermeister would if all the sugar were removed. It's aged in oak barrels for at least a year, and boasts a list of over forty ingredients, most of which have never been made public, though the company admits to myrrh, chamomile, cardamom,

aloe, gentian root and plenty of saffron. Other rumoured ingredients have over the years included codeine, quinine, echinacea, ginseng, St. John's wort and even wormwood, so it's little wonder Fernet has been considered a cure-all for everything from menstrual cramps to cholera over the years, and was one of the only alcoholic drinks that remained legal in the U.S. during prohibition.

The scarcity of Fernet-Branca in Toronto's drinking establishments is curious, especially considering the popularity of 'Jäger shots' among the city's partygoers. One might imagine that shots of Fernet could be the grown-up equivalent, but other bitters such as Campari or Amaro are considerably easier to find. Fernet is carried by the LCBO only in select locations – oddly, the Galleria Mall location at Dupont and Dufferin seems to have over forty bottles in stock at any given time (luckily, it's my local branch). Still, nothing in the drink's history explains what it's doing in a cocktail called 'the Toronto'; Fernet-Branca's connection to Canada is essentially non-existent.

The history of the Toronto cocktail is as murky as the Fernet itself. The earliest cocktail guides to include the recipe are *Esquire's Handbook for Hosts* (published in 1949), and in the witty and rakishly written *The Fine Art of Mixing Drinks* by David A. Embury, a classic cocktail tome that first came out in 1948.

While it might be reasonable to deduce that the Toronto was a WWII-era cocktail, invented in the 1940s and first recorded in print towards the end of the decade, very little information exists to prove or disprove the theory. When I inquired about the Toronto cocktail with Robert Hess, a cocktail expert, co-founder of the Museum of the American Cocktail, online-TV-show host and the man who recently wrote the introduction for the reissue of Embury's long-out-of-print classic, he said that while he is familiar with the Toronto cocktail, he could tell me nothing about its origins. Several inquiries with seasoned bartenders, cocktail scholars and drink bloggers yielded the same result: nobody seems to know where the Toronto comes from, though many admit it's pretty good, once you acquire the taste.

In Toronto itself, the Toronto is virtually unknown. An internet search for bars that serve the cocktail dug up the Uva Wine bar in Vancouver's Moda Hotel, and Seattle's classy Zig Zag Café. Some old-fashioned sleuthing – an enthusiastic but not exhaustive tour of Toronto bars – uncovered the sad fact

that nobody in Toronto knows that there is such a thing as *the* Toronto. Or, if they do, they don't have the supplies to make one. In fact, with some swankier exceptions among the hotel bars and high-end cocktail bistros, it's hard enough to find a place that can even make a decent old-fashioned.

What, then, is Torontonian about the Toronto, a drink made with American whiskey, an Italian digestif, Venezuelan bitters and some sugar water? The answer seems obvious: in more ways than one, the Toronto is a perfect potable representation of our city. For a city that used to be called Muddy York, a foggy brown drink seems an appropriate cocktail ambassador. Like our citizens, the ingredients come from all over the world. The waves of complex flavour that arise from the pairing of Fernet and rye can be overwhelming to the palate – it's a densely populated drink, a bit like our quickly expanding, condo-filled town. It's not particularly beautiful to look at – and let's face it, Toronto is no pageant queen. And yet, the concoction results in one of the most complex, unique and interesting flavours in the cocktail world. It's an acquired taste, but once you get to know and understand its rich palate, it inspires fervent devotion.

If our palate for its strange flavours is nurtured and developed, I believe the Toronto has the potential to become the *In the Skin of a Lion* of cocktails – a poignant reminder of the varied histories that make up our city, a beautifully nostalgic yet utterly modern expression of our current diversity and, above all, a challenging and unique symbol of the city – a flavour all our own. The more Torontos I consumed while researching the drink, the more delicious they tasted. Through my cocktail goggles, the city itself took on a new shine, and I became convinced that we should embrace and champion this drinkable representation of our urban persona. If the Manhattan is world-famous and imbued with the classy, cosmopolitan, urbane character of its namesake city, then the Toronto is its homely (but oddly seductive) cousin, existing in relative obscurity, strange tasting and difficult to recommend. And yet there's something strangely alluring about the Toronto. Like our city, the cocktail is a secret knockout – the one who doesn't appear beautiful at first glance, but if you look closely, becomes the hottest babe in the room.

David Alexander **The tofu revolution: Toronto's vegetarians from 1945 to 2009 and beyond**

If I had looked into a crystal ball in 2003 and seen that five years later I'd be executive director of the Toronto Vegetarian Association, I would have had some questions: Should I trust this crystal ball? Is my future set in stone or is this one of those future-that-could-be predictions? And what the heck is a vegetarian association?

In 2003, I wasn't vegetarian, I didn't live in Toronto, and if you had asked me about a vegetarian association, I might have guessed it was a small group of people who shared bad tofu and argued about which vegetable is the most exciting.

In fact, the Toronto Vegetarian Association has been providing information and support for almost seventy years. It boasts more than 1,000 members, hundreds of volunteers and three full-time staff – including me. As for bad tofu, there's no such thing, just bad tofu preparation. And the most exciting vegetable is probably the common onion or perhaps the aubergine … but I digress.

The course of my life changed in 2005 when a persistent friend and farm-animal sympathizer convinced me to see *Peaceable Kingdom*, a film that documents the tragic conditions for animals at factory farms and the folks who take it upon themselves to give shelter to those who've survived abuse, escaped captivity or been left for dead.

My friend was an animal activist, freshly inspired by the TVA's annual vegetarian food fair in Toronto. A few months and many tofus later, I would find myself looking at a job posting and thinking, So what the heck am I getting myself into?

Toronto's vegetarian movement can be traced back to 1945, when a small group of middle-aged, middle-class British immigrants incorporated the Toronto Vegetarian Association. The group was interested in shaking things up in the city. It started by organizing lectures, writing letters to businesses to request vegetarian options and sending soy grits and vegetable oils to war-torn Europe.

The group drew connections between vegetarianism and movements for nuclear disarmament, world peace and ending hunger around the world. They took a holistic approach to health and healing and emphasized Christian, do-unto-others ideals. They started meeting for dinner to share resources and discuss what it would take to build a totally vegetarian society.

This small group of dedicated people would persist in building support for the city's burgeoning vegetarian community through the 1950s, 60s and 70s as their small group became a modest movement.

When Peter McQueen became vegetarian in 1975, there were, he estimates, two or three vegetarian restaurants in Toronto. 'And I knew of one,' he says. 'A Tex-Mex vegetarian restaurant across from the reference library on Yonge Street.'

McQueen was fourteen when he became interested in the environment and started to question the ethics of killing animals for food. He didn't know any vegetarians and had no access to the kind of support that can be found online today, so it wasn't until he came across a book called *Diet for a Small Planet* that he resolved to change his diet.

Within a year, McQueen found the Toronto Vegetarian Association. 'Although no one at the meeting was my age, it was still useful.' In fact, many of the people he met there were in their seventies or eighties.

'By the time I came along there was a need and an interest to revitalize the organization,' recalls McQueen, who would go on to serve as a long-time member of the TVA's board of directors.

McQueen marks the ten years from 1985 to 1995 as a period of change for vegetarians in Toronto. By the end of the 1980s, there was an expansion in the number of veg restaurants and veggie-friendly offerings at other restaurants. Lifelong vegetarian Nimisha Raja started noticing 'things like tofu becoming more widely available instead of having to search for it in the corner of a health food store.' Some of the restaurants didn't last, but the overall effect was an expansion of choice.

And with a new generation of activists, there was an expansion in activities coordinated by the folks at the TVA. In 1984, the association held the city's first major vegetarian event.

Visitors to the TVA's first Vegetarian Information Fair – held at the Board of Education building at 155 College Street – enjoyed exhibits and talks about vegetarianism as well as a day's worth of cooking demonstrations. 'We were looking to put on an event that was more than just a potluck or talk,' recalls McQueen. But, as exciting as the first event was, the organizers thought they could do a better job marketing the fair. The popularity of the cooking demos prompted the idea of using food as the carrot to draw people to the event.

In its second year, visitors to the refashioned, relocated and renamed Vegetarian Food Fair experienced even more

food sampling and cooking demonstrations because of the event's new location at the Kensington Market campus of George Brown College. The result: attendance doubled from 250 to 500, which packed the small space.

Now in search of an even larger venue, the organizers learned that Harbourfront Centre had been looking to initiate a health fair. Harbourfront was pleased to partner with an organization willing to coordinate event programming, so the Vegetarian Food Fair moved there in 1986 and the expanded one-day festival attracted nearly 3,000 people.

The fair now attracts 15,000–20,000 visitors each year, some vegetarian, some just curious, providing information and support about how people can incorporate healthy, plant-based meals into their diets.

The event also features presentations from the hottest cookbook authors, nutrition researchers and activists engaged in promoting alternatives to a troubling system of factory farming that sees animals as commodities and chooses profit over compassion.

'Over the years I've heard from people who became veg because of the Food Fair or came across it and it helped,' says McQueen. 'It also helps to give new businesses a start,' by providing a platform to showcase products, making it easier for businesses to connect with eager new customers.

The Toronto Vegetarian Association – whose membership had grown from about 400 in the 1970s to over 1,000 by the mid-1990s – was charting a different course than other vegetarian groups in North America, who generally limited their efforts to organizing monthly social events. In the next few years, the association launched a directory of vegetarian shops and restaurants. 'As we promoted vegetarianism and the places food was served, more people started to eat at them and the market grew,' McQueen says.

Finding the TVA helped Shing Tong realize her vision of opening a vegetarian restaurant. She recalls that one volunteer, Steve Leckie, was particularly helpful in providing resources and expertise in starting her business. 'It was very reassuring,' she remembers.

She wanted to show people the variety of food that vegetarians can make using simple ingredients. 'Maybe I would help people go vegetarian,' she remembers thinking, 'help people make the transition easier.'

'It took time to build a reputation by word of mouth,' she recalls. Exposure in the Vegetarian Directory and at the Vegetarian Food Fair proved helpful, and Health Haven lasted for ten years at its Etobicoke location. Five years ago, Tong decided to move it downtown to Baldwin Village: 'Our lease was up and there were a lot of requests from downtown customers to move the business.'

In its new location, the restaurant began displaying paintings and photographs by local artists and took on a fitting new moniker: Vegetarian Haven.

Things in Toronto have come a long way for Nimisha Raja since her university days, when her two lunch options were an egg-salad sandwich or a plate of salad.

Raja moved to Toronto from Kenya in May 1970 at the age of seven. Vegetarian from birth, she remembers being 'plunked into the public school system in a homogeneous school,' where she was one of a handful of non-white kids; she and her brother were the only vegetarians. 'I felt like I was dropped here from a different planet. In Kenya, I went to a school that was mostly Hindu, so everyone was vegetarian.'

The new environment was bewildering, but Raja can't recall ever being tempted to try meat. 'Hindus believe in the non-violence principle, ahimsa,' she explains. 'I was raised with that principle at the forefront that we do not need to kill to have food. The non-violence message was so deeply ingrained, I never saw meat as food.'

But in school her vegetarianism became an issue at every turn. Her parents would have to write notes to teachers and pack lunches for school trips. At birthday parties, she would eat ahead of time or, when lucky, be treated to grilled cheese sandwiches. 'Or I would wait until it was cake time,' she recalls.

'In terms of it becoming less alienating, it's only been in the last ten years,' Raja estimates. 'There's been a raising of the veggie consciousness because it permeates our city.' She cites the exponential proliferation of vegetarian and veg-friendly restaurants in Toronto and the availability of alternative products like silken tofu, tempeh and soy milk in the city's mainstream grocery stores.

Raja credits some of this progress to the work of the TVA, which has played a crucial role in supporting these businesses and trying to get the word out. But she also believes that multiculturalism has played a role in Toronto's elevated level

of vegetarian awareness. The wide variety of vegetarian restaurants is testament to that fact – from pure vegetarian Buddhist and Indian eateries to Ethiopian, Thai and Middle Eastern restaurants that feature a variety of vegetarian options.

'These ethnic cuisines have such a wide array of vegetarian choices,' she says. 'It's made being veg in Toronto so much easier than it was when I was growing up.'

City councillor Glenn De Baeremaeker has seen a big change since going veg twenty-five years ago. 'I think my friends saw me as the weird guy at the end of the table who doesn't eat meat,' he recalls. The people of Toronto have become more respectful of vegetarians and vegans in particular.

De Baeremaeker's work on council gives him hope that the city's interest in food issues is growing. 'In the City of Toronto we're talking about local food procurement,' he explains. While the concept has been around for a long time in textbooks and journals, De Baeremaeker explains that it used to seem like a utopian pipe dream. 'Now it's feasible.'

He sees this not only as an example of people's growing awareness about food issues, but also as a positive development for vegetarians. Like others, De Baeremaeker sees a natural synergy between vegetarian eating, urban agriculture and local farmers' markets. Eating local in Toronto is an automatic shift towards plant-based foods.

Other forces have also helped make the city a hotbed for herbivores.

By the time Lauren Corman came to Toronto in 1999, the Annual Vegetarian Food Fair was North America's largest free vegetarian festival, and had grown to include music, world-class speakers and way more delicious food. But while the fair was larger than anything going on in Winnipeg, the community she encountered in Toronto didn't seem connected to other social movements.

She began hosting the *Animal Voices* radio program on CIUT several years ago. One of her main goals for the show was 'to put the animal-rights movement and the vegetarian, vegan movements into conversation with other social and environmental movements.'

Though the show has grown to be international in its scope and audience, *Animal Voices* often features local activists, chefs and business owners. Episodes have featured local cookbook author Siu Moffat's fair-trade vegan truffles

and socially conscious animal-friendly stores like Panacea and Global Aware.

Animal Voices also has a variety of local flavour to report on. The City of Toronto is now home to seventy-seven vegetarian restaurants and North America's largest vegetarian food fair, and each year sees new annual cook-offs, concerts and other public events.

'Food seems to be the one thing that does bring people together,' says Steve Fish, organizer of the annual Vegan Chili Cook-Off and owner of Left Feet, a sweatshop-free vegan footwear store. 'Everything else seems to divide people.'

The Chili Cook-Off, which happens during Toronto's chilly mid-winter, draws entries from restaurants, businesses and self-confessed amateurs. With more than twenty entries in 2009, there's a chili for everyone from chocolate lovers to spice demons. Plus, keeping in the spirit of connecting vegetarianism to other social causes, money raised at this event supports Toronto's Out of the Cold program.

Chili isn't the only thing pitting Toronto's culinary amateurs against each other. With the support of the TVA, an annual event called the Totally Fabulous Vegan Bake-Off has been established to disprove the occasionally accurate assessment of vegan baking as bland, dry and flavourless.

'I felt like World Vegetarian Day called for a party that would demonstrate how wonderful it is to be living in a way that really celebrates and values life,' explains Lisa Pitman, who organized the first Vegan Bake-Off in 2008. 'Most big parties in our culture revolve around food.'

For Pitman, it's also important to counter the negative stereotypes. 'Sometimes vegans and vegetarians are portrayed in the media as being dour and cantankerous,' she says. 'Animal abuse, planetary destruction and lifestyle-related diseases are all very serious issues.' The bake-off is an opportunity to have some fun.

For Pitman, who has lived in Calgary and Guelph, the Toronto movement stands out for its commitment to outreach and support of volunteers. 'People seem to really celebrate vegetarianism here in a way I haven't experienced before,' she says. 'I think that's a good sign that there is more growth on the horizon.'

Having spent three years working with activists, business owners, social conveners and passionate volunteers, I've learned that Toronto's vegetarian community is more than just a small group of folks writing letters and meeting for dinner.

This is a full-fledged movement, on course to challenge the entire city to reconsider how we think about our food.

These days, Nimisha Raja runs Evolving Appetites, which she founded 'as a service to help people adopt a healthier lifestyle,' through talks on healthy eating, cooking classes and an e-newsletter.

She would like to see Toronto follow Chicago's example: that city's health commissioner decided to go vegetarian for a month and challenged members of the public to join him – particularly those from his own African-American community, which suffers from higher rates of heart disease and type-2 diabetes. 'I'm inspired by what Gandhi said: lead by example and become the change you want to see,' Raja says.

Activists want to see vegetarianism continue to permeate the City of Toronto. Shing Tong envisions a Veggietown in the style of Chinatown or Little Italy. 'I would like to make the whole street vegetarian,' she declares. In fact, this is the sort of hub that has popped up around the headquarters of PETA in Norfolk, Virginia.

Business owner Steve Fish wants to see more outreach from those already committed to veg living. 'The next big challenge is getting outside of that group and reaching out to the masses,' he says. 'And somehow have some fun doing it.' He sees an opportunity for activists to work with artists, musicians and culinary artists to put on 'more parties,' as he says.

Tong and Fish both feel veg activists need to think bigger. My conversations with both led in the same direction: a seven-day, multi-venue street festival in the style of Toronto's successful Pride celebrations. Tong believes this is the kind of event that will help advocacy and build Toronto's international reputation as a place to invest in vegetarian businesses.

Lisa Pitman reports that she is starting to see more local events pop up, but she wants to fill up the calendar with bake-offs, cook-offs, festivals and concerts. 'Not everyone would see a vegan bake-off as activism,' she admits. 'But if we don't take time to have fun in a park on a fall afternoon then we won't have the energy to tackle life's bigger challenges.'

Lauren Corman sees an opportunity as the City of Toronto changes its archaic street-vending bylaws, which, until recently, allowed street vendors to sell only hot-dog-shaped products. Reform would open this market up for vegetarian foods like samosas, falafels and burritos.

Peter McQueen wants to see veggie foods and resources become more broadly available across the city. With the right

resources, it's easy for someone living downtown to find specialty tofu, fresh fruits and vegetables and even restaurants that specialize in vegetarian foods. McQueen worries about neighbourhoods where finding any healthy food options is a daily struggle. He's hopeful for new initiatives like the Ontario Vegetarian Food Bank, which serves communities in Scarborough and North York.

Today, when I look into my crystal ball, I see boundless potential. A growing group of activists and business owners, bloggers and social conveners, volunteers and professionals all working to promote vegetarianism in Toronto. People from a multitude of cultures and motivations replacing the meat in their diet with delicious plant-based foods on a part- or fulltime basis. A city on the verge of what can only be described as a cultural Vegaissance.

I see monthly lectures geared to diehards, non-veggies and new vegetarians. People encouraging restaurants to add more and more vegetarian and vegan options. Veggielicious celebrations at dozens of restaurants and Vegan Drinks bringing activists together to connect and grow together.

I see a vegetarian week that rivals the Taste of Danforth in Toronto's imagination. An international veggie laureate being named each year to promote the many joys and benefits of veg living. A Veggie Village where foodies can go for healthy, eco-friendly meals, and a vegetarian resource centre with a kitchen for cooking classes, a bookstore for consumers and an activist headquarters for students.

I see compassion for farm animals as a cause taken up by Toronto's members of parliament. Omnivores cutting out meat one day of each week (then two, then three, then four) at the urging of environmentalists and public health authorities.

I see a vegetarian mayor, not preaching to the masses, but living as a shining example that vegetarians are interested in building a just and thriving city capable of feeding all of its citizens in a sustainable and healthy manner.

But more than anything else, what I see right now is a city on the verge of breakthrough, communities waiting to be engaged in the important project of building a healthier, greener, more compassionate city, and a public that's ready to rethink the way we eat.

Ilona Burkot,
Laura Burr &
Jane Lac

Putting a price tag on healthy eating in Toronto

Ripened fruit, richly coloured vegetables, dark loaves of bread pebbled with seeds and grains, creamy dairy products and delicate cuts of fish: this is what we're told healthy eating looks like. We're supposed to eat vegetables, drink milk, grill lean meats and lightly spread non-hydrogenated margarine on whole-grain toast. But it's not cheap. For many families, a diet of this nutrient-dense, healthy food is simply too expensive.

There are many obstacles to getting nutritious foods into a home, including access to healthy groceries, transportation, motivation to eat well and knowledge about what to buy and how to prepare it. For example, in busy Toronto life, you may know which foods are 'good for you,' but getting stuck on the TTC leaves you little time to shop and cook at home, making it difficult to eat well on a daily basis. And even if all these barriers can be overcome, the cost of healthy food can still discourage or prevent families from achieving a balanced diet full of the nutrients important for life-long health.

It's not a surprise that cost determines what foods find their way onto our plates and, consequently, affect our health. For that reason, each year Toronto Public Health calculates and publishes the *Cost of the Nutritious Food Basket*. The NFB tells us how much it costs for the average person or family to purchase food staples at a grocery store in Toronto. It is based on the cost of sixty-six food items from surveys and research that show what Torontonians frequently eat – convenience food items, such as premade sauces, frozen dinners, restaurant, takeout and fast foods are not included.

So, what is the magic number?

For 2008, the average cost of healthy food for a family of four was $136.28 per week. For you, this number may seem high or low, but how does it compare to other urban cities? You decide …

> Montreal: $155.00 per week
> Ottawa: $166.00 per week
> Winnipeg: $171.00 per week
> Edmonton: $154.85 per week
> Halifax: $149.73 per week

Toronto food costs look favourable against other cities, though a direct comparison is hard without considering other factors such as inflation, housing, transportation and other costs of living.

The current NFB, however, is not based on healthy eating recommendations laid out in (Eating Well With) Canada's Food Guide (CFG). Since 1942, Canadian families and health professionals have used the food guide as a resource to guide nutritious food choices. But little attention has been given to what it would actually cost a family to meet these recommendations.

In January 2008, a group of registered dietitians determined the cost associated with eating according to CFG in Toronto. A seven-day plan of meals for a family of two parents and two children was designed and then reviewed by eight dietitians. Every day, each family member had to eat the recommended number of servings from each food group. Following CFG, grain products chosen were mainly whole grain, lower-fat foods were used, vegetables and fruits of all colours were included, and tofu, lentils and beans were alternative protein sources. Convenience and preparation time were considered when designing the menu; for example, work-intensive breakfast items were planned for the weekend, and dinner leftovers were used for lunches the following day. Meals could be prepared by an individual with modest food-preparation skills and would require only basic kitchen equipment and appliances.

The meal plan consisted of a variety of meals and snacks, such as whole-wheat pancakes, tofu-vegetable stir-fry, whole-wheat muffins, berry smoothies, hummus with pita bread, whole fresh fruit and vegetables, and fish fingers. Items in this family's grocery cart included: twenty apples, four pears, one bunch of spinach, one cucumber, two heads of romaine lettuce, one jar of pasta sauce, one loaf of whole-wheat bread, a 500-gram package of whole-wheat pasta, ten litres of 1% milk, one can of chickpeas, 400 grams of lean ground beef, a dozen eggs and two cans of tuna. After the nutritious meals were planned, the total amount of food required for the week was determined and the cost was assessed by averaging prices from a variety of stores in Toronto.

The price tag on the CFG grocery cart for a family of four was $186.02 for one week – $49.74 more than the 2008 NFB price of $136.28. For a family of four earning the median household income in the Greater Toronto Area of $6,175 per month, this translates into 12 percent of their monthly income.

For many families, though, this is out of reach. To follow the CFG meal plan, a family of four earning minimum wage ($8.75 per hour[1] for forty hours per week, $1,400 per month) would spend a whopping 37 percent of their monthly income

1 Minimum wage in 2009 is $9.50, but it was $8.75 in 2008, when the NFB was calculated. The NFB for 2009 was not yet available at the time of publication.

on healthy foods, while a family of four receiving Ontario Works and associated benefits would spend 45 percent of their monthly income. The percentage of income spent on food is similar if food costs are calculated using NFB: a minimum-wage-earning family of four and one receiving Ontario Works would spend 27 and 33 percent of household income, respectively.[2] This percentage of monthly income is shocking – sufficient volumes of nutritious foods are clearly unaffordable for some families.

2 Toronto Public Health. Board of Health Report. *The Cost of the Nutritious Food Basket in Toronto.* 2008.

We took a look at the average household income of all Toronto neighbourhoods and then calculated the percentage of income needed to purchase food to follow the CFG meal plan. Families across the city would need to shell out anywhere from 1.5 percent to a striking 25.3 percent of household income to achieve healthy eating recommendations. In centrally located areas in the GTA such as Regent Park (72), North St. James Town (74), Thorncliffe Park (55), Flemingdon Park (44), Little Portugal (84), South Parkdale (85), Crescent Town (61) and Oakridge (121), the portion of income necessary to purchase healthy food is on average 19.8 percent. There are additional clusters of communities outside the central core where a mean of 16.4 percent of income would have to be used for healthy food items.

Evidently, many families within the GTA would need to use a considerable portion of their income to eat according to CFG. This is unreasonable – even impossible – as it would mean sacrificing other necessities like housing, water, electricity, transportation and clothing, which eat up a large amount of household income. Typically, only the leftover funds are spent on food, where it is possible to stretch a dollar and buy low-budget items, such as boxed macaroni and canned soups. But while these will fill you up, they will leave you with a nutritionally deficient diet.

Over fourteen years ago, the Toronto Food Policy Council stated, 'The Canadian health care system, although committed to optimal nutrition in concept, has failed to invest adequately in the provision of a nourishing affordable diet as a health promotion measure.'[3] Individuals deprived of a wholesome diet – often because of its prohibitive cost – are much more prone to poor perinatal outcomes, failure to achieve full developmental and growth potential, and chronic diseases including osteoporosis, heart disease, hypertension and Type 2 diabetes. Making healthy foods more accessible would help prevent many chronic diseases, improving the health of

3 David McKeown, *Food Security: Implications for Early Years Populations.* Toronto Public Health, 2006, p. 33.

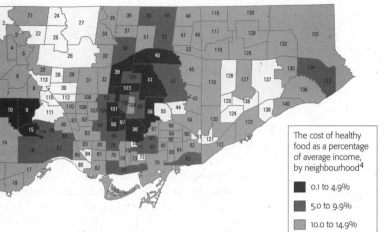

The cost of healthy food as a percentage of average income, by neighbourhood[4]

- ■ 0.1 to 4.9%
- ■ 5.0 to 9.9%
- ■ 10.0 to 14.9%
- □ over 15%

1 West Humber-Clairville
2 Mount Olive-Silverstone-Jamestown
3 Thistletown-Beaumond Heights
4 Rexdale-Kipling
5 Elms-Old Rexdale
6 Kingsview Village-The Westway
7 Willowridge-Martingrove-Richview
8 Humber Heights-Westmount
9 Edenbridge-Humber Valley
10 Princess-Rosethorn
11 Eringate-Centennial-West Deane
12 Markland Wood
13 Etobicoke West Mall
14 Islington-City Centre West
15 Kingsway South
16 Stonegate-Queensway
17 Mimico
18 New Toronto
19 Long Branch
20 Alderwood
21 Humber Summit
22 Humbermede
23 Pelmo Park-Humberlea
24 Black Creek
25 Glenfield-Jane Heights
26 Downsview-Roding-CFB
27 York University Heights
28 Rustic
29 Maple Leaf
30 Brookhaven-Amesbury
31 Yorkdale-Glen Park
32 Englemount-Lawrence
33 Clanton Park

34 Bathurst Manor
35 Westminster-Branson
36 Newtonbrook West
37 Willowdale West
38 Lansing-Westgate
39 Bedford Park-Nortown
40 St. Andrew-Windfields
41 Bridle Path-Sunnybrook-York Mills
42 Banbury-Don Mills
43 Victoria Village
44 Flemingdon Park
45 Parkwoods-Donalda
46 Pleasant View
47 Don Valley Village
48 Hillcrest Village
49 Bayview Woods-Steeles
50 Newtonbrook East
51 Willowdale East
52 Bayview Village
53 Henry Farm
54 O'Connor-Parkview
55 Thorncliffe Park
56 Leaside-Bennington
57 Broadview North
58 Old East York
59 Danforth Village - East York
60 Woodbine-Lumsden
61 Crescent Town
62 East End-Danforth
63 The Beaches
64 Woodbine Corridor
65 Greenwood-Coxwell
66 Danforth Village-Toronto
67 Playter Estates-Danforth
68 North Riverdale
69 Blake-Jones
70 South Riverdale

71 Cabbagetown-South St. James Town
72 Regent Park
73 Moss Park
74 North St. James Town
75 Church-Yonge Corridor
76 Bay Street Corridor
77 Waterfront Communities-The Island
78 Kensington-Chinatown
79 University
80 Palmerston-Little Italy
81 Trinity-Bellwoods
82 Niagara
83 Dufferin Grove
84 Little Portugal
85 South Parkdale
86 Roncesvalles
87 High Park-Swansea
88 High Park North
89 Runnymede-Bloor West Village
90 Junction Area
91 Weston-Pellam Park
92 Corso Italia-Davenport
93 Dovercourt-Wallace Emerson-Junction
94 Wychwood
95 Annex
96 Casa Loma
97 Yonge-St.Clair
98 Rosedale-Moore Park
99 Mount Pleasant East
100 Yonge-Eglinton
101 Forest Hill South
102 Forest Hill North
103 Lawrence Park South
104 Mount Pleasant West
105 Lawrence Park North

106 Humewood-Cedarvale
107 Oakwood-Vaughan
108 Briar Hill-Belgravia
109 Caledonia-Fairbank
110 Keelesdale-Eglinton West
111 Rockcliffe-Smythe
112 Beechborough-Greenbrook
113 Weston
114 Lambton Baby Point
115 Mount Dennis
116 Steeles
117 L'Amoreaux
118 Tam O'Shanter-Sullivan
119 Wexford/Maryvale
120 Clairlea-Birchmount
121 Oakridge
122 Birchcliffe-Cliffside
123 Cliffcrest
124 Kennedy Park
125 Ionview
126 Dorset Park
127 Bendale
128 Agincourt South-Malvern West
129 Agincourt North
130 Milliken
131 Rouge
132 Malvern
133 Centennial Scarborough
134 Highland Creek
135 Morningside
136 West Hill
137 Woburn
138 Eglinton East
139 Scarborough Village
140 Guildwood

4 Map and community information downloaded on March 14, 2009, from: www.toronto.ca/ demographics/profiles_map_and_index.htm

Torontonians and reducing strain on an overburdened health-care system.

The purpose of putting a price tag on healthy eating is to draw attention to the fact that many Toronto families do not have $186.02 per week ($9,673.04 per year) to buy 190 servings of fruits and vegetables, 172 servings of grain products, seventy servings of milk products and fifty-six servings of meat and alternatives per week. Every year the NFB brings attention to how poverty affects health. In 2008 it stated explicitly that 'The absence of effective action to correct this situation leaves the clear implication that malnutrition and poor health are acceptable consequences of official government policy.'[5]

5 The Cost of the Nutritious Food Basket in Toronto.

It is a long and arduous road to change government policy and achieve buy-in from stakeholders. There are ubiquitous media reports and pervasive talk around buying local and organic, and about artisanal cheeses, breads, preserves and a multitude of other foodstuffs. Yet a growing number of our fellow citizens lack the resources and, above all, money, to buy basic healthy food – artisanal or not!

As practicing dietitians, we encounter many families who have difficulty obtaining sufficient healthy food to support wellness, ameliorate nutrition-related problems and prevent disease. For these households, policy changes and programs may be too few, too far away or perhaps out of reach. And so we use our expertise, personal experience and passion to offer families practical and applicable strategies to overcome food prices (even if only by a few cents) and come closer to achieving a healthy diet. Here we share these with you:

1. Buy in season: strawberries in the summer and squash in the winter.
2. Look for store specials and clip coupons. Many grocery stores stash booklets of coupons among their shelves: stock up, it's free money!
3. Prepare foods at home whenever possible. Look at the difference between a tuna sandwich with tomato made at home and one from a takeout restaurant:

	Homemade	Takeout
Time	8 min prep time	10 min wait time
Cost	$1.70	$5.17
Calories	253	530
Fat	6 grams	30 grams
Sat. fat/ Trans fat	1 gram/0 grams	7 grams/0.5 grams

Healthy meal and snack ideas for the whole family

	Monday	Tuesday	Wednesday	Thursday	Friday	Saturday	Sunday
Breakfast	Bran flakes Milk Banana	Oatmeal Applesauce Milk	Bagel with margarine Fruit and yogurt smoothie	Whole-wheat toast Peanut butter Juice	Whole-wheat bread Scrambled egg Orange Milk	Whole-wheat pancakes Low-fat yogurt Grapefruit sections Milk	English muffin with cheese Egg Canned peach slices
Snack	Whole-grain muffin Pear	Banana Milk	Whole-grain muffin Orange	Low-fat yogurt Clementines	Apple	Grapes	Banana
Lunch	Bean and vegetable soup Whole-wheat crackers Carrot sticks Milk	Tuna-salad sandwich on whole wheat	Leftover stir-fry Whole-wheat tortilla	Three-bean salad Whole-wheat pita Milk	Leftover pasta with tomato meat sauce	Dal Brown rice Broccoli Canned pear slices Milk	Grilled cheese sandwich Garden salad
Snack	Apple	Whole-wheat crackers	Apple Peanut butter	Banana	Kiwi fruit	Carrot and celery sticks	Hummus Whole-wheat pita Carrot sticks, milk
Dinner	Oven-baked tilapia Brown rice pilaf Garden salad	Vegetable and tofu stir-fry Whole-wheat pasta	Vegetarian bean chili Whole-wheat bread Garden salad Milk	Whole-wheat pasta Tomato meat sauce Broccoli Corn	Homemade fish fingers Sweet potato Peas	Grilled lemon chicken Whole-wheat pasta Corn and peas	Chicken Tikka Masala Naan Low-fat pudding
Snack	Raisins	Fruit and almond crisp Low-fat vanilla yogurt	Tomato salad Cheddar cheese cubes	Chocolate-chip banana bread Apple Milk	Toasted whole-wheat pita with cheese	Almonds (unsalted)	Kiwi fruit

4. Make your own frozen dinners: prepare large portions and freeze for another day.
5. Grow your own: look into community gardens or plant vegetables and herbs on your balcony or in the backyard.
6. Buy in bulk when possible. Share a bushel of tomatoes with friends or neighbours!
7. Look into community programs near your neighbourhood that teach cooking skills and how to make healthy meals from simple ingredients. Seek out free recipe booklets at grocery stores and tap into TV programs that showcase easy-to-prepare recipes.
8. For cheaper protein sources, try meat alternatives such as beans, lentils, chickpeas, tofu and eggs.
9. Can it: canned or frozen fruits and veggies can be cheaper, especially during off-season.
10. Buy cheaper cuts of meat: when prepared well, these can be just as delicious as tenderloin.
11. Organic foods are not necessarily healthier and are much pricier.
12. Avoid prepackaged and processed foods. While they might be quicker, they will drain dollars from your bank account.
13. Share cooking skills and recipe ideas among friends and family.
14. The outside perimeter of the grocery store is the best place to start: it's where you'll find whole fresh fruits and vegetables, meats, dairy and whole grains and will help you avoid prepackaged foods.
15. Although preparing meals from scratch takes time, use it as time to spend with your family and to pass on cooking skills and recipes to the next generation of healthy eaters.
16. Plan meals ahead. Take time on the weekend to chop up vegetables for the week.
17. Save your change: make your own coffee or tea at home or at work. Just one large coffee a day adds up to over $550 a year for one person! The money you save can go towards meals.

Though we have focused on the effects of food costs on health and nutrition, this exercise would be incomplete without bringing awareness to other, equally important, facets of

eating that are affected by rising grocery bills. Food plays an important social and cultural role in all of our lives. All three of us have fond memories that centre on food and eating with family and friends: Thanksgiving dinner with a perfectly roasted turkey, birthday parties with decadent desserts, tables laden with home-cooked dishes at family barbecues and everyday gatherings at the kitchen table all elicit warmth, comfort and togetherness. In addition to bringing family and friends together and marking important social occasions, food is also an integral part of our cultures and heritage. Today, the cost and availability of cooking ingredients can make it challenging for families to maintain time-honoured and culturally vital, food-centred practices. For some families, putting food on the table is not pleasurable but a cause of stress and worry.

Food and eating should be nourishing for both body and soul. Over time, however, compromised access to good food affects not only our physical health but also our mental, emotional, cultural and spiritual well-being.

There is no simple solution to reducing food prices and making healthy eating more affordable. It is our hope that renewed interest in food affordability and recent advocacy by health organizations will focus attention on this increasingly important issue in Toronto.

Joshna
Maharaj **Cooking for a change: The role of chefs in
grassroots and global communities**

In film, television, print and web media, and in conversations
around the table, food has increasingly filled our cultural
space over the last few years. From the rise of celebrity chefs
and their restaurants to school lunch programs and contamination incidents on farms and in factories, people are talking
about food and making important personal connections. Now
is the time to embrace new and more sustainable ideas about
growing, cooking and eating food. The well-being of our
planet, our health and our economy are at stake, and we all
have some responsibility to act. During my time as the chef at
the Stop Community Food Centre, I've discovered that much
of what we think is new is actually a return to the way things
once were, a reconnection to abandoned tradition. While in
many households the home kitchen is no longer the primary
source of nutrition, we still intuitively understand the need
to cook and eat at home.

But what about outside the home? Who are the people who
move this domestic tradition into a very public, social context?
They are cooks and chefs, and they work in restaurants, cafés,
hospitals, schools, catering kitchens, community centres,
hotels and street carts all over this city. You can identify them by
distinguishing features including tired, bloodshot eyes, scarred
forearms and a ceaseless willingness to talk about food.

As a chef, I'm constantly thinking about how I connect
with the people I feed, and how that relationship changes over
time. We understand the roles of doctors, bankers, engineers,
bus drivers, police officers and business people in keeping our
city functioning, but we sometimes neglect the role of the
people who keep our city fed and nourished. The programming
at the Stop attempts to invest in communities both within and
beyond the walls of the program space. My work as a chef in
this context has challenged me to think about how I fit into our
community, and the role I can play in our mandate to connect
people more securely to good, healthy food.

Researching the role and tradition of the chef throughout
history, I discovered that while there are countless volumes of
work about *how* to be a chef, very little has been written about
what it means to be a chef, and the relationship chefs have
with the people they cook for. Here's what I think: on a very
basic level, chefs rely on community. We need hungry people

to feed, and can be considered providers of nutrition and pleasure. On a more complex level, chefs are also social and cultural communicators who can influence social, style, cultural and market trends, all through buying, cooking and serving food.

Every human needs to eat. Food is one of our top collective priorities, our strongest common denominator. It is therefore irrefutably political. In his book *A History of Cooks and Cooking*, Michael Symons writes that 'food is used to uphold and teach ideologies that reinforce the existing social order.' What's most exciting about this statement is that, if chefs, through food, have the power to engage with the existing social order, we also have the power to change it.

Within the confines of their restaurants, chefs can engage with politics in how we write our menus, who we purchase our raw ingredients from and how we treat our staff. The untapped opportunity lies in the possibilities that exist outside our restaurants, where chefs can be leaders, teachers and activists. The tradition of maintaining distance from the world, which once ensured a chef's status, now renders us out of touch with our community. As food issues become more critical, chefs have an obligation to get connected to their communities, and to lead and advocate on behalf of good food.

Chefs are natural allies of food security because, in one way or another, we all work in the service of food. The same passionate fervour that inspires beautiful food should also render lack of access to that food unacceptable, and foster an understanding that feeding someone is about meeting a very basic human need first, and turning a profit second. Recently, chefs have enjoyed unprecedented celebrity at local, national and global levels. Through cookbooks, television shows, blogs and customized cookware, we get into people's homes and participate in their lives in an important way. And so many people visit our restaurants and use our recipes for their celebrations. They ask our advice and debate and engage with us – the professionals. We build empires, write books and get a round of applause for adding garlic or pork fat to a dish, but very few of us actually talk about the real politics of food. With looming environmental and economic crises, a rise in poverty in the developed world and a host of other social and political challenges, our food supply has never been more threatened. Why don't we try to nurture local food cultures and economies with our work? Our celebrity can inspire others to do the same, and that's when change happens.

Chefs in Toronto, in particular, have a unique opportunity to advocate for healthy, sustainable food. Older cities like New York, San Francisco, Paris and London are lauded as the homes of great food traditions, but there is something distinct and compelling about the youthful diversity of Toronto's food scene. Whether it's a noodle soup in Chinatown, early-morning croissants in Leslieville or a marathon tasting menu on King Street, Toronto has confirmed itself as a source of authentic flavour and culinary mastery. And this style is not exclusively rooted in the French tradition; it embraces the many other ways that people on this planet approach cooking and flavour. Chefs here make dishes from one part of the world with flavours from another, somehow finding harmony on the plate. And we serve this wide range of food to an equally diverse community. It is on this platform of reputation, celebrity and cultural awareness that we can be a voice for social change.

At the Stop, I've witnessed the transformation that can happen in a non-profit kitchen with a trained chef at the helm. My elevated food skills, the result of professional training and general nerdiness, enable us to do better things with the humble ingredients we have, bringing pleasure and wholesome eating into what is often a bleak food experience. We've been able to eliminate all processed and packaged food from our menus, right down to the vinaigrettes for our salads, which are now all made in-house by volunteers. In our community kitchens program, I've witnessed the excitement that grows in participants when they learn to cook something they love to eat, or reconstruct something they've eaten in a restaurant. I've also seen the joy and discovery of new Canadians learning to cook with ingredients they didn't have access to in their home countries. Sharing my food skills has been one of the most rewarding parts of the job – it has enabled me to go beyond offering a plate of food to building capacity in our community and getting people excited about food and cooking. I've noticed a lift in some community members' sense of themselves as a result of their experiences in the kitchen. These newly acquired kitchen skills have helped many participants feel empowered and equipped to feed themselves and their families, even on minimal or non-existent budgets. Having a trained chef in our grassroots kitchen sends a clear message that well-prepared, delicious food is for everyone, not just those who can afford it.

One of the most powerful ways that chefs can effect change is in how we source our raw ingredients. A conscious

decision to support local farmers goes a great distance to stimulate local economies while getting better quality food onto more tables in homes and restaurants. While our food budget is limited at the Stop, we use the purchasing power we do have conscientiously and in support of a more sustainable food system. In our quest to build and strengthen communities, embracing farmers is essential. We support a vision of a local food system that is truly accessible to everyone, and making direct connections with producers is an important step in that effort. By offering community members local, seasonal fresh food, we help farmers support their farms and families. For our community of urban dwellers, having a connection to farms outside the city is a much more authentic way to live, reminding us of the reality of our interdependence.

Frugality and the efficient use of ingredients are guiding values in most kitchens, for economic reasons and also out of respect for the food itself. Learning to adapt recipes so they meet the Stop's philosophy that food should be healthy, affordable and delicious has been amazingly rewarding. On top of the food we source from local providers, there's a constant stream of surprise donations at the Stop, plus the continuous delight of produce from our own garden. This has led to experimentation and creativity in the kitchen, marked, thankfully, by more triumphs than disasters. These experiments have allowed us to put our twist on many classic recipes: using mashed butternut squash to top a shepherd's pie instead of potatoes, for example, or a bumper crop of zucchini from our garden as the noodles for a lasagna. One Saturday, we received a large donation of smoked fish from one of our market vendors, sending me poring through cookbooks to create a recipe for our own smoked fish pie, which was a huge hit with community members. Holding our food to this healthy, affordable and delicious standard while still reflecting the diversity of our community has opened the door for us to develop our own style and culture of cooking.

I don't suppose this sounds much different from the creativity and improvisation found in any professional kitchen, but for a non-profit community food organization, it's a pioneering effort. This was not something I anticipated when I started working at the Stop; it was amazing to discover that I could still legitimately grow my skills as a chef and sustain my passion for food in that very different kitchen context.

One of the most important elements of working for change is looking ahead to what we will pass on to future generations. With the same spirit with which we embrace the kids in the Stop's kitchens and gardens, I think about students in cooking school who are still forming their understanding of food and cooking. One way to engage with the idea of chefs as agents of social change is to include this message in chef-school curriculum. Alongside knife skills, foundations of flavour and food costing and theory, we should also introduce classes that address sustainability, making farm connections and the responsibility chefs have to their community.

Currently, students in the Italian program at the George Brown Chef School have the option of taking a Slow Food course, which introduces them to the history and principles of Slow Food, an international organization working to promote a more sustainable food system while nurturing traditional wisdom in kitchens and on farms. This is an important first step in a larger effort required to rethink how we train chefs. There is honour and responsibility in working in a kitchen, and when young chefs graduate from chef school, they need the tools and awareness to uphold this standard in a more holistic way.

One of the things I've learned in my young career as a chef is that it's amazing how little people really think about food until you inspire them. As professional cooks, we can be that inspiration. To my colleagues in kitchens around this city: I urge you to think about the political and social impact of your work and your food. Think about how people are eating when they're not sitting at your table. In the same way your community supports your restaurant, your restaurant can support your community by creating space for discussion.

What can you do? Take a stand, familiarize yourself with the issues and have an informed opinion. Make pamphlets and literature available to your diners, collect signatures on petitions, hold a town-hall-style discussion on local food issues or even offer up your restaurant as a pickup location for Foodshare's Good Food Box. Plant a kitchen garden or host a preserving workshop. Treat your staff well and manage them with care. Take a group of kids to a farmers' market, then cook something together. Get connected with community organizations and support their programs.

Food is sacred and, as chefs, we are custodians of this important cultural tradition. I realize these big ideas will only add to your long hours in the kitchen, and are perhaps only

indirectly tied to your bottom line, but good food needs a champion, and it makes sense that chefs answer this call. As people start talking, learning and sharing ideas, momentum will grow, and our restaurants will become hubs of grassroots food excitement. The city will buzz and a thriving, engaged food culture will emerge. Let's start a conversation about food, through our menus and our community connections. The rewards of this relationship move both ways.

In my work, the most touching feedback I receive is when someone tells me they've tried one of my recipes, it turned out well and they're excited to try more. As chefs in this social, economic and environmental climate, we can no longer think of our work as simply cooking and selling food. It's one thing to see a community group rally at Queen's Park and call for a better standard of living for low-income people, but just imagine the impact of a community of chefs dressed in their whites standing beside that community group, pots and pans in hand, echoing that call for change.

Now, more than ever, chefs must work together to offer people a more balanced and dynamic way to engage with food. The kind of real change we're looking for will require lots of energy to achieve, and while it won't happen overnight, we are all surely worth the effort.

Jamie
Bradburn

Not loafing around: Bread in Toronto

E DIFFERENCE IN STRENGTH.

GOOD BREAD

tween Good and Poor Bread

ery great. The size of a loaf don't count,
the amount of nourishment it contains
. Our bread is made from the finest west-
flour and is baked in such a way as to
in all its most nutritious elements.

he Tait, Bredin Co.
(LIMITED).   y246
744-746 YONGE STREET.
elephone 3133.

The Evening Telegram,
Feb. 2, 1900.

1 Charles Davies, *Bread Men*
(Toronto, Key Porter Books,
1987), pp. 21–22.

Bread lovers have it good in Toronto. From the wave of European-inspired artisan loaves that followed the success of ACE Bakery in the 1990s to the staple breads of each culture in the city, Torontonians can sample a wide range of high-quality loaves. Even the long-maligned standard grocery-store selection has improved, with the major chains carrying a wider selection of styles and ingredients in their breads than just white, brown, Wonder and the occasional ethnic specialty offered a couple of decades ago.

In nineteenth-century Toronto, most families made their own bread at home, so commercial bakers faced a challenge in weaning housewives off their homemade loaves. Consumers needed to be convinced that baking was drudgery and that buying premade loaves would save time and improve one's health. The friendly neighbourhood bread man was a key weapon in the baker's arsenal – his charm could make or break a company's livelihood.

What was the daily grind like for a bread delivery man in the 1880s, when future moguls like a teenage George Weston entered the business?

From the moment the boy hitched the horse to his dark-panelled covered cart in the morning, the day was a slow, measured ritual. The cart wound along dusty, tree-lined streets; at each stop he carried his wood and metal tray filled with an assortment of unwrapped bread and cakes up to the kitchen door. He chatted politely with matrons, indulged small children with treats or occasionally flirted with pretty young housekeepers who exchanged tickets for bread. On he would go, plying his trade along streets where every hedge, every alleyway, every dog's hiding place, became reassuringly familiar. After the oppressive heat and sometimes cloyingly sweet aromas of the bakeshop, the horse cart was a pleasure in comparatively foul weather.[1]

By 1900, local bakeries battled for customers in the city's seven daily newspapers. Competition was fiercest in the *Evening Telegram*, where half a dozen bakers boldly boasted of the superiority of their products to readers who picked up a copy of the paper on their way home for dinner. Subtlety was a foreign concept in a field where bakers like H. C. Tomlin proclaimed that their bread 'is very good – immeasurably better than most bread you buy,' without any evidence to back up their proclamations. Who needed official customer surveys or reliable nutritional data?

L: The Evening Telegram, *Feb. 24, 1900.* *R:* The Evening Telegram, *March 8, 1900.*

BEATS ALL OTHER FOOD
That is how it earned the title "The Staff of
Life."

THE BEST BREAD
is necessary if you would be healthy and
happy. Our bread makes rosy cheeks and
strong muscles. Our

Health Brown Bread
has no equal, neither in the ingredients used,
the process of manufacture, or in health-pro-
ducing properties.

The Tait-Bredin Co., Limited
744-746 Yonge Street.
Tel. 3133.   y215

THE ARTIST
here made the mistake of picturing our friend
carrying home a loaf of rye bread; instead it
should be a loaf of our

HEALTH BROWN BREAD
and then no one would have wondered at his
rotundity of make up. Just try it yourself and
make note of your muscular development.

THE TAIT-BREDIN CO.,   y246
Tel. 3133.   744 and 746 YONGE ST.

    The purity of the product was stressed, whether it was
high-quality ingredients or the hygiene of the production
facilities. Skilled labour was a key point of many ads – Tait-
Bredin noted in one *Evening Telegram* spot that 'even the best
ingredients would be rendered unfit for food if we employed
poor workmen.' Consumers were assured that each baker's
goods were made by qualified employees fully devoted to
furthering the craft, as opposed to the housewife for whom
baking was only one of seventy-eight tasks to be accomplished
during the day.

    Among the battling bakeries of 1900, Yonge Street–based
Tait-Bredin stands out for the bizarre illustrations used in its
ads. Eager to show the nutritional strength of its products,
especially for its 'Health Brown Bread,' Tait-Bredin's advertising depicted spindly-legged loaves accomplishing feats like
running in a race along a viaduct, lifting heavy barbells to
make 'Poor Bread' feel bad and punching out ambulatory
steaks and potatoes to prove bread's nutritional strength. It
also felt no shame in slamming overweight Torontonians who
bought hefty loaves of other types of bread – if the portly figure
in one ad had chosen Tait-Bredin's brown instead of a human-
length log of rye, 'no one would have wondered at his rotundity of make up.'[2] The company's products may have helped
the stamina of proprietor Mark Bredin, whose busy schedule
included a couple of terms on city council.

    By contrast, George Weston's ads in 1900 used quaint,
genteel imagery, employing cherubs, children, eighteenth-

2 *The Evening Telegram,*
March 8, 1900.

century servants and Dickensian figures. The latter were used to back up a claim that the 'golden opinions of the oldest residents of Toronto' valued Weston bread for its digestive qualities. Palatability was the only selling point that Queen-and-Portland-based R. F. Dale used for his ads, while H. C. Tomlin stressed his wares provided the most sustenance for 'the brain worker, the muscular worker, and for children.'

The fervour of 1900 gradually faded, with rumours of the largest local players uniting to form a conglomerate. It took a decade, but in 1911 Bredin, Tomlin and Weston, along with bakers from Montreal and Winnipeg, merged their interests to form Canada Bread. Weston pulled out to re-establish his own eponymous firm in the early 1920s, forming the base from which a manufacturing and retailing empire was built on both sides of the Atlantic, including familiar names like Wonder Bread and Loblaws. Canada Bread carried on and, under the ownership of Maple Leaf Foods, continues to stock many of the brand-name baked goods in Canadian grocery stores.

With consolidation came conformity, as the enriched white loaf rushed to the front of the pack. Bread men vanished

L: The Evening Telegram, Feb. 24, 1900.
R: The Evening Telegram, March 20, 1900.

from city streets as Torontonians began to purchase their bread from supermarkets or neighbourhood specialty bakeries. By the end of the 1980s, apart from the occasional choice of crusty Italian or Portuguese loaves or a chewy Jewish rye, the local grocery-store bread section had only variations of mushy enriched white or brown bread made by corporations. Smaller family-run bakeries had run into higher operating costs that put many out of business.

By the early 1990s, consumers were looking for something more than the homogenized product found on most shelves. When Martin Connell and Lynda Haynes opened ACE Bakery on King Street West in 1993, they quickly discovered there was a large local audience willing to pay a premium price for higher-quality baguettes. According to Haynes, their customers 'were cutting back on expensive trips and other big-budget items, but they wanted to go on buying flowers, good bread and great cheese.'[3] ACE products soon made their way onto restaurant tables and supermarket shelves, and demand for its breads eventually led to a large production facility in North York.

3 Doug Burn, "On the Rise," *Food in Canada*, January/February 2007, p. 28.

The past decade has seen many artisanal bakeries and manufacturers emerge around the city. The philosophy behind this wave of bread makers may best be defined by ShaSha Bread Co. founder ShaSha Navazesh: 'We would rather be making a few good things than making a lot of not-so-good things.'[4] A greater diversity of ingredients are used for customers with a wider taste palate than the brown and white of old, while a lower dependency on preservatives and healthier grains attract the health-conscious, thus serving diners in the mood for a grape-skin baguette or a spelt-laden loaf. Neighbourhood artisan bakers are setting up shop in established higher-income residential areas (e.g., Epi Breads in Leaside, Thobor's in North Toronto) or up-and-coming sections of the city with an ideal customer base, such as Leslieville, Brick Street Bakery's choice for a second location.

4 Quoted in Dan Pelton, 'Rollin' in Dough,' *Canadian Packaging*, September 2004, p. 14.

The industry giants that descended from Toronto's early battling bakers are trying to draw back customers by expanding their lines to include knockoffs of artisan loaves and nutrient-enriched versions of the old staples. As Haynes once said in an interview, 'Once you've tasted real bread, how can you eat Wonder bread again?'[5]

5 Quoted in Sandra Eagle, 'Aces High: A Passion for Great Bread is the Driving Force Behind this Toronto Bakery.' *Food in Canada*, January/February 2002, p. 32.

Liz
Clayton

Viva la (coffee) revolución!

Glossary

Chemex: A staple of '50s kitchens, this stylish and super-simple coffee maker brews coffee in a paper filter in an hourglass-shaped carafe. It's recently come back into fashion for its ease of use and clean-tasting cup.

Clover: One of the most innovative (and expensive, and hotly debated) coffee machines of the modern age, this piston-driven, futuristic device is a fully automated coffee brewer. It was perhaps best known for its $13,000 price tag — at least until Starbucks bought the company and availability became scarce.

French Press: This plunger-based dispenser brews coffee in three to four minutes, producing a rich (and sometimes sludgy) brew that's become a favourite.

It all went down rather innocently, in a place you might not have expected. The class lines of proletariat Canadian coffee versus the frou-frou frappuccino crowd were drawn across the lobby of a hospital.

Toronto General Hospital once firmly held the middle ground – Canadian-owned, proud but not fancy – in the form of a modest Second Cup kiosk. But lobby renovations in 2003 eschewed the moderate for a choice between extremes. At the University Avenue entrance now stands a Starbucks – pendant lamps, chocolate-dipped biscotti, maple tables and all. The lineups swell with surgeons and the kind of hospital visitors who look like they've just happened to stop in at the ICU on their way to the ROM. Walk a little further in, though, up a couple stairs – it's always worth it to save a buck – and there stands the bastion of honest Canadiana itself, a Tim Horton's. (Though the chain only recently ventured into the downown core from the Ontarian side-roads it dominates, its arrival in Toronto proper was immediately embraced.) Queued up here are the ranks of the real: the families visiting en masse who grab double-doubles for the drive back to Brampton, the med students, the hospital's janitorial staff.

The class divide of those getting their fix on is staggering and highly visible, and it speaks not only about money and class but questions Canadianism itself. If Timmy's is the national emblem, is upgrading to a venti rejecting the country itself? And in Toronto, a burg whose country snipes about it behind its back in every other city and province, what does it mean to formally turn one's back on the homegrown coffee of the working class – even if it's now owned by Wendy's? And isn't the choice between the two poles a depressing lesson in the lesser of evils?

But now there is a true psycho-economic middle ground – the independent café culture of the city, slowly extending its tendrils in the past few years to blossom beyond niche nerdism into viable neighbourhood strongholds, so much more Torontonian than anything a big-box corporate café could serve up. The city's indie cafés, stealthily piggybacking on the success of chain stores like Starbucks, Second Cup and Timothy's, have actually co-opted the tide of 'fancy coffee' drinkers who can now return to their own corners for cups of legitimate local craft at increasingly high quality.

The groundwork for this was laid in the subculture, of course. To the bohemian Kensingtonites we owe I Deal Coffee and Moonbean; to the bike messengers we owe Jet Fuel on Parliament. These cafés proved the viability of true independents in what a decade ago was a cluttery, not-too-coffee-centric landscape, where only pioneers like I Deal and Bloor West Village's Coffee Tree had the nerve to roast their own beans. But an international revolution was taking shape in the post-Starbucks landscape of independent coffee. And it didn't really crash onto Toronto's shores until Stuart Ross went to Italy, and then Seattle, to spend time with espresso legend David Schomer, and brought back the gospel of the emerging 'third wave' of specialty coffee. In 2003, he opened, in an odd little brick modern building just off the Church Street strip, Bulldog Coffee – catering mostly to gay dogwalkers and what would become the city's first real coffee-connoiseur elite. Bulldog offered up an espresso called Super Bar, roasted in nearby Concord, and was the first place in town you could see latte art – hearts or leaves designed through careful pouring of textured milk on the top of your espresso drink.

Soon enough – as tends to happen in any niche industry – Bulldog's acolytes and employees began to splinter off. Barista Matthew Taylor teamed up with the owners of a cozy breakfast place in Corktown to open Mercury Organic Espresso Bar in 2005. Another former employee of Ross's, Ed Lynds, opened up a shop called Dark Horse not too far down the road with his partner, Deanna Zunde, soon after. Suddenly, what had happened successfully in cities like Vancouver, Portland, Seattle and San Francisco had spread east. Toronto was joining an international movement – and also creating a local one.

And with the new movement came a new culture, some of which was met with resistance. At Mercury, drip coffee simply wasn't on the menu. Espresso in a to-go cup wasn't either.

'It's a city that was ready for it,' says Douglas Tiller, one of Mercury's owners. 'Overall, I think Torontonians are relatively adventurous, and quite receptive to new ideas. I think a lot of that is how you broach that with people. You can try and educate someone if you don't make them feel like you're talking down to them or preaching to them.

'As far as things that we do every day, not doing drip coffee was sort of a tough sell to a lot of people. And people don't seem to understand why they can't get an espresso to go. We tell them we don't have the proper cups to put them in, but that's really just our excuse. It's taste: putting a shot of espresso

Pourover: A very simple method of brewing drip coffee by simply suspending a filter cone above a cup – some cafés have special equipment to suspend four or five at a time, or you can make it by the cup with a plastic or ceramic cone dripper at home.

Syphon Brewer: A traditional Japanese brewing method that's become repopularized in the U.S., this process involves heating water in a bottom carafe, via flame or high-powered halogen heater, which then rises into a top carafe where the coffee is brewed. Once the heat is cut, the coffee syphons down through a filter into a lower carafe through vacuum suction. The skill of syphoning is so involved, there are even 'Syphonista' championships!

Triple-Tall Caramel Macchiato: A misnamed coffee drink from Starbucks that has caused baristas around the world to have to explain to people that a 'macchiato' is not, in fact, a 20-ounce drink topped with candy syrup.

Blondie's
1378 Queen St. W
416.532.7410

Bulldog Coffee
89 Granby St.
(at Church St.)
416.923.3469

Crema
3079 Dundas St. W
(at Quebec Ave.)
416.767.3131

Dark Horse
682 Queen St. E
(at Broadview Ave.)
647.436.3460

Dark Horse II
215 Spadina Ave.
416.979.1200

Grinder
126 Main St.
(at Gerrard St.)
416.901.0290

Hank's (in the Wine Bar)
9½ Church St.
647.288.0670

in a paper to-go cup just ruins the taste. It's not a drink that you draw out over time – you get it, and you drink it, and it's gone,' explains Tiller. 'Why not just take that two minutes to drink an espresso, enjoy it the way it's best enjoyed, and then leave the shop?'

Bringing that level of attention to taste and detail to Toronto's coffee sphere built a culinary bridge. Coffee lovers, foodies and the receptive everyday drinker began to find a point of intersection. Cafés that connected neighbourhoods, like Dark Horse and Mercury, were joined by Manic Coffee on the College strip, the Common out in Dufferin Grove, Crema in the Junction, and Hank's – a joint venture between an espresso bar and the Jamie Kennedy Wine Bar, which truly marked the tipping point of independent coffee's serious arrival in Toronto.

Manic Coffee owner Matt Lee feels the independent scene offers something to Torontonians that chains at either end of the spectrum can't.

'People feel the need to identify with something that's a little more unique, that kind of moulds to their own personalities. A specialty coffee store is putting down something new, and a smaller shop will involve the community a lot more in decisions and how it does everything,' says Lee, whose store offers a continually rotating selection of high-end coffees prepared one cup at a time on a $13,000-price-tagged brewing device called the Clover.

'Toronto, I felt, was becoming too commercial, moving towards a lot of big boxes, and I think the birth of the new café scene has been really instrumental in developing the community – having a place where everybody can meet every day, relatively affordably, rather than a big box,' says Lee, pausing to add, 'and also having something that tastes better, right?'

'When Manic introduced the Clover, that really took people aback,' says Sam James, who has done barista stints at Manic, Hank's and Dark Horse. James has also stood out in the larger coffee landscape – in the improbable-sounding world of barista competitions, James has taken regional championship titles for his prowess at preparing espressos, cappuccinos and signature drinks on a competition circuit that extends well beyond Toronto to a global level in an attempt to elevate and celebrate the craft.

'I think people were oblivious to the options of French press or hand drip and these individual by-the-cup, brew-to-order methods of doing coffee,' says James. 'The Clover really put coffee on a platform and introduced people to freshly

made coffee one cup at a time. It was a really good intro
duction, and we can introduce these classic manual
methods of how we're doing things as well.'

Though James is excited to describe the nuances of
single-origin, carefully sourced and roasted coffees and
Torontonians' receptivity to learning, he is also quick to note
coffee's innate democratic appeal: whether you want to
appreciate it on a so-called higher level or at Coffee Time,
the door is open to everyone.

'Where wine is too noble and too classist, you can apply a
lot of the same appreciation to coffee without having to break
the bank or pretend that you're of a certain class that can
afford to be a wine drinker. With coffee you're like, hey, who
doesn't drink coffee?' says James.

And it's through that truth that worlds of taste and
community join together: even across the citified lanes of a
humble country.

'Though we are a sort of working-class society, there's a lot
in our society who aren't your typical working-class Timmy's
customers, and those are the people that look for a little more,'
says Mercury's Tiller. 'That's where specialty coffee fits in.'

So to those looking for a little more – in terms of taste, and
of investing in their community – this new wave of coffee fills
that void. Specialty stores have built upon a landscape of inde-
pendence, and the exchange of excitement and ideas that
define a city. From the European roots of cafés as microcosm
centres to the modern urbanist notion of the café as the 'third
space' between work and home, Toronto's cafés have redefined
the neighbourhoods they themselves were defined by. More
than just fixie cyclist hangouts and post-baby-yoga meet
spots, these shops attract true cross-sections of Canadians
coexisting in the most unusual, and often inspiring, ways. By
building ties through taste and through creating the melting
pots of conversation that exist in the transitional space of
neighbourhood cafés, these shops go far beyond the button-
push drug delivery of the big boxes and share something new –
at both a higher level and one that is grassroots. It's not anti-
nationalist to skip over Timmy's – it just might be a civic duty.

Manic Coffee
426 College St.
(at Bathurst St.)
416.966.3888

Mercury Espresso Bar
915 Queen St. E
(east of Logan Ave.)
647.435.4779

Pennylick's
281 Augusta Ave. (in
Kensington Market)
416.348.0909

Sam James Coffee Bar
297 Harbord St.
(at Manning Ave.)
647.341.2572

Erik Rutherford

When a gastronomic wonder is served in Toronto, does anybody taste it?

I am one of those Torontonians who likes to propagate the idea that I live in a gastronomic mecca. Whenever a new acquaintance makes polite conversation about Toronto, I'll hear myself say, 'Oh yeah, Toronto is an amazing city for food, one of the best in the world. You can find anything. Torontonians really know how to eat.' Etc.

The thing is, I am never really sure if what I am saying is true. It does seem an unlikely historical turn that this workaday city – a city built by stern, abstemious people with a puritan distrust of sensuality – should register on the global gastronomic radar at all. After all, though I'm no gastronome, I do know that good cuisine entails good eaters. You only serve it because people will appreciate it, which is why the greatest chefs tend to stick to magnet cities like London, Paris and New York. So, even if generations of immigrants have done wonders to evolve the local palate, as in many cities, I don't see why we Torontonians would be any more discerning than our fellow North Americans. Is there some mysterious ingredient in the drinking water that makes us prefer the fancy to the plain, the spicy to the bland and the haute to the hearty?

I decided to approach a few of the city's French chefs and ask what they think of us as eaters. I figure if anyone has the authority to draw a portrait of culinary Toronto, it's the guys from France: not only is their cuisine the Western world's gastronomic polestar, it is also a reliable litmus test of gastronomic savvy – all those dissimulations of brains and guts, and not so dissimulated tongues, tripes and trotters, are daunting to the uninitiated and are bound to betray a culinary imposter. Are Torontonians adventurous, discerning eaters? Do chefs coming to Toronto have to raise their game, or do they find themselves patronizing the patrons?

I speak first to Laurent Brion, chef and co-owner of Tati Bistro. We sit at the long bar with espressos and look over the day's menu: escargots in garlic butter, steak tartare, duck confit, cassoulet, bouillabaisse – nothing too intimidating, though I'm a little surprised to see duck gizzard salad.

'Do many customers order that?' I ask.

'A few. It's not a big seller. I like it so I offer it.'

'Shouldn't you be saying, *they* like it so I offer it?'

Brion laughs. 'I just make real French food here, like in France: andouillettes, frogs' legs, kidneys. People will say to me, 'Ah, wonderful, I can't find that anywhere else.' There are a lot of sophisticated gourmands in this city who want the real stuff. In a way, when you open a French restaurant abroad, you have to pay even more attention to the quality of the products and how they're made because people are skeptical.'

Brion's bistro looks as authentic as the menu; with its wood-panelled facade, little candlelit tables and slate menu boards, Tati would sit just as comfortably on the rue Oberkampf in Paris as it does on the Harbord restaurant strip. 'The secret I've finally learned from my years in Toronto,' Brion tells me, 'is not to anticipate what people want. The only thing I do is simplify the menu. A chef who prepares a complicated meal presented on a complicated menu is asking for trouble in this city.'

Brion hails from Poitou in southwest France.[1] He arrived in Toronto in the 1980s after working kitchens in Poitiers, Paris and Bermuda. In late 2007, he left Teatro, where he had been executive chef, and opened Tati.

'When I first started working in French restaurants here twenty years ago, Tati would have been impossible,' he says. 'Back then, eighty percent of our clientele had never even tasted a fresh oyster. When I'd put sweetbread on the menu, clients would ask for "a slice." Or they'd ask for crème caramel with the caramel on the side, as if you could separate the two! That doesn't happen anymore. There's been a huge evolution because we've been teaching Torontonians food.'

'Who's "we"?' I ask.

'Oh, many chefs.' He rattles off a few names, among them Scot Woods of Lucien; Didier Leroy of Didier; Jean-Pierre Challet, ex-chef at Le Select and the Fifth, who now runs a high-end catering kitchen from an address on Harbord; and Marc Thuet, whose restaurant is now called Conviction in lieu of the previous Bite Me (possibly the most unfortunate name ever for a restaurant, though I did once see a fondue place in Edinburgh called Dip Your Bits).

'Chefs have got the suppliers to step up, too,' Brion continues. 'Now you can actually find the things you need. Decent bread, quality meat. We have bavette on the menu. Ten years ago bavette was impossible to find. All you could get was tough flank steak. By showing butchers exactly what we want, we have it, but it's a slow evolution. Only two weeks ago a butcher came here to sell me some meat, and he had never

1 Poitou is known for its Chabichou du Poitou, a dessert goat cheese. In April 2009, Brion and his partner, Whitney Brown, opened a cheese and gourmet food boutique on Harbord, just west of Tati, called Chabichou.

heard of bavette before. Two weeks ago! He asked me to show him how to get the cut. The butcher! That's what I mean by educating.'

Across the street at the elegant Loire, chef Jean-Charles Dupoire is chopping golden beets in preparation for evening service. I stand at the kitchen serving window and put in many of the same questions.

'The young chefs in the city work more and more with local suppliers,' Dupoire says, 'and that relationship benefits everybody. Ontario farmers are more consistent and more concerned with quality than before. I think pretty soon Ontario cheese will be able to compete with cheese from Quebec. We're even happy now with the bread we get.'

Dupoire believes Toronto's best chefs are slowly introducing the French idea of *terroir*. 'Respect for place, for the local soil, that's why there's so much diversity back home. Charcuterie, for example, is different in every region of France. Diversity is the richness of French cuisine. Let's do that here in Canada. Let's get to know the taste of each region.'

Dupoire's personal terroir is the wine, cheese and charcuterie from around his hometown of Tours, at the edge of the Loire Valley. He moved to Toronto in 2001 and took on the kitchen at Epic in the Fairmont Royal York. At the time, his childhood friend, Sylvain Brissonet, was already in Toronto, the sommelier at Langdon Hall. Seven years later they saw an opportunity to open a restaurant together. Choosing the name was easy: Loire.

Canadians, Dupoire explains, are unaccustomed to making the link between soil, roots and place. '*Toujours le vin sent son terroir*,' goes an old French proverb, but even when it comes to wine, Canadians are more likely to notice the grape variety on a wine label than the region the wine is from.

I point out that a lot of the dishes on Dupoire's menu aren't really the kind you'd find in Tours: carrot-coriander risotto, mussels steamed in Steamwhistle beer, seared rainbow trout with burnt lemon sauce and Chinese greens (Dupoire purchases the bok choy and lemons on Spadina).

'French cooking is not just a list of dishes,' Dupoire reminds me. 'It's a technique, a set of values, just as terroir is a philosophy of practice and a sensibility. What is nice in Toronto is that French chefs feel free to give their French roots some new flavours, and to adapt local products to their own style.'

'And do you not have to adapt your dishes to the style of your customers?'

'In a restaurant like this, no, not really. When I worked at the hotel, I had to think about what I was serving. That was a bit of a problem. I sometimes had ten customers a day who would request their own dish. But here that doesn't happen. I can even serve calf liver and beef tongue. If I am inventive, people will order it. I have no complaint with the way people in Toronto eat.'

The next day, I meet with Jean-Pierre Centeno, chef and owner of Gamelle on College Street.[2] I tell him what I've been hearing: chefs working in Toronto today can find the quality local ingredients they need to make whatever crazy French dishes they want, and they can do it in full confidence their food will be properly valued. On the other hand, chefs are culinary teachers, educating their suppliers and customers in the ways of gastronomy. Isn't there a contradiction here?

'Both portraits are fair,' Centeno says. 'It's true there are diners in Toronto with highly discriminating tastes; they are people who have been to the best restaurants – here, in New York, in Paris. But that's just it. In France, gastronomy permeates the whole culture. Whatever background you come from, you inherit this reverence for cuisine, from school, from everywhere, even if you don't eat gastro-level food. But here, culinary education comes from the world of restaurants and nowhere else, which means gastronomy really only concerns the upper layers of society.'

I pull out a cartoon from the *New Yorker* that shows a disgruntled celebrity chef cooking for his wife and two kids, who are waiting impatiently at the kitchen table.[3] The son and daughter are saying, 'Yuck! What smells so disgusting?' and 'Why can't we just order pizza like everyone else?' The chef's wife, looking bored, says, 'Whatever it is you're making, it sure is using a lot of pots and pans.'

Centeno laughs: 'Definitely, definitely!' Just then his daughter calls, and as if to corroborate the cartoon, she tries to talk her way out of lunch at the restaurant. The exchange is spirited but Centeno holds firm. 'I try to show good cuisine to my kids,' he says, putting the phone down. 'I say, you can eat the processed stuff which you like because it has sugar, or you can have this: it tastes good, but it's also good for you.'

I glance over at the lunch menu; it's late morning and I am beginning to feel hungry: fricassée d'escargots and entrecôte grillée with truffle mashed potatoes. Lucky girl!

'My daughter,' says Centeno, 'she's got the North American palate, which is very simple: sweet and sour. That's the first

2 Sadly, shortly after I interviewed Jean-Pierre, Gamelle closed. Its website, www.gamelle. com, cites the state of the economy and the high prices of quality ingredients as reasons for the closure.

3 I found this cartoon on page 164 of a brilliant book by Priscilla Parkhurst Ferguson called *Accounting for Taste: The Triumph of French Cuisine* (Chicago: The University of Chicago Press, 2004). She says that French cuisine acts as both our culinary consciousness and conscience.

thing I was told when I came to Toronto. You put something sweet and add a little sourness to it and the customers are going to love it.'

As a child in Spain, Centeno spent most of his free time in the kitchen helping his mother, who was a chef in retirement homes. The family was part of anti-Franco activities and at the end of the war fled to France. Centeno continued his culinary apprenticeship in restaurants in France, Greece and Spain. When he moved to Toronto in 1978, the city was a 'culinary no-man's land.'

'And now, thirty years later? Has Toronto arrived? Is it a gastronomic mecca?'

'The city has definitely leapfrogged a lot, thanks to what Europe and other culinary parts of the world have brought in. But it's actually happened very fast so there are pieces missing. I think people still have trouble putting things in perspective.'

'Which means?'

'Well, if I say it, I'm going to get snapped for it. I'll put it this way: Torontonian diners are a bit juvenile. I would say they tend to follow fads. They forget it's okay to eat things or in places that other people don't like. A few years ago the big fad was tuna; now it's charcuterie. Right now in Toronto you've got places serving charcuterie and they haven't even got kitchens. Meanwhile, great chefs are working their hearts out, using local products, to make the real thing. That's what I mean by juvenile. But you know, at the same time, I think Europe is becoming more like North America than the other way around.'

Brion and Dupoire also grumble about fads. The consensus seems to be that fads are insidious because they turn an ingredient or dish into a fetish, and this is anathema to French cuisine, which traditionally is much more about practice than product. So I can't help but ask: what is French cuisine?

All three answer in more or less the same way, by narrating the various stages of a French meal – an idealized and possibly mythical French meal. From what I can gather, it runs something like this: fresh, high-quality local produce is meticulously prepared under the supervision of a chef who has devoted innumerable hours to the kitchen, initially as obedient child with his/her grandmother, then as disciplined apprentice under a culinary master. Friends, family and invited guests gather around the table, among them passionate, sophisticated sensualists with long experience of gastronomic

indulgence. The table is set in the customary order, a symbol of civilization itself. Suitable wine is abundantly consumed. Conviviality and excess are reined in by courtesy and chatter. The food is elaborately presented. Slow, attentive eating begins, a series of gustatory moments expertly savoured. The meal lasts for hours.

Brion, Dupoire and Centeno quietly acknowledge that they are inheritors of all the nostalgia and authority that comes with this forever elusive culinary narrative, the loss of which haunts the French to such an extent that Sarkozy has been petitioning UNESCO since February 2008 to formally declare French gastronomy a world cultural treasure (an honour until now bestowed only upon dying practices such as Armenian duduk music and Ugandan barkcloth making).[4]

Whether or not the French culinary tradition is disappearing, it continues to loom like a disapproving eye over the world's culinary practices, which always fall short of its fabled heights, especially on this side of the Atlantic. Here we are haunted not by the loss of culinary tradition, but by the lack of it. According to caricature, we are either culinary incults raised on the 'cuisine' of speed and convenience, or health-obsessed vitamin poppers who put taste a distant second to nutritional value, preferring the German adage 'You are what you eat' to Brillat-Savarin's 'Tell me what you eat, and I will tell you who you are' – rather than recognizing food as a vector of social character and status, we see it as fuel, part of a physiological process instead of a gastronomic one.

Do Torontonian diners resemble these caricatures? I have asked Brion, Dupoire and Centeno, but I am especially eager to hear what Jason Bangerter has to say. He is chef at L'Auberge du Pommier, Toronto's haute-est venue for French haute cuisine. Though nestled among squat glass office blocks on the west side of a desolate stretch of Yonge Street, on the inside this faux country inn has Michelin-star sobriety and elegance. The high-tech induction kitchen is spotless, spacious and bustling. Bangerter proudly calls it 'the hottest kitchen in Canada' and I am convinced.

Surely in this restaurant meals are not rushed, diners are not counting calories and bombarding the chef with silly requests.

'No, no, I get requests all the time,' Bangerter laughs. 'And if someone wants something changed I change it, no questions asked. Today at lunch someone ordered a beautiful ocean

4 Under the Safeguarding of Intangible Cultural Heritage program of UNESCO (www.unesco.org/culture/ich/index.php?pg=home)

trout with a herb garden salad and a sauce Bois Boudran, a lovely dish, light on fat, very healthy – and she wanted everything separated on the plate, none of the elements touching each other. I had people calling for a nine-course gastronomic tasting menu that was not just vegan, but raw! No fish, no meat, nothing cooked. Here it's all about the guest.'

'But that shows lack of respect for the chef, doesn't it?' I say. 'The French fathers of the table seem to say that the chef and eater share responsibilities. The chef serves the terroir by understanding and using it well; the eater serves the chef by tasting well. There's a kind of culinary contract, isn't there?'

I pull out Brillat-Savarin's other famous aphorism – 'Animals fill themselves; people eat; the intelligent person alone knows how to eat' – and ask Bangerter if he thinks it's wrong to indulge people who 'don't know how to eat.'

'No, of course not! I never say, this is the bling, you eat it. I remember one time in Paris I ordered a steak for lunch and asked for a Coke. The waitress said, 'No, sorry, that's poison,' and she brought me water instead. Another time I asked for milk with my espresso. A waiter told me flat out, 'No, that's not done.' That wouldn't fly here. In Toronto, like in all of North America, it's a service relationship to food. It's not like France, where diners might come in with a whole set of expectations, even prejudices. Here it's turned round. Diners come to a restaurant like this not so much to test out, but to discover.'

Bangerter reminds me that we're not in the nineteenth century. Yes, chefs serve but they also teach, and it's all right if diners dictate as they learn. A shallow knowledge of ways of French culinary history and tradition should not be seen as a lack of 'intelligence,' but rather as an opportunity to develop a unique Canadian cuisine.

'Chefs working in Toronto just have to transmit the passion and the knowledge, and it's accessible to everybody. The kind of gastronomes you're talking about are rare here. The rest have never seen a truffle. But that's not a bad thing. It means Canadian cuisine can begin to emerge out of these older European traditions, and eventually it will evolve to the level of French cuisine.' He smiles. 'Just give us a few more centuries.'

I wonder if Bangerter's openness and optimism have to do with the fact he was born and raised in Canada. He was a young trainee just out of George Brown College when he joined the brigade at the King Edward Hotel. Five years later he went via the Meridian in Paris to apprentice under Swiss master Anton Mosimann in London. Then, in 2002, he was

invited back to Toronto by owners of L'Auberge to become *chef de cuisine*.

After chatting for an hour or so, Bangerter tells me I've found my answers. Yes, Torontonians worry more about the butter and cream content of their dishes. Yes, they spend only one to two hours at dinner. Yes, they break the supposed culinary contract. But they fill the best restaurants and they are ready to enjoy.

'We don't have the same volume of well-versed high-end clientele as Paris or New York, or the three-star Michelin restaurants where you drop a grand or two. That's not going to happen for a long while. But we do pretty well. Look around here. You say Toronto has this big reputation, but actually I think Toronto doesn't get enough credit.'

That evening I enjoy a six-course tasting menu at L'Auberge with my friend Anne-Michèle, a true gourmet. We are given royal treatment by Joel Centeno, head waiter and, as it turns out, Jean-Pierre Centeno's brother. Every dish passes the Anne-Michèle test with flying colours. Me? I'm no gastronome, but the *homard glaçage* was a gastronomic wonder, and I'm pretty sure I tasted it.

Karen Hines   **My filthy hand**

I dig my filthy hand into a stainless-steel bin of iceberg lettuce. I grab a salad-sized clump and dump it beside a steaming crepe Bretonne. I take a couple of tomato wedges with the same filthy fingers from an adjacent stainless-steel bin. I slip the tomato wedges in on the side, and dress the salad with a creamy vinaigrette from an oily ladle that has been handled by the eight other filthy-handed girls who are on the floor with me this shift. I wipe my greasy, lettucey, tomato-y hand on the greasy, lettucey, tomato-y dishcloth that is set out beside the salad dressing. It needs changing, but we're in a full-on post–*Apocalypse Now* rush. Dazed patrons have filled the patio. They have just endured a two-and-a-half-hour trek through hell and they are hungry and thirsty for crepes and iced tea.

It is Yorkville, 1979. I am fourteen. I am too young to watch *Apocalypse Now*. I have lied about my age to get this job, in this outdoor café, across the street from Checkers disco, just down the street from the Rainbow Room and around the corner from Parachute, where you can buy duds like they wear in Devo. It's a killer summer job for a teenager, and I'm making about 300 bucks a week. This will pay for my dance classes for the year and for vintage dresses so I can be Magenta at the *Rocky Horror Picture Show* screenings that I sneak into with my friends and that occupy the centre of my universe.

My right hand is my tray hand, which means my left hand (the filthy hand, the lettuce and tomato hand) does all the intricate work. My filthy hand is not visibly filthy, but I have been slinging crepes and iced tea for about three hours now without a break or a wash. I have been handling bills and dealing change, taking my customers' filthy money from their filthy fingers with mine, and digging my filthy hand down into the depths of my black nylon waitress apron to hunt around for quarters, nickels and dimes. I keep the incoming twenties in an exotic Asian silk billfold that is greasy and grey in the spots where I finger it most. I have to set the billfold down on my tray to make the change. The tray is sometimes damp, often slick with vinaigrette and grimy with ashes from dirty ashtrays (which I regularly wipe clean with the filthy ashtray cloth). Once I'm done making change, I pick up some dirty plates, throw them on my tray and head back to pick up more crepes and make more salad with my filthy hand.

My right hand is also filthy, but not from money: it is filthy because it lives, spread-fingered, at the bottom of my tray, which I set down only when I have to, when I slide it onto the dish-pit shelf where we pile the dirty dishes once we scrape them clean with the knives and forks that have been in the hands of our mouth-wiping customers, and only after we have discarded their napkins with our fingers. I use both hands for the dish-scraping and napkin-tossing. Then I pick up my filthy tray, pick up my fresh order, dig my filthy hand back down into the iceberg lettuce bin and grab a perfect clump of leaves with economy, precision and a kind of yogic flow.

I am ignorant, yes, but I am not malevolent. I am young and fresh and I like my job and my customers. So do my bosses and all my fellow waitresses, one of whom is putting herself through school and will become a genetic scientist. Another is soon to break out as an award-winning film star known for her intelligent choices. Another will become my family doctor. This is 1979, eons before Purell. We don't think in terms of E. coli and salmonella and 'pathways of transmission.' None of us knows that all those one- and two-dollar bills are covered with fecal matter and are hotbeds for Giardia – we just don't think like that. Our hands are simply 'dirty.' It's way faster to grab the lettuce by hand and, during a rush, every second counts. We figure what the customers don't know won't hurt them. We don't intend to be disrespectful: the reality is that at the end of our wearying shift we will be provided with a half-price meal that includes all the salad we can eat. We will dump that salad on our own plates with our filthy hands and we will eat it without a care. We will also eat dinner rolls with our fingers as we count out our filthy money and add up our tips.

I worked at that café for four summers, and I can say with certainty that I never missed a day of work due to illness. I don't recall the other girls missing any either, except one who got sick from eating eggs Benedict at a swank restaurant we went to late one night after a shift, just for fun (Toronto's trendier joints were just learning about eggs Benedict – that they sell well, but not that you shouldn't let hollandaise sit around till three in the morning). But none of us got sick from our filthy hands, and we never got any complaints of sickness from our customers, some of whom were regulars and dined on our filthy salads throughout the season. Towards the end of my third summer there, we did switch over to salad tongs,

which were awkward to use and sometimes thrown aside at the height of a rush by those of us who had learned to measure by feel.

I have a slight case of emetophobia (the fear of vomit or of vomiting). This condition usually has to do with issues of control; some would suggest the fear of vomiting is the direct result of holding on to the delusion that one is in control. Weirdly, though, I am not afraid of restaurants. Or rather, I refuse to be afraid of restaurants. I spend a lot of time alone when I work, and I like going to places that bustle and have pretty lighting.

I doubt there are many restaurants today that encourage bare-fisted salad serving, but I'm certain a lot of servers cut their customers' sourdough with the same fingers they have just made change with. I'm also pretty certain that the server who hands me my water glass by its rim has also been handling other customers' dirty glasses by their rims. But I drink the water because I want to live in the world, and after half a glass of wine, you can even find me diving into those bowls of nuts and pretzels they set out at hotel bars – nuts and pretzels that you know are crawling with microbes from the hands of other half-drunk, caution-to-the-wind-throwing patrons. I don't believe they throw those snacks away between tables, and despite my heightened awareness, I am often guilty of poking through for the almonds. I Purell first, but I doubt that everyone else who's poked through that bowl did. Also, I know enough to know that if a server gets slammed with a rush, the stainless-steel pretzel scoop may be tossed aside in favour of the quicker, defter, filthy hand.

For me, going to restaurants is a lot like driving even though you know the odds. I like to think I'm stronger because of all the filthy hands. I like to think it's all the filthy hands that will counteract the damage that overuse of antibiotics and, yes, Purell have done to us and to the world. I like to think my filthy hand has been just one of many filthy hands that will be the immune-boosting salvation of all humankind during the next great plague. Still, I shudder when my waitress touches her own mouth ...

I called Toronto Public Health recently, curious to know if seeing a server touching her own mouth during an inspection would be enough to slap a joint with one of Toronto's dreaded 'yellow cards.' The gentleman I spoke with wasn't sure, he said. But he did tell me that servers are exempt from food-handler

regulations – the ones that require food handlers to wash their hands regularly, whatever 'regularly' means – he couldn't say exactly. I told the gentleman that I consider the young woman who fingers all the lemon wedges, then shoves one onto the rim of my glass, a 'food handler.' He chuckled and acknowledged that there is indeed a 'lack of control' with regard to servers, that the pressure is on 'the operator' (the restaurant) to police their staff. Food handlers have to spend an entire day (!) learning about food safety; servers do not, but the folks at Toronto Public Health are far less concerned with that waitress coughing over my pasta or touching the rim of my glass with her filthy fingers than they are with, say, rats or warm refrigerators. I asked, 'But what if my waitress was still shedding her last week's Norwalk virus, touched her mouth, then touched my lemon?' The gentleman chuckled again and made reference to the good old days when servers had to be X-rayed for tuberculosis and wear hairnets, then tried to reassure me by citing incubation periods and optimum environments for various viruses and pathogens. He said that 'populations' of pathogens significant enough to cause illness are not likely to grow in a few minutes on a fingered lemon wedge. That even well-fingered pretzels are an inhospitable environment unless the pretzels are sodden, like, say, from somebody sneezing on them. When I asked the inevitable N1H1 question, he coolly laid out the stats, which indicate that the dreaded flu is transmitted only through person-to-person contact. Well, if my contact with that lemon-wedging, rim-fingering, bread-cutting, mouth-touching waitress isn't person-to-person, I don't know what is. I thanked the chuckling gentleman and hung up with my phobia in full bloom.

I know too much now. I long for simpler times.

It is one a.m., August 1979. The *Apocalypse Now* crowd is heading out. They're still hollow-eyed, but they're filled with crepes and filthy salad now and seem a little cheerier. The Checkers disco crowd is pouring in. The cooks throw down a heaping plate of slightly burned crepes with maple syrup to keep us going. Eight waitresses share two forks and the crepes are devoured in minutes. Some of us eat with our fingers.

Secondo

John Lorinc **Walking towards the schnitzel**

My father, John, was a big walker, which made him something of an oddity in the car-oriented world of 1960s and 70s Lawrence Park. An immigrant with an accent (my parents left Hungary as refugees in 1956), his voice marked him as different from the day he and my mother bought their house. And in the period prior to mass-marketed health and environmental awareness, there weren't many adults roaming the sidewalks of our leafy neighbourhood, especially after dinner, which is when he liked to go for a stroll. The whole family would take a walk, or he'd go out on his own, regardless of the weather. Sometimes a car would stop, the driver inquiring if he needed a lift.

My father wove his ambulatory inclinations into our lives. Early ski lessons at the resorts north of Toronto included a stint of trekking *up* the hill in full equipment, a character-building activity I found both tedious and mortifying. In the spring and the fall, we donned Tyrolean-style knapsacks and leather boots and walked the Bruce Trail, then a new amenity upon which one could hike for long stretches before encountering another human being.

And from the time my sister and I were about eight or nine, my parents liked to while away a Saturday by walking us all the way downtown, past the sleepy shops on Yonge Street north of Eglinton, through the saddle of Mount Pleasant Cemetery and on down the St. Clair hill towards Yorkville. The prize at the end of these long treks was a wiener schnitzel, followed by the promise of a subway ride uptown for those with sore feet.

At the time, Toronto's best Hungarian cafés and pastry joints were located on that stretch of Bloor west of Bay: Jack and Jill, in the then ultra-fashionable Colonnade; the Cake Master, in a walk-down on Yorkville; Marika's, in the bowels of an office building opposite the Manulife Centre; and, of course, the Coffee Mill, a storied café patronized by Yorkville literati such as George Jonas and Barbara Amiel, and which *NOW* magazine once dubbed 'the Drake of its day.' A few blocks down Bay sat the dolled-up Csarda House (now the site of Bistro 990). Further west, the 'goulash archipelago' – Corona, Continental, Country Style and the smoky backroom of the Blue Danube Room – catered to the budget-conscious.

This concentration of Magyar eateries was no accident. Many of the thousands of Hungarians who'd fled to Canada

during the 1956 revolution settled in the cheap apartments
and rooming houses in the east Annex. They flocked to these
cafés because there they could order proper espresso and
soak up some faux European ambience in a metropolis that
didn't yet understand the fine points of big-city living.

The only way to properly experience a city is to walk its
streets, because only the pace and perspective of pedestrian
movement allows one to absorb the tastes and smells of an
urban neighbourhood, with its workaday shops, the easily
overlooked quirks of its architecture and what Jane Jacobs
described as the 'ballet' that occurs on the sidewalks.

I can backdate my affection for Toronto's urbanism to these
schnitzel-focused outings with my parents, which began in the
sleepy environs of North Toronto and terminated two hours
later in the liveliest part of a city in the throes of a cosmopolitan
flowering. A bit further south from Yorkville, towards College,
the City, in the 1970s, had closed off several blocks to traffic,
transforming Yonge into a pedestrian mall teeming with
people, all of them walking and soaking up the atmosphere
(and smoking dope). That stretch included retail landmarks
such as the original Coles, an over-lit literary emporium (now a
Shopper's Drug Mart) where I'd find a corner and flip through
Time-Life picture books; Mr. Gamesway's Ark, a warren-like
games store in the sandstone post office at Charles Street
that now houses a Starbucks on the first floor and a gym on the
second; and Hercules, the dusty army surplus store at Glouces-
ter that's now a dusty sex shop.

On one occasion, I remember, we met a young woman
named Beverly, a colleague of my father's at Humber Memo-
rial Hospital, where he worked as a pathologist. She invited
us into her house, a rambling semi in the residential streets
sandwiched between Yonge and Bay. The place was filled with
odd thrift-shop treasures, including a pair of scavenged
barber chairs with swivelling red leather seats and chrome
pump pedals that made them rise to the appropriate height.
For a kid from staid Lawrence Park, the sight of a living room
so decorated offered a glimpse into a parallel universe accessible only to those lucky enough to live south of Bloor.

From her place, we made our way back to Jack and Jill,
where you could sit in semicircular booths on red leather
banquet seats. Afterwards, my parents might take us into the
Coffee Mill or Cake Master for dessert and coffee. The Coffee
Mill, founded in 1963 by Martha von Heczey, was originally

located in the Lowthian Mews, on Bloor West. Its focal point was a fountain with a bronze statuette, surrounded by wrought-iron tables. Sitting there on a sunny afternoon, my sister and I would get a sugar cube dunked in coffee, along with palacsinta, a thin pancake filled with cottage cheese or apricot jam. Nearby, at the Cake Master, I admired the display cases filled with sweets – marzipan frogs or inverted cake cones dipped in chocolate – but dreaded the chatty owner. She knew my parents, and my sister and I were always subjected to cheek pinches and dreary waits as they bantered in Hungarian.

In most of these restaurants, the schnitzel came in one of two sizes: large or huge. Schnitzel is veal, pork or, occasionally, chicken breast that has been pounded into a thin sheet (thinner is better). It wears a coat of amber-coloured breading that, when done properly, should readily fall away from the meat in swaths. A lemon slice always sits on top of the meat, which is typically served with a starch and what passes for vegetables in Hungarian cuisine – pickled beets, coleslaw or thinly sliced cucumbers drowning in a puddle of sugar-laced vinegar.

At the age of ten or eleven, I still couldn't finish the typical portion, especially the ones served at Country Style, which had, and still serves, the city's largest schnitzels, Frisbee-sized slabs of veal that dangle shamelessly over the edge of an oval plate. But once I hit my teens, I acquired the stamina to down the whole thing, including the roasted potatoes, the slices of pillowy rye that preceded the feast, and dessert. I see those meals now as a kind a milestone of early adolescence – a warm-up for the late-night pizzas and midnight diner meals consumed during that perpetually ravenous phase that characterizes one's late teens and early twenties.

My father died when I was entering Grade 7, and our family discontinued those walks to Yorkville. Adolescence was upon me, and I preferred to spend time with my friends. However, when as a family we wanted to go out to eat Hungarian, my mother always took us to the Country Style on Bloor just east of Bathurst. Her own friends all had their preferred schnitzel joints. Some swore by the Continental, others were devoted to the Corona. Truth was, the food didn't differ much from one to the next. The joke was that there was a huge common kitchen under Bloor Street, cranking out fried food for all those places.

In contrast to the laid-back sophistication of the Coffee Mill (which moved to 99 Yorkville in 1973) or the folksy kitsch of the Csarda House on Bay, with its peasant tapestries and fiddle players, Country Style presented a study in efficient turnover, value for money and minimalist decor. Eight bucks for half a square foot of meat, which was plunked down in front of you within minutes of placing the order. What else could a hungry teenager want?

In the mid-1970s, the owners punched out the back wall and relocated the kitchen to create a few more seats. But Country Style has scarcely changed since then, although it's been sold twice. There's a framed photo of the Hungarian parliament building on one wall, as well as a map and some knick-knacks. One enters through a small vestibule, which is curtained off in the winter. At the front, there's a counter and a display case for desserts. The tables, covered with red-and-white-checked tablecloths, are arranged in tight rows, with a few cramped cubbies on one side, presumably for couples out on a date. There's a highway down the middle where harried, gruff waitresses wearing open-heeled lace-up leather boots schlep plates heaped with food. The kitchen is at the back; after years of eating at this restaurant, I've always figured it's best not to peek inside.

Venturing out for dinner, we came as a family, or with my grandmother, or after a day of hiking or skiing, with friends in tow. The regulars – older, obese Hungarian men, their wispy hair brushed straight back – sat at the counter, hunched over a dish of something fattening and sipping soda laced with cherry syrup. The restaurant was usually full, so you had to stand among the regulars as they ate. But you didn't have to wait for long because the pressure to eat and leave was enormous. The waitresses briskly waved each set of new patrons to their tables and slapped down menus, clunky folios with padded, maroon exteriors. We rarely opened them, however. Everyone knew they'd be ordering a wiener schnitzel.

In the past decade, almost all the Hungarian restaurants along Bloor have closed, except the Coffee Mill at one end, and the Country Style at the other. 'The secret of my staying power is simple,' von Heczey once confided to a reporter. 'I try not to change too much.' The Country Style, for its part, won the war of attrition that played out in the Annex. Many of the Hungarian regulars are gone, having succumbed, no doubt, to the heart disease that will kill anyone whose diet includes nothing but schnitzel. Despite that loss, the restaurant still

does a brisk business feeding hungry university students and other carnivores.

As for myself, I have maintained my habit of walking regularly to the Annex (now from a home on St. Clair West), but my destination tends to be a bookstore or café with a hot spot. My wife and I have two sons, and we've introduced them to the pleasures of relentlessly pounded, artfully breaded, deep-fried meat – although we consider schnitzel dinners a guilty pleasure rather than a staple, for all the obvious reasons. Our sons, Jacob and Sammy, also love Vietnamese, Ethiopian, Japanese, Italian, Szechuan, Middle Eastern and whatever else this city's kitchens offer up. But when these big-city kids are really hungry, they ask for Country Style. And, cleaving to tradition, they don't bother reading the menu. As of this writing, they're still a bit young to manage a whole serving. But I'm pretty sure that that particular rite of passage is just around the corner.

My mother's wiener schnitzel recipe (and my technique)

Begin with about eight slices of boneless pork (veal cutlets or chicken breasts also work). Trim away the fat and pound each slice, on both sides, with a meat tenderizer, using the textured surface. This is a noisy process and if you are doing it correctly, flecks of raw meat will splatter around the working surface. When starting with a centimetre-thick slice of pork, you should pound the meat until it has doubled in size, and then cut it into two pieces.

Pile the flattened meat onto a cutting board. Pour about two cups of white flour on a dinner plate. Pour about two cups of breadcrumbs on a second plate. Take four eggs, break them into a soup bowl and whip them with a bit of water until blended.

Arrange the flour, eggs and water next to the cutting board with the meat, and then put out a second cutting board or another plate for the breaded slices.

The way to remember the order is that it's reverse alphabetical: flour, eggs, bread crumbs. Dredge, dunk, bread, then stack the coated raw meat in a pile. The ends of your fingers will be covered with sticky lumps of flour.

Only after all the meat has been breaded, pour half a bottle of canola oil in a frying pan about five centimetres deep. The oil should come halfway up the pan, deep enough that you can submerge each schnitzel. Turn the burner to high and wait until the oil gets hot (drop in a clump of breadcrumbs to see if it sizzles).

Depending on the size of the meat slices, carefully put three or four in at once using a fork. After a couple of minutes, or once the breading has turned a golden brown, turn over and fry each one a bit more. Meanwhile, turn the oven on to about 250°F.

Remove the fried schnitzels and place them on two or three sheets of paper towel. Put another sheet on top to soak up the excess oil. Give them a bit of a squeeze. Use fresh paper towel for each new tranche. Once this process is completed, put the schnitzels onto a baking sheet in the oven to keep them warm until you're ready to eat.

Squeeze lemon on each slice. Save leftovers for sandwiches. Don't eat this too often.

Gary
Wilkins

Making space for agriculture

When you think of conservation authorities in Ontario, agriculture is usually not the first thing that comes to mind. This is probably particularly true for the jurisdiction of the Toronto and Region Conservation Authority, the most populated area in Canada. People generally associate conservation authorities with parks, flood and erosion control, resource management, or their experiences as children at one of the outdoor education centres operated by conservation authorities. However, TRCA has been involved with agriculture since its inception in 1957. In fact, agriculture was even part of the conservation lexicon of TRCA's predecessor, the Humber Valley Conservation Authority, established in 1948.

At present, TRCA is the largest public landowner in the Greater Toronto Area. Since 1948, it has acquired over 16,000 hectares of land for a variety of purposes. Some of this land is flood plain and is maintained as such, some represents the core and linkages of the terrestrial natural heritage system, some is used for recreation and education and some continues to be used for agricultural purposes.

Over the years, TRCA's agricultural initiatives have been varied. In its first year as an organization, TRCA co-operated with the provincial Department of Agriculture and the Ontario Agricultural College to conduct land-judging competitions during which farmers and other rural residents learned how to properly manage local soils. Then, in 1959, TRCA initiated two new private landowner assistance programs. The first provided technical and financial assistance to farmers for the construction of grass waterways, farm ponds and drainage projects. Thankfully, the promotion of land drainage as a beneficial management practice ended because it became apparent that such action contributed to the loss of valuable wetland habitats and upset the balance of overland runoff to watercourses, causing increased stream flow and erosion.

As a result of the spread of Dutch elm disease in the 1950s, TRCA also adopted a tree-replacement program to provide trees for farm lanes and windbreaks, and to enhance the attractiveness of the rural landscape. In 1959–60, pasture and strip-cropping demonstrations were undertaken on some TRCA properties. Hydro-seeding experiments were also carried out to determine the most economical methods for establishing cover on the unproductive and highly erodable slopes of the Oak Ridges Moraine.

By 1963, TRCA had made considerable progress on one of its major agricultural projects: the development of the farm at the Albion Hills Conservation Area, in the Town of Caledon. The farm provided excellent demonstrations of wise agricultural practices. The hallmark of the farm was its partnership with the neighbouring outdoor education centre, where students were instructed on farm practices, animal husbandry and environmental management. By 1971, demand had grown so much for the program that the farm opened for the first time on a day-use basis to students not attending the on-site residential outdoor education centre. In 1978, a new dairy barn for forty cows was constructed, and the Milk Marketing Board approved a milk production quota for the operation. Unfortunately, the dairy farm closed in 2008, unable to cover the cost of much-needed infrastructure improvements to eliminate environmental problems caused by barnyard runoff. However, during the lifetime of the farm, thousands of students saw first-hand where their food came from.

In the late 1980s and 1990s, TRCA and the Ministry of the Environment began working with rural landowners to heighten public awareness of the sources and causes of rural water pollution. Since 2000, TRCA's Rural Clean Water Program has partnered with the agricultural community to reduce direct and non-point source pollution on agricultural and rural lands. Today the program provides technical and financial assistance to landowners to implement a range of voluntary management practices to improve water quality. These practices include buffer strips, chemical storage, clean-water diversion, integrated pest management, livestock access restriction to watercourses, manure storage and handling, milk house wash-water disposal, septic system repair and upgrade, well decommissioning and tree planting.

While agricultural use of TRCA land has always been compatible with the organization's goals, it has remained an interim activity, discontinued when the land was needed for another purpose, such as reforestation. And although it has always been involved in agriculture, TRCA has never employed staff to farm its productive farmland. For the past fifty-two years, TRCA's agricultural land has been rented to others on an annual basis for the farming of conventional crops such as corn, soybeans and alfalfa, as well as livestock pasturing and dairy and beef production. However, its agricultural land rentals have declined over the past twenty-five years,

mainly because short-term leases provide no incentives for farmers to make personal investments to implement long-term and often costly beneficial management practices. Lack of accessibility to TRCA-owned farmland due to land fragmentation, small plot sizes, congested roadways and urbanization has also contributed to the decline of agricultural use of the lands.

In an attempt to reverse this trend, TRCA adopted a new vision in 2003, dubbed *The Living City*. This new corporate vision acknowledges that 'the quality of life on Earth is being determined in rapidly expanding city regions,' and delineates a new objective for TRCA that challenges the organization to contribute more to achieving sustainable communities. TRCA started to seriously re-examine agriculture as an important and legitimate long-term use of some of its land, and as a way it can help make a contribution to better city-building and sustainable communities. In other words, TRCA acknowledged it could play a meaningful role in the evolution of a new kind of agriculture in the GTA by preserving some of its large land inventory for local, near-urban agricultural opportunities.

In 2008, the conservation authority adopted a policy that requires staff to give serious consideration to agriculture when discussing the future use of TRCA land. Staff is now authorized to negotiate five-year land leases instead of one-year terms, to promote local food production and to seek local food procurement for TRCA facilities. New opportunities utilizing smaller land parcels, innovative techniques and intensive agricultural production methods are being created. TRCA now faces new challenges such as finding new partners and growing new kinds of crops that satisfy the public's desire for locally grown products and caters to changing demographics.

TRCA has initiated several new agricultural projects on its properties in the last five years. The first, started in 2003, is the Toronto Urban Farm, located on three hectares of TRCA-owned property near the southeast corner of Jane Street and Steeles Avenue, opposite the Black Creek Pioneer Village. This is one of Toronto's most vulnerable and stigmatized communities. Although there are many community services in the area, none integrate child and youth development, food security, environmental stewardship, health promotion, recreation and social entrepreneurship like the Toronto Urban Farm.

The farm is operated by Toronto Parks staff as an extension of their Community Gardens Program, which offers services

Toronto Urban Farm (near Jane St. and Steeles Ave.).

that support city-wide urban agriculture. The objectives of this project are ambitious:

- to create meaningful employment opportunities for local youth;
- to enable youth to develop leadership and entrepreneurial skills;
- to increase participants' knowledge and skills in organic farming and environmental stewardship;
- to increase public awareness and build community capacity to address local food security;
- to promote healthy nutrition and active lifestyles;
- to increase the availability of heirloom vegetables and other plant species;
- to generate and disseminate knowledge in sustainable agriculture and community development.

TRCA's second urban agriculture project is being undertaken at the Claireville Conservation Area in Brampton. In 2008, a lease agreement was reached between TRCA and FarmStart, a not-for-profit organization that receives provincial and federal support to coordinate farm facilities, resources and linkages important to new and young farmers. The project will also develop effective land tenure and stewardship arrangements, explore emerging local and direct farm market opportunities, support a new generation of farmers and promote innovative and sustainable business models. The lease gives FarmStart custodianship of fifteen hectares at the Claireville Conservation Area. This joint endeavour aims to help new farmers

McVean Farm, Claireville Conservation Area, Brampton.

McVean Farm.

TRCA staff at the Allotment Gardens, Downsview Park.

establish ecologically sustainable and economically viable agricultural enterprises to supply markets in the GTA, conduct agricultural research and demonstration facilities, and offer new farmer-training programs.

FarmStart will maintain the highest standards of stewardship over the land, overseeing wild areas and shelterbelts in conjunction with the existing woodlots and riparian areas. The agricultural portion of the land will be transitioned to organic certification over the first three years of the lease. With the assistance of TRCA staff, an environmental farm plan will be put into place to guide the development of the new farm facility. FarmStart will take a phased approach to developing the infrastructure needed to support new farmers on the site. Fencing of borders will be completed to protect crops from vandalism and theft, and to separate public demonstration areas from the agricultural plots dedicated to crop and livestock production, farmer training and research. A reliable water supply and irrigation system was installed in 2009. Future facilities will include greenhouses, windmills, storage sheds and meeting spaces. The historic Double English Wheat Barn is also being considered as part of the operation for storage, training and heritage interpretation.

By 2012, the new farm facility is expected to be fully operational, and will feature a dynamic research and demonstration facility, a training farm and twelve or more new farm enterprises. The value of new crops such as okra, bitter gourd and a variety of eggplants, beets and chilies – crops chosen to cater to the area's growing South Asian community – will be higher in both volume and dollar value than historic cash crops such as corn, soybeans and wheat, while still maintaining and improving soil fertility and cultivation practices. Research and demonstration plots will illustrate sustainable farming practices such as low till/no till, trash mulch systems, all-season unheated greenhouse production and water conservation practices. Wind and solar-generated energy will power equipment and educational displays and demonstrations. In addition, outreach and educational planning will increase public awareness of sustainable farming practices and food distribution.

By encouraging new farmers, local food production and community engagement, this farm project will allow people to access and connect to the source of their food and to understand and value the land on which it is grown and those who have grown it. In addition to car, the site is accessible by foot,

The Living City Campus at the Kortright Centre, Vaughan. bicycle and public transportation, which will help to reduce greenhouse gas emissions. The proximity of the site to town will also attract community use and stewardship as people come to buy their food, walk the trails and bring groups of children for educational and fun, food-oriented programs.

The third urban agriculture project being pursued by TRCA is at the Living City Campus at the Kortright Centre in Vaughan. The campus is an evolution of the existing outdoor education program that has served TRCA so well for thirty years. TRCA's plans for the centre will broaden the scope of programming from its focus on environmental education to a more holistic approach that will include near-urban agriculture. The farm will use bio-intensive farming methods and 'high tunnel' greenhouses to produce vegetables year-round. When fully developed, the farm will be a certified organic vegetable operation with direct market sales.

Finally, as mentioned earlier, the farm at the Albion Hills Conservation Area was a dairy operation and partnered with the neighbouring outdoor education centre for decades to educate visitors to the area. This operation has ceased, but a new partnership is being sought to carry on the agricultural

tradition of the property. In the meantime, TRCA continues to make space for agriculture on its land, promotes the growing of local food and requires local food procurement in the kitchens of its education centres. TRCA's target is to purchase 40 percent of its food requirements from local sources by 2012.

Perhaps one of the biggest challenges for agriculture is the difficulty of protecting the land base from competing uses. The revised Ontario Provincial Policy Statement, Places to Grow Act and Greenbelt Plan, all adopted in 2005, provide stronger support of the protection of agricultural land. These planning tools will need to be enforced and upheld by governments as each comes due for review. Municipal governments must make provisions in their official plans to protect the land base for agriculture and other secondary and agriculture-related uses that support the industry.

Some municipalities, such as the Region of Peel, are updating their agricultural policies in 2009. Caledon has already made significant advancement in its policies to protect agriculture. In the future, local bylaws will have to reflect the need to accommodate diverse agricultural use not only in rural areas, but in urban areas as well. Practitioners and proponents of urban agriculture such as community gardens and allotment plots will need to look for more space through community retrofits and new community design. On an individual level, life-skills training is needed in the techniques of growing food in ordinary places such as back-yards, on balconies, in school yards or workplaces. Wide-spread individual commitment is necessary to ensure that local urban agriculture can make a significant contribution to healthy, sustainable communities in the future.

Stéphanie
Verge

The Love(ly) Bug:
An ode to bees in the era of Colony Collapse Disorder, wasp invasions and rooftop apiaries

An old Polish folk tale says that when God created bees, the Devil shot back with wasps. Those of us who suffered through 2009's wasp invasion (and the attendant 'Toronto's so WASPY' hilarity) would likely agree. Decks, patios, stoops: nowhere was safe from the incessant weaving and bobbing. After an unseasonably cool and rainy June and July, it seemed cruel to have to deal with hordes of yellow jackets just as our own jackets were finally coming off. Of course, the pesky wasp's almost unparalleled ability to irritate isn't its only unsavoury trait – wasps fall infinitely short when compared with the industrious bee. They are garbage-loving carnivores, not honey-making flower children. And while the sting of a bee may smart as much as the sting of a wasp, the wasp's utter lack of poetry makes it seem all the more vicious.

The first time I was stung was, nevertheless, by a bee, on a sweltering, blue-skied day on my friend's farm. We were pretending I had died from some tragic, unnamed disease and had roped his younger brother and my younger sister into playing our mourning children. As they lay me down in the funeral (hay) wagon, hands folded in my lap, I felt a sharp pinch on the underside of my arm. I sprang up, panicked, slapping frantically, smearing a fuzzy blob into my skin as I did so. We sprinted up the path to the house, where my friend's German grandmother told me to stop my hollering – it was just a bee, after all – before she got out the calamine lotion and handed me a cookie. How much weight her Teutonic no-nonsense attitude and baked goods carried with my six-year-old self is hard to measure, but I did grow into one of those people who only half-heartedly wave their hand through the air to discourage hovering insects. No leaping out of my chair in a frenetic bid to escape, no sitting statue-still chanting 'bread and butter' under my breath on repeat. But as for her off-the-cuff 'it's just a bee' dismissal, she couldn't have been more wrong.

Whether or not Albert Einstein actually uttered the prediction, much attributed to him, that humanity would die a hungry death in four mere years should bees cease to exist is a subject of debate – a brilliant physicist yes, entomologist not so much. Regardless, this statement has been regurgitated over and over since 2006, when American beekeepers started

reporting massive and mysterious losses. Hives were being abandoned by their tenants, and there were no dead adult bees to be found – they had simply vanished, leaving the queen alone, surrounded by her immature brood and facing a bleak future.

The exact reason for the mass exodus and its after-effects, a.k.a. Colony Collapse Disorder, is still uncertain, with theories ranging from heavy pesticide use to the proliferation of cellular technology. CCD does seem to be a bigger problem in industrialized countries where the use of pesticides and the practice of monocropping are widespread, but most experts point to a combination of elements. Like humans and other social creatures, bees are highly susceptible to stress, which compromises their immune system and leaves them open to disease and death. Being trucked across the country to pollinate large crops – blueberries, canola, alfalfa, say – throughout the year is disorienting, and saddles the bees with a form of insect jetlag. Overcrowding of hives, being forced to feed off the same types of crops, bee-blood–loving varroa mites, Nosema parasites, noxious pesticides, contaminated water sources, global warming – these are all threats to the creatures that hold one of the keys to our survival.

To grasp the gravity of the situation, all you have to do is play a quick game of Let's Pretend. Imagine a world without almonds. No problem, unless you're an almond farmer in California and owner of a crop that depends on half of the honeybees in the U.S. A world without cucumbers – sigh, goodbye, Hendrick's? Easy enough. Take a page from Douglas Coupland's apocalyptic new book, *Generation A*, and imagine a world without heroin – no bees means no pollinated poppies. Done. Okay, now imagine a world without a third of the food currently available to us. When fruits, vegetables and flowers can't be pollinated, what are our alternatives? When the bees disappear, what happens to us?

Certain historians believe that Moravian missionaries brought bees into Canada through Kent County at the end of the eighteenth century, even though others say bees were being kept in the British American colonies back in the mid-1600s. Regardless of the timing, bees have existed in Canada for well over 200 years. And even though the full brunt of CCD hasn't been felt in this country, Canadian hive losses have almost doubled over the past few years due to elevated winter and spring mortality. Honeybees and their powers of pollination represent $1.7 billion to the fruit and vegetable industry in

Canada. Any significant loss in the bee world is going to be keenly felt by those who grow and consume produce, driving up prices and leading to yet another set of problems.

These and further developments in the food world have led to an explosion of curiosity surrounding urban ecology and locavorism. With so much of our sustenance coming from other places, the cost of getting our meals to our tables is both fiscal and environmental. Local beekeeping cuts down on the transportation side of things, not to mention the question of excess packaging. While certain cities do allow urban beekeeping – Vancouver lifted its ban in 2005 – Toronto isn't among them. The Ontario Bees Act effectively rules out beekeeping in most urban areas by disallowing hives within thirty metres of a residence.

The Royal York's executive chef, David Garcelon, shows off some of the hotel's industrious rooftop dwellers.

But that didn't discourage David Garcelon, the executive chef at the Fairmont Royal York. A high-profile believer in environmental stewardship in the city, Garcelon nurtures a herb, fruit and veggie garden that was planted on the rooftop of the fourteen-floor hotel over a decade ago. When he noticed how many bees were showing up for the plentiful and varied sky-high grub, he contacted the Toronto Beekeepers Co-operative to find out about adding hives to his concrete breadbasket, which is elevated enough in comparison to surrounding buildings to meet the province's thirty-metre rule. The hotel started off with three hives in 2008 – the hives are tended by hotel staff and members of the co-op, which also keeps twenty hives at the Evergreen Brick Works in the Don Valley as part of an initiative with FoodShare – and was able to harvest 160 kilograms of honey by the fall. They doubled their numbers in the summer of 2009 and are likely to meet the hotel's honey needs (approximately 450 kilograms) in short order. The hotel's 300,000 bees forage within a 3.5-kilometre radius that includes the pastoral properties on Toronto Island. Between Garcelon's alpine strawberries, tomatoes, mint, lavender, et al., and the island goods, these inner-city bees are better off than their country cousins, who are forced to feed on sprawling, homogeneous crops. And their joy is contagious: anyone who's ever tried the cheese and honey plate at Epic or detected the sweet amber presence in their Library Bar cocktail can't dispute the pluses of having happy, healthy bees.

Garcelon and his co-op compatriots may be the area's most high-profile bee enthusiasts, but they certainly aren't alone. The Ontario Beekeepers' Association, based in Milton, has been around since 1881 and represents over 3,000

The Toronto Beekeepers Co-operative's Cathy Kozma tends to the hives while Garcelon looks on.

Garcelon and members of the co-op take a peek.

beekeepers. The Toronto District Beekeepers' Association was formed thirty years later and now works out of the Kortright Centre for Conservation in Vaughan, where members help spread the gospel through educational programs. Things have changed immeasurably since local naturalist and author Charles Sauriol (*Remembering the Don, A Beeman's Journey*) started keeping hives in the Don Valley in the 1940s.

Despite the recent surge in enthusiasm for urban agriculture, the notion of growing food downtown remains a foreign one for many city dwellers. And laws like those in the Bees Act do little to make the general populace more familiar or more comfortable with the concept. Yet with the help of a resourceful few, metropolis-loving bees will keep coming. Guelph, a municipality known for its abundance of enviro pilot projects, is going ahead with Pollinator Park, a landfill turned meadow of wildflowers and grasses known to attract bees, butterflies and other pollinators. And regardless of rules and regulations, covert apiaries dot backyards across Toronto, kept safe by tall hedges and knowing neighbours placated by the promise of a taste of the season's harvest.

While the bee's sticky endgame is undeniably delicious, our attraction to bees isn't limited to our tastebuds. Humanity's long-held fascination with the little buzzers runs deep – they've had a grip on our collective imagination for eons. According to the Bible, bees flitted around the Garden of Eden. Ancient Egyptians left the fruits of their labour in the tombs of dead relatives. They inhabited Leo Tolstoy's books, brain and backyard. Sarah Ferguson had them embroidered on the seventeen-foot-long train she had made for her wedding to Prince Andrew, a nod to her family crest.

So why the apis love affair? Well, it's impossible not to admire the bee's dogged determination. As civilization builders, they are a potent testament to the power of organization and discipline over free-wheeling chaos. Every member of the hive has a role to play and they are single-minded in their devotion to the task at hand. When hard at work, bees are difficult to distract – they just want to be left alone to make honey, their sole goal. That the machinations of such a complex, intertwined society is inherently captivating to us, the most social of creatures, is hardly surprising. It's how much we take away from them that remains to be seen.

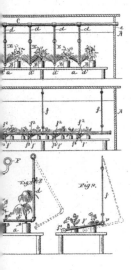

Mark
Fram

Greenhouse Toronto, once upon a time

The basic food position of 1914

A century ago, what is today the almost completely filled-in official twenty-first-century *city* of Toronto was the almost completely filled-in *countryside* of Toronto. The city centre was a small district of commerce and industry where a web of factory-lined railways converged alongside the piers of a modest port. This core was surrounded by irregular chunks and waves of suburban houses interwoven with flood-prone ravines, breweries, fields, orchards, sand pits and brickyards, out to the old official city limits of 1914. Beyond were mingled small towns, villages, rail junctions, country churches and schoolhouses, small working farms and urban outposts like factories, sanatoriums and even a prison farm. Suburbia and exurbia were not at all empty tracts. Very faint traces of that old suburban landscape survive, in road and subdivision alignments, a few place names and some curiously old houses.

It was this pre-modern suburbia, inner and outer, that mostly fed itself and the Toronto it surrounded. No more, of course. Today, it's a global, almost placeless, food network that feeds both city and suburb, mostly from afar.

The vintage greenhouses in the margins on pages 140, 142, 146 and 147 date between 1884 and 1917.

Market gardens and greenhouses within the city and inner suburbs once produced a lot of Toronto's vegetables and even some of its fruit, alongside processors of poultry, dairy, eggs and meat. Supported by a rural rail network far more intricate than today's, alongside local warehouses and granaries, the immediate region could provide kitchens with everything except citrus, even through winter, almost daily. This might not have been the wide-ranging larder now available in supermarkets, specialty shops and even corner stores, but the system satisfied most everyone's diet a century ago at a fairly high standard, and with an astonishing variety that has been forgotten: we can now get kiwis and avocados whenever we want, but the hundreds of local varieties of apples have shrunk to a mere handful.

Perhaps it's not such a coincidence that the rise and fall of urban market gardening in both quantity and variety since the early twentieth century parallels another early twentieth-century phenomenon, the electric car. No typo: the early *twentieth* century. The twenty-first-century world may look upon the electric car as a futuristic environment-saving innovation, but it's not at all new. There were electric runabouts on the road in quantity before World War I. For that matter,

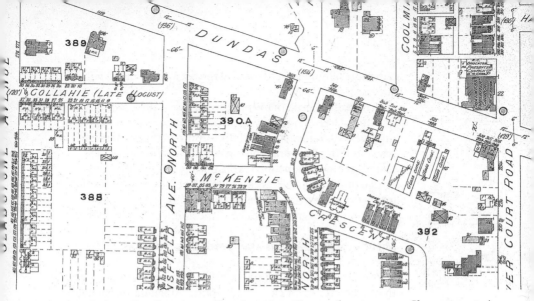

electric (not diesel) trains radiated out into Toronto's country-side, too. And there were electric-lit and ventilated green-houses. These all vanished long enough ago that they seem new ideas today, not the comebacks they really are.

Glass conservatories in the evolving suburbs of 1892, at the corner of Dundas and Dovercourt streets.

Suburbia versus countryside

Even while the old, inexorable and supposedly invisible hand of the property market plows under the gardens sooner or later, until not so long ago there were always small margins and interstices in older residential locales – some well within city limits – where vegetables, flowers and seed stock could be grown and sold. In some residential suburbs that now sprout tract houses or condo towers, there were commercial 'growing operations' not so long ago, though only a few people might now remember them first-hand.

But it's no longer just the real-estate market that fore-dooms the local veggie patch. Since the 1950s, market gardens, orchards and greenhouses for food or flowers have been typically classified as industries, even as environmental hazards, and they are no longer permitted anywhere near where people live or play. The modernist green city promoted recreation parks and front lawns over vegetable plots and greenhouses. Even its successor, the post-modernist (morally) green city, prefers back-to-nature wetlands and ravines over swimming beaches and toboggan slopes, never mind food. Apart from window boxes, personal gardens and yards that are rarely more than diminutive turf farms, today's 'growing city' comprises a precious few historic glasshouses, a scattering

of remote allotment gardens and the occasional newfangled 'green roof.'

There aren't even many pictures of those older ordinary growing places, though there are often inadvertent glimpses of unremarked, vanished suburban Toronto in the corners and backgrounds of unremarkable photos. The remains of the history of food production inside the city are quite literally buried under asphalt and concrete. What follows is some of the bits of evidence of the places where the city once cultivated itself. Comeback from the past = innovation for tomorrow?

Might's market gardens and Goad's greenhouses

To trace this buried civilization calls for a paper archaeology of maps, directories and financial reports. Albeit disconnected, some richly informative archival records that survive show us where these places were, who operated them and how they fit their neighbourhoods.

It has to be said that these old documents contradict the easy claims that twenty-first-century personal computing, data networks and Twitter have transformed us so radically. In truth, the new century is no more an obsessive-compulsive compiler of everyday data on everyone and everything than the twentieth – or even the nineteenth. The Victorian world was no less an information aggregator and hoarder than Google. Not all the old data may survive, but while we may lack photos in quantities worthy of Flickr, we often have names and addresses (courtesy of the Might's Directory Co. and others), maps (from the Charles E. Goad Co.), property and business arrangements (from local tax-assessment records), credit ratings (from Dun & Bradstreet) and even family biographies (from ninety- and hundred-year old censuses).

(opposite) By 1914, even though the city was expanding in all directions, greenhouses, dairies and orchards were still mixed in with houses and workplaces, as here in the east end of the city between Logan and Carlaw avenues north of Gerrard St. There were still greenhouses here in the mid-1930s.

Nicely enough, the commercial directories and maps – sources for the examples offered here – didn't stop at the official edge of the city. They show different forms and scales of greenhouse development around the city's fringes. There were certainly a few private conservatories attached to stately homes, and the public glasshouses at Allan Gardens that survive today. But it's the wide variety of stand-alone operations documented in the directories and insurance maps that is far more revealing of the ingenuity and complexity of the period.

Throughout the city proper and on its edges there were rambling complexes, modest single sheds, open plots, mixed orchards and acres of glass roof. Some were full-service

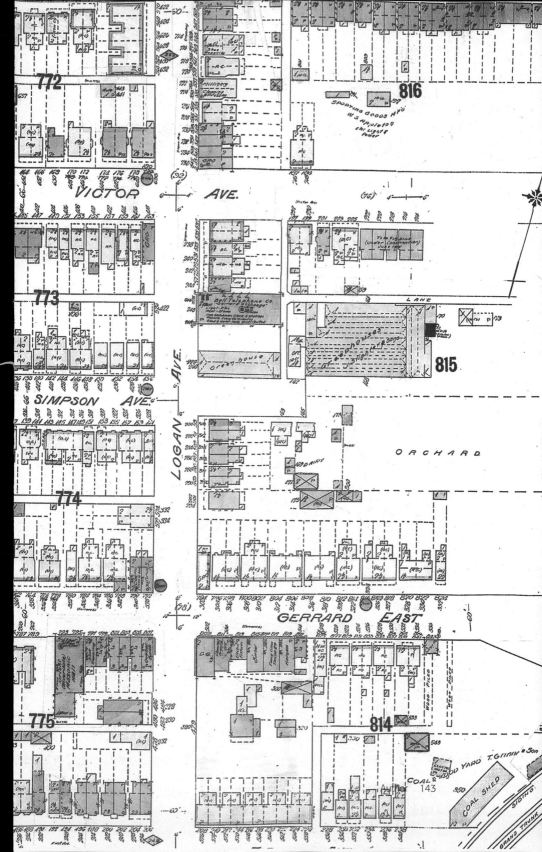

The numbers of business directory listings for 'market gardens' inside and close to the city:

| 1900: 242 | 1903: 234 | 1908: 169 | 1914: 162 | 1917: 170 | 1922: 134 |

After 1900 the numbers decline, as refrigeration and transportation technologies supplant 'freshness,' as other urban activities push up land prices, and as new suburbanites turn up their noses (literally) at the rough realities of farming in their new neighbourhoods. The decline stops temporarily during wartime. Even so, only about half of the 1917 market gardeners are the same people and locations as they were three years earlier. It is a tough business.

What follows are the full directory listings during World War I. The market gardens that remained in place are highlighted. Even in wartime, suburban expansion is evident in the rapid occupation of Cedarvale, Fairbank and Lambton Mills for commercial gardens, bypassing stalwarts like Humber Bay and Todmorden. Almost all would be displaced by the real-estate booms of the 1920s, leaving only a few small yards and greenhouses like those in the city proper.

1914	1917		1914	1917		1914	1917
CITY				Lightfoot Chas, 88 Awde		Ryan Bros, 754 Ossington av	
Athersich Wm H, 942 Logan av	Athersich Wm H, 942 Logan av		Lightfoot S & Sons, 24-30 and 21-25 St Lawrence Mkt	Lightfoot S & Sons, 24-30 and 21-25 St Lawrence Mkt		Sharpley Charles. 564 Christie	Sharpley Charles, 564 Christie
Avery Thos, 124 Broadway av	Avery Thos, 124 Broadway av			Linse Henry, north side Moore av		Shephard George, 121 Arundel	Shephard George, 121 Arundel
Bamford James, 27-33 St Lawrence Mkt	Bamford James, 27-33 St Lawrence Mkt			McCulloch Harold, s s Blythwood rd 2nd e of 451			Shimkofsky Moses, 26 Fairlawn av
Bamford John, 40 St Lawrence Mkt	Bamford John, 40 St Lawrence Mkt					Shuter Albert W, 1099 Davenport rd	
	Bullyment Mance, 262 Runnymede rd		MacNamara Frank, 789 Davenport rd	MacNamara Frank, 789 Davenport rd		Stevens Chas, 1927 Dufferin	Stevens Chas, 1927 Dufferin
Butler Leonard, 1063 Pape av			MacNamara John W, 699 Davenport rd	MacNamara John W, 699 Davenport rd		Symes Geo, n s Symes rd 1 w Glen Scarlett rd	Symes Geo, n s Symes rd 1 w Glen Scarlett rd
Byers Wm, 983 Davenport rd	Byers Wm, 983 Davenport rd			Macnamara Patk, 1199 Shaw		Tofani Bros, 665 Eastern av	Tofani Bros, 665 Eastern av
Callicott Joseph, 911 Davenport rd			Miller Bernard W, 1969 Dufferin	Miller Bernard W, 1969 Dufferin		Topping Chas, 32 St Lawrence Mt and 715 Bathurst	Topping Chas (Mrs Maria Topping), 32 St Lawrence Mkt and 715 Bathurst
	Callicot Joseph, 45 Hammond pl		Mills J H, 379 Danforth av	Mills J H, 379 Danforth av			
Conboy Jas, 849 Ossington av	Conboy Jas, 849 Ossington av		Millsom Wm, 370 Soudan av			**CEDARVALE**	
	Corcoran James, 1296 Dufferin		Nicholson George L, 327 Pape av	Nicholson George L, 327 Pape av			Barker Robt
Corcoran M & J, 1292 Dufferin			Phillips Geo A, 667 St Clair av w	Phillips Geo A, 667 St Clair av w			Bell James
	Davis Henry, n s Blythwood rd 1 w of Bayview av		Preston Roger, 680 Danforth av	Preston Roger, 680 Danforth av		Bell Walter	
			Punnett Richard, 646 Christie				Bennett Wm
France Arthur, 131 Jones av			Reed Henry E, 1 Chatham av	Reed Henry E, 1 Chatham av			Daniels Fredk
Gummitt Wm E, 46 Helena av			Reed Wm E, 71 Chatham av	Reed Wm E, 71 Chatham av			Daniels James & Sons
Hong Ling, 1128 Shaw	Hong Ling, 1128 Shaw		Richardson James, 398 Greenwood av				Daniels Wm H
	Johnston Robert, 2 Belcourt rd			Rutledge Oscar E, s s Blythwood rd 1st e of 451			Daniels and Sons
	Kidd Wm, 256 Broadway av					Garbutt James	Garbutt James
Lightfoot Chas, 16 Awde							Graziano Bros
							Jennings Bros
							McGregor Robt
							McKay Thos C
							Magee Harold A

1914	1917
Stapley Percy R	
Tustin James	

EARLSCOURT

1914	1917
Avery Geo A	
Maybee Theophilus J	
Miller Bernard W	

FAIRBANK

1914	1917
Anderson Wm J	
Bowers Geo	
	Curtis Chas
Fowler Geo H	
Jones Wm	
	Moody Wm
	O'Hara James
	O'Hara John
	Privett Arthur
	Waterman Ernest
	Wilcox Bros

HUMBER BAY

1914	1917
Allen Joseph W	Allen Joseph W
Aymer Chas	
Aymer George	
Barrow John	
	Bell Albert
Bell Percy A	
Bradley Lewis T	Bradley Lewis
Brown John G	Brown John G
Burbidge Ernest	Burbidge Ernest
Clarke Alex	
Clarke John	
	Collins Chas
Collins James	Collins Jas
Collins Wm	
Cowley Wm	
Cox Joseph	Cox Joseph
Cox Saml	Cox Saml
Crowhurst Ernest	
Dandridge James	Dandridge James
Dickson John	Dickson John
Edton Thos	
Elford Isaac	Elford Isaac
Elford Wm	Elford Wm
Forsythe James	Forsythe James
Gill John	
Greenfield Chas	Greenfield Chas
Grigsby Amos	Grigsby Amos
Grigsby Wm	Grigsby Wm
	Hanley Robt
	Harris Wm
Holmes Wm	
Hunt Herbert	
Kent Wm	Kent Wm
	Lizzard David
Magrath John	
Major Rupert	Major Rupert E
	Morehouse Wm
North Geo	North Geo
North Harry	North Harry
North Wm	North Wm
Parker Walter	Parker Walter C
Pycock James	Pycock James
Reeves Frank	Reeves Frank
Reid Ralph L	
Rowett Ernest	Rowett Ernest
Rowett Geo H	
	Rowett Herbert
	Rowett John H
Rush Geo	Rush Geo W
Rush Joseph	Rush Joseph W
Smith Henry S	Smith Henry S
Stephens John	

1914	1917
Stocks James	
Temple Andrew	
	Tiffin Dalton A
Tizzard David	
Todd James	Todd James
Todd Joseph	
	Todd Wm
Webb Arthur	
Whitworth Edwd	Whitworth Edw
	Whitworth Geo
Whitworth John	
Wixson Thos	
Wright David	

LAMBTON MILLS

1914	1917
	Ashton Lawrence
	Atkinson Wm
	Banham Wm
	Banks Edwd
	Bannon John P
	Barr Saml
	Carlton Arthur
	Cornish Frank
	Jeanes Leonard
	Marx Carl
	Milligan John J
	Pressley Thos
	Wilson Geo
	Woods Albert

LITTLE YORK

1914	1917
	Jones Joseph J

MIMICO

1914	1917
Davey James	Davey James
Dickson John	

MOUNT DENNIS

1914	1917
	Aikins Thos
Barton Edwin	
	Buchel Albert, 55 Lambton av
Crayden Thos R	
Dabbs Chas H	
Davis Albert	Davis Albert
Lodge James	
	McCutcheon Andrew
	McCutcheon Thos J
	Marshall Chas W
	Mason Alfred
	Mason Wm
Maxted Stephen	Maxted Stephen
	Pordage Edward G
Pordage John	Pordage John
Robinson Alfred	
	Spence Percy
Syme James A	Syme James A
Wilds Horace	
Yetman Chas	Yetman Chas
Yetman Henry	Yetman Henry

OAKWOOD

1914	1917
	Coates Geo
	Graham Bernard

TODMORDEN

1914	1917
Anderson Wm	
Athersich Wm	
Barker Robert	
Barron Alex	Barron Alex
	Bateman Wm

1914	1917
Bee Wm	Bee Wm
Bell James	
Bell Robert	
	Boorne Leonard
Bradley Thomas	Bradley Thomas
	Brayman Thos
	Bunce John S, 15 Plains rd
Byers Joseph	Byers Joseph
Carwardine Bros	Carwardine Bros
Clark James F	Clark James F
	Collins Francis
Collins Joseph	Collins Joseph
	Constable Alex
Cosburn Chas	Cosburn Bros
Cosburn Robt	
	Curtis Geo H
Daniels Fred	
Daniels James	
Daniels W H	
Dart John	Dart John & Son
Dart Joseph	Dart Joseph
Dart Joseph Jr	
Dunn Wm W	Dunn Wm W
Graziano Bros	
Griffin Fredk	
	Griffin & Enston
Hare Bros	Hare Bros
Hoskin John	
Inward George	
Jennings Bros	Jennings Bros
Leamen Christopher J	Leaman & Son
	McCauley James & Sons
McGregor James A	
McKay Frances M Mrs	
McKay John	
McKay T C	McKay T Chas, 925 Greenwood av
Magee Earl E	
Magee Everett	
Monk Geo	
Mortimer James	
Roberts Robt W.	
Segriff Bros	Segriff Bros
Segriff John R	
Simpson Charles	Simpson Charles
Smith Edward	Smith Edward
Somers Bernard	Somers Bernard
	Stevens & Son
Tomlin George	Tomlin George
Tustin James	
Ward Wm	Ward & Son
Westwood John	
	Westwood Percy
Whitnell Isaac	
	Willett Frances, 1125 Donlands av

WESTON

1914	1917
Best John	Best John
Eagle Edwd	
Harris Patk	Harris Patrick
Redmond Michl	
Redmond Thos	
Willie Lena Mrs	

WYCHWOOD

1914	1917
	Corner Walter J
	Graham Thos
	Groves Chas

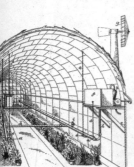

retail-market-garden-florist businesses with main-street frontages and city-wide delivery networks. Some greenhouses temporarily occupied prospective house lots for a few years, others for decades. Some greenhouses were squeezed into back lanes of working-class districts. Occasionally their traces can be made out today as a break in the continuity of adjacent houses of a certain age, or in newer structures of odd configuration, or even as still-empty lots. For instance, along upper Christie Street across from Artscape's renovated Wychwood Barns, a big surface parking lot is easy to imagine as what it once was, one of a set of market gardens and greenhouses that used to line the street.

The sample maps and lists here show bits of Toronto at the outbreak of World War I. This seems to have been the peak of urban growing, in range and variety. Most of the gardens and greenhouses evident in 1914–16 disappeared by the 1930s. Thanks to the improvement of both city streets and rural roads that began in the 1920s, the biggest operations, whether florists or winter-vegetable growers, were able to consolidate themselves as wholesale operations far from Toronto's tight spaces and dirty air, near places like Brampton or along the lakeshore. At the same time, the continentalization of food production, accelerated by improved rail and refrigeration offered fresh produce in the midst of Canadian winters. And the expansion of chain stores, branded processed food and cheap canned vegetables year-round pushed out the small-scale local growers and their labels.

The grow-ops of tomorrow?

The modern-day successors to the World War I market gardeners at Todmorden and Humber Bay now cultivate the reclaimed bogs of the Holland Marsh and the shrinking fruitlands of the Niagara Peninsula. Although in any given summer, at least until they're finally paved over, there may still be a few pick-your-own plots of strawberries or sweet corn closer by for the lucky few in the northeast corner of Scarborough.

On the other hand, the local greenhouses of olden days vanished decades ago, eliminated by refrigerated greens from irrigated fields in California and Mexico, and greenhouses in Florida, Arizona and even Almería, Spain.

Even if we could have them back, is there room? For open-air market gardens, not really. Toronto's official plans call for 'intensification' within the amalgamated megacity – meaning

hundreds of thousands of new dwellings – so it's hard to imagine much room for serious cultivation. Even the rapidly filling 905 municipalities aren't planning to retain more than perfunctory space for food production.

Greenhouses are another story, though their comeback would have different problems. There is certainly the technology and the rooftop space for high-intensity greenhouse cultivation (*pace* today's grow-ops).[1] But governments haven't been interested in pushing either the capital investments or the regulatory overhauls needed to accommodate and encourage substantial food production right in the city and right on top of buildings. Despite high oil prices in 2008 warning of the imminent end of cheap long-distance transport, it's wind turbines and solar panels rather than local tomatoes that seem to be the sexy icons of future self-sufficiency.

1 See Graeme Stewart's 'The suburban slab: Retrofitting our concrete legacy for a sustainable future' and Mark Fram's 'Planning walking zoning greening' in *Green-TOpia: Towards a Sustainable Toronto* (Toronto: Coach House Books, 2007).

The cold reality is that on average, albeit with a lot of grumbling, Toronto's local economy – used to a relatively small proportion of household expense for food over the past half century – can absorb higher food costs, up to a certain point anyway. (Unhappily, unless political priorities change radically, the average is just that, average, and the less-well-off might have to eat even less well than they do now.) Greenhouse complexes as local food factories are unlikely unless worldwide transportation costs soar almost exponentially and rewrite the equations. Until then, Toronto can hardly compete with Almería.

In any case, Toronto is unlikely to want to return to Victorian diets or even today's locavore restraints. Torontonians themselves are now, after all, as globalized as the globe itself, with faces, tastes, appetites and enthusiasms no longer bound by western Europe. Local greenhouses would have to grow a great deal more than tomatoes and cucumbers. But you have to ask, why not?

So here's a new basic food position for the next decade or two. Growing food within and close by the city has proven successful in the past. Once upon a time, in hundreds of small market plots and greenhouses, Toronto *did* grow and process a lot of what it sat down to eat – not to forget the flowers and foliage that pleased the eye and delighted the table. To recover some of that old-time self-reliance, and improve on it, doesn't require expensive invention from scratch. It's been done. Now it's just a matter of some pragmatic adaptation. That's the unremarkable and kind of creativity that cautious old Toronto should still be good at.

Iara Lessa &
Cecilia Rocha

Nourishing belonging:
Food in the lives of new immigrants in T.O.

At the first sign of unsettledness, some people run to the kitchen to cook themselves something soothing, to search for 'comfort food.' This comforting effect of food brought us to think about the relationship between food and settlement. As immigrants ourselves – we were both born in Belo Horizonte, Brazil, and we met in Toronto, where we've both lived for over twenty-five years – we are very aware of the hardships of the re-rooting process. We often share stories about growing roots in Canada and how we felt when, in the past, the things we longed to eat were impossible to find. Today, things seem different: at Dundas and Dufferin, you can find almost any Brazilian ingredient. We've often wondered if it is easier for recent immigrants to Toronto to belong here when the world is so much more connected.

These queries stirred us to undertake a research project supported by CERIS – the Ontario Metropolis Centre. We talked to forty-five women from different origins who had immigrated to Toronto in the last five years about the roles their food practices and habits have played in their search for respect, participation and belonging in this new society. These new immigrants were recruited for the study primarily through agencies delivering ESL programs and through FoodShare, a community agency working with food issues in Toronto, and our partner in the research project.

Food both represents us and singles us out

Food is often associated with newcomers and their settlement and homemaking practices. Many immigrants are represented in receiving nations by the images of the rich and fragrant foods they cook and the traditional food stocks of their home-lands. Canada's policy of multiculturalism emphasizes diversity and tolerance, and promotes fairs and cultural festivals as tools of integration and symbols of Canadians' acceptance of newcomers and their cultures. The exoticism of foreign dishes comes to symbolize cosmopolitanism, global integration and acceptance of others.

Globally, practices surrounding the purchase, preparation, consumption and disposal of food are commonly accepted as central cultural signs. Food is thought of as central to family interactions, as a conduit for social regulation and

as a reaffirmation of family and community. Within many societies, including Canada, women are still in charge of preparing food and feeding the family and, in many cases, their sense of self and identity is bound to these roles. Food is seen as key to the formation of personal and group identity and figures significantly and symbolically in the life cycles, histories and social traditions of different social groups. Food practices are a marker of one's social location and ethnic identity and constitute a good vantage point from which to examine class, racialization and gender relations.

While food can function as a kind of cultural shorthand and allow for a celebration of harmony and the integration of communities, it also sometimes represents a battle of interests and power among diverse practices. In a 2008 article published in the *Journal of Intercultural Studies* titled 'Alimentary Agents: Food, Cultural Theory and Multiculturalism,' media and cultural studies professor Ben Highmore looked at the practice of curry consumption in Britain, and speculated on its parallels with a continuation of the colonial battles undertaken in the subcontinent.

Likewise, Australian writer and philosopher Mary Zournazi proposed, in her article 'The Queen Victoria of Bush Cuisine: Foreign Incorporation and Oral Consumption Within the Nation,' that food provides consumptive metaphors for processes encompassed by immigration such as the swallowing up of foreign bodies, the devouring and assimilation of their differences and the gradual digestion of othered bodies into an imaginary body politic. This brings to mind the conflicts that occur over odours and techniques of unfamiliar cuisines. The foreignness of smells and preparation habits is often invoked against the settlement of racialized immigrants and results in calls for the urgency of education about 'national' standards and strict public-health policies. Fears of infection and contamination through foreign food are as old as immigration itself. Food, argues UBC professor Sneja Gunew in her introduction to a special issue of the *Journal of Intercultural Studies*, lies at the very heart of colonialist incorporation and co-optation. Through food, immigrants can be celebrated, but also singled out, rejected and crushed.

Diasporic healing: soothing loss and longing

The food narratives of newcomer women collected in our interviews gave concrete form to the nostalgic longing for a

home left somewhere else. Carmen, a forty-year-old Peruvian woman, illustrated the expression of this longing: 'I keep a little bit of the maize. If it stays in your kitchen always, in a line there … and in a jar, you still see it and feel that time you ate it, you know … you had that taste … And if you finish that … (sigh) …'

Salma, a new Canadian originally from Bangladesh explained, 'I miss a lot of vegetables in the morning. In my home country, there are vegetables that we do not find here. At breakfast here there is a lot of bread.

As Gunew puts it, 'In the "ethnic" or diasporan text, food traditionally functions to mark the memory of another kind of corporeality, of the body moving through a different daily repertoire of the senses.'

These narratives of loss and longing express and acknowledge feelings associated with uprooting, and allow for an empathetic connection with another world and its communities. They also seem to enable groups in the diaspora to recount and perhaps exhaust the negative effects of loss. The possibility of producing small comforts offers the opportunity, even if only temporary, to bridge geographic and temporal gaps through memory and sensory satisfaction. Annia, who came from Budapest two years ago, put it this way:

> On Sunday, when we were at our home, we were very happy. We were reminded of our country and our meals together. There's a store here on Danforth that has fish. It is fresh and tastes very, very good. And so when we brought fish from this store … we prepare in our home and its very good taste. So those are those small things that remind [us of] our country or make me feel a little bit …

The idea that cooking our homeland's foods erases space and time and keeps home alive came up repeatedly in our research meetings. When you're a newcomer, your life is marked by the ongoing search for familiar ingredients, by the desire for a connection to home and the possibility of finding fragments of memories of the homeland. All this embodies a hope for settlement and re-grounding. And, among its many soothing effects, food composes a list of tangible desires and dreams. It provides a reason to call family to inquire about cooking tips, different aspects of recipes and preparation. It is a focus for communication with relatives and friends who bring food back from visits to the homeland. Food helps to

bridge distances, feeds memory, gives concrete ways to express loss, soothes the nostalgic longing and offers hope for recreating the familiar in a strange land.

Food in processes of othering and exclusion

The cost of food is 'a definite item in the budget here,' said Sania, one of our interviewees from India. While certain foods may be more affordable in Toronto, in many cases the cost of food has had a strong marginalizing effect on the lives of the women interviewed. Angela, a twenty-five-year-old South African woman, said, 'When we came we just looked in the stores ... All those vegetables we liked ... The prices are not a lot more but ... we did not have good jobs ... Only my husband was working.'

Many of the women we spoke to negotiate food cost through ingredient substitution, long travels to find better prices and hours scrutinizing ads. Many have gained their knowledge of city streets and geography through expeditions to procure affordable food that came to their attention through flyers, television or word of mouth in the community. For some, the search leads to the unprecedented and often humiliating experience of being the recipient of donated food. Food Banks Canada reports that 46 percent of their clients in 2008 were born outside of Canada, and that 47 percent of that group have been in Canada for more than ten years. Half of their clients come from households with children and, not surprisingly, given the country's current immigration policies, 37 percent of them have graduated from college or university.

But cost is not all that has to be circumvented. The women with whom we talked remarked on the segregation, jokes, shame and discrimination their husbands and children suffer at work and at school. In many cases, these environments were described as non-accepting of different foods and quick to castigate those who eat their home food in the integrated spaces ruled by mainstream norms. 'So that was the thing my husband felt,' recounted Sonja, a newcomer from Pakistan. 'At work they say, "What is this? What is that? It smells bad. You better wash after." So, you know, I thought, "Don't take our food. Chapati is bread, it is okay."'

While multiculturalism publicizes and emphasizes the food of the other, these foods are often not welcomed into mainstream society. Many women worry about the risk of being segregated and crossing the tenuous line of tolerance

encouraged by multiculturalism. A mother recounted that she had to carry out a lengthy battle at her son's daycare after the staff refused to feed the child what she sent for lunch. These food narratives demonstrate the strong racializing subtext of immigrants' settlement and, on the most primary level, urgently call for cultural-awareness training and policies that will ensure an environment in which newcomers can develop positive roots and interactions.

Re-rooting home: Integrating the loss of home into a transformed new life

These negative encounters may be mediated by positive situations that encourage newcomers to start setting down roots in new soil. Some immigrant women in our study proudly recounted stories of the discovery of new foods and ingredients from around the world and the creation of integrated recipes. 'I feel proud,' said Nadia, a mother from Iran. 'You know those puff pastry sheets that you can buy from the shop? They have a recipe using cranberries or blueberries for filling. But I made patties, meat patties or vegetable patties, with those. Then everybody loved it in my family, and also my neighbours.'

The creation of new food and food habits occurs through several dispersed and subtle changes: buying an unknown vegetable from the supermarket, getting a new recipe from a colleague, following the suggestions of one's children, watching a television program. The incorporation of prepared foods also offers convenience and speed. This can mean the acquisition of some Western dietary habits and the introduction of new dishes into family meals. In many cases, the women we interviewed discovered the convenience of, for example, prepared chapatis, tortillas and several complete dishes from their homelands. In many cases, these foods were not commercially available there, usually prepared by hired help or extended family and shared among a few families. Buying prepared home foods incorporated changes in the traditional preparation while allowing, despite the extreme time pressures of routines in their new country, a continuing connection with the familiar.

By introducing these innovations into the home, women are creating a hybrid or borderland space that can mitigate the prejudice they experience in their interactions with mainstream institutions. The resulting ambiguity of the home space

comforts family members and helps them to deal with discrimination, facilitating the negotiation of ethnic identity and belonging. Offering favourite traditional foods, unique hybrid dishes and surprising new foods can transform the home into a distinctive space that exists in the present but also in the re-lived experiences evoked by the tastes of the homeland. These spaces of hybridization forge ways to resist acculturation and assert a valued identity. In addition, in using food as a repository of culture, the women we interviewed make a conscious effort to ensure that their children will not forget the tastes, traditions and festivities of their homeland. 'When I prepare Indian food, it's more like I am passing the culture my kids never saw to them, their background, what we have back home, so that they know their roots. They did not drop out of the sky – they came from some traditions,' explained Rachika, a thirty-nine-year-old newcomer from Pakistan.

These experiences seem to help move immigrant families beyond feelings of loss and longing into a space where they can develop relationships with their new surroundings. Using food as an intermediary, they can increase their capacity to enact the detailed and complex work that settlement entails. However, this engagement can only occur in the presence of a minimum of resources: cooking requires housing, equipment and utensils; affordable, available and adequate ingredients; and time and peace of mind to be able to make use of the powerful resource. Practices of hybridity are an outcome of a supportive context that allows for these basic needs to be met while fostering the emergence of a greater sense of belonging and promoting a re-rooting that reinforces familiar homeland practices and activities.

Food, then, is profoundly implicated in opening possibilities of formulating relations and attachments with a new environment. It is an important part of the creative activities involved in reconstructing one's culture and traditions as a viable and empowering legacy that makes possible a transformed future.

References

Highmore, Ben. 'Alimentary Agents: Food, Cultural Theory and Multiculturalism,' *Journal of Intercultural Studies*, 29(4), 2008. pp. 381–398.

Gunew, Sneja. 'Introduction: Multicultural Translations of Food, Bodies, Language.' *Journal of Intercultural Studies* 21(3), 2000. pp 227–237.

Zournazi, Mary. 'The Queen Victoria of Bush Cuisine: Foreign Incorporation and Oral Consumption within the Nation." *Communal/Plural* 4(1), 1994. pp. 79–89.

Food Banks Canada, 'HungerCount 2008.' (Food Banks Canada, 2008).

Kate Carraway &
Peter Maynard

An unmovable feast

Most of the time it's bad service, and not bad food, that makes for a bad dining experience. Disappointing service ruins the food, it ruins the ambience and it ruins the lifestyle fantasy we chase by venturing out of our own kitchens, to be cooked for and served by other people, professional people. While food tends to subsume our thoughts about dining out, service is probably the most meaningful element of a meal.

In Toronto, a city used to apologizing for itself, especially for its failures to appear 'world-class,' restaurants often demonstrate this institutional low self-esteem by providing overwhelmingly and comically bad service. Some of Toronto's finest restaurants feature service that ranges from hand-wringingly obsequious to ignorant, haughty and just plain rude. The overarching attitudes and practices of food service in Toronto contradict what the city's kitchens are capable of. There is a tremendous amount and diversity of talent here, and the chefs in the better, more prestigious establishments are often as famous as their restaurants. Food in Toronto is a big deal. Still, the gap between the talent in the kitchen and the talent at the front of the house undermines not only these restaurants but also our city.

Eating out carries with it a reasonable expectation of good service, and that expectation implies a few specific things. Typically, the server is the patron's only connection to the kitchen, and he or she should be familiar with every dish, including the primary ingredients, where the ingredients were sourced and what the cooking process is. For instance, Simon Bower, the co-proprietor of Lucien on Wellington Street, has his servers recite ingredients when a dish is presented to a patron; at other establishments, he says, 'a lot of waiters are interested in bluffing, and it's very visible and very transparent.' Servers should also know their way around their restaurant's wine list, whether or not there is a somme-lier. This knowledge should be tempered with discretion; above all, good service is self-effacing. According to local food writer Shaun Smith, 'What you want is someone who is prepared, knowledgeable and engaged with the task at hand, who anticipates the patron's needs and is striving to make sure the dining experience is pleasant. The best do this without being intrusive or showing effort. The dining room is about the patron. As soon as a server puts his or her needs before the patron's needs, they are on the road to failure.'

Chris McDonald, the chef at Cava on Yonge Street, says, 'Things work better when the waiter is in control. When the customers are in control of the dining experience, things start going sideways. If the waiter can be in control of the points of service and the dining experience, then things can be orchestrated in a fashion that reflects the house style.' When something goes wrong with the service, the whole restaurant is implicated.

The biggest hurdle in establishing a dining culture in Toronto that's comparable to those in the major cities we aspire to match is that we collectively and culturally belittle service industry jobs. In Europe, service-sector work is standardized and professionalized in a way that it's not here; the European model is based on a long history of doing things right and according to tradition rather than striving for trendy newness. As McDonald explains, 'In Europe, it's different. You have two or three generations that go to the same restaurant, and two or three generations that are operating the same restaurant. It happens in Montreal as well. There are restaurants that have been there forever.'

Often, the countries with the most firmly established class systems are the ones where professional service people have less class anxiety, particularly less than in a status-obsessed city like Toronto. In Berlin, working as a clerk in a bookstore isn't considered pejorative the way it is in Toronto. There is a certain dignity and mastery in European service and in some other North American cities that's lacking here. Understandably, Toronto servers are informed and influenced by Toronto's second-class standards, and end up reinforcing them by being rude, pretentious and unconvincing in their work, undermining the efforts of the kitchen they're representing. In Toronto, servers often insinuate themselves into a customer's meal in a way that's cloying and irritating; in Paris, an average dining experience is brutally efficient but quietly polite; New York's reputation for snobbery is often legitimate, but the quality of the service still tends to be more professional. Cava's McDonald grew up in New York, and says, 'I think there is a level of ease that we don't have here, where the people who are in the service industry recognize that they're in the service industry and have a certain ease talking to their patrons, whether that's a candy store or a shoe store or a restaurant. You walk into a juice bar in New York City and the counter help who has never seen you before will say, "Those are great shoes." It's just a different way of dealing with strangers.'

What could be the basis for a strong service culture in Toronto ends up being a liability. In a city that's composed of conflicting, mashed-together cultures and social notions, there is a natural confusion and ambiguity about the role of servers, about whether they're supposed to be servants or experts. A similar confusion is found in expense-account restaurants that maintain a duty-bound relationship between server and customer, and server and kitchen. There, the mores are so conservative and old-school that there remains a sense that waiters and waitresses are the help, which is no better than the implicit and explicit contempt found elsewhere.

As a city that is constantly agonizing about how it measures up to the first-tier cities of the world, Toronto generally fares pretty miserably: the local attitude about our failings is precisely this constant fear of international scrutiny that squelches any broad opportunities for levity and originality. The size of the city has something to do with this. Toronto really is between big and major. Says Chris McDonald, 'We have a problem here compared to a lot of the cities that you might compare us to: we have next to no tourism, certainly no culinary tourism. Without any tourism, you end up with the same people, the same fish in your fishbowl … It's good to have people on vacation, or business people on an expense account, in your restaurant. You need new blood all the time. You have to compare us to Columbus, Ohio, [not] Chicago or Montreal or New York.' *Toronto Star* food writer Corey Mintz says, 'The only dining city I can really compare Toronto with is New York, which is not fair. The biggest difference I notice is that high-volume restaurants in New York are more efficient. But you can only get to that level when you can depend on constant clientele.' Adds Lucien's Simon Bower, 'It seems that the restaurant community in New York raises the bar on each other because the competition is so fierce; the chefs raise the standards, they execute things better. The service is expected. New Yorkers are tough. World-class business travellers are tough.'

What makes for strong service culture in Paris, New York and other 'world-class' cities can't be done on a smaller scale and shouldn't be attempted. But Toronto does have an opportunity to revisit and evaluate its approach, to use its citizens' constant self-evaluation to demand better by instituting dignity in service jobs. This all has to be preceded by a commitment to professionalism and a respect for the trade.

The best servers in the city clearly take the job seriously, and seem to genuinely enjoy participating in the ritualized environment and luxury experience. So, too, should restaurant patrons.

Bad service is also the fault of our restaurant reviewers, who act as the liaison between a restaurant and its potential patrons. Usually, criticism will be squarely about the food (with perhaps a few bitchy lines about service) – there is rarely a correlation made between the service and the kitchen, as if each succeeds or fails independent of the other. 'Because there is no universal standard set by an outside body, such as Michelin, little critical attention is paid to the minutiae of fine service that can make a good restaurant great, and a great restaurant brilliant,' says Shaun Smith. 'I think one reason for these failings is that we don't have a rating system in place that factors in service to a very significant degree. That is, the restaurants are policing themselves.' If a dish sits on the pass for too long, sauces congeal, frites get soggy. Customers, too, are responsible for the problem, when they patronize the restaurants that don't emphasize service, as are servers who use the kind of vulgar mental arithmetic that evaluates a customer's bill and tip potential in advance. There's a lot of begrudging that goes on in the kitchen. Even if the servers tip out to kitchen staff, they're getting most of the discretionary money, and in a lot of ways they're doing the least work. Bower says, 'There should be no such thing as an automatic gratuity, or no such thing as the waiter perceiving what the gratuity should be. The service should dictate what the customer should leave as a tip.' Paradoxically, in France, where a gratuity is included on the bill, service has a higher standard. With an added, semi-optional 15 percent gratuity in place in Toronto, servers slack off.

There are many professional servers in Toronto who are educated about food and understand their professional function. And, certainly, restaurants that provide consistently good service will benefit. 'Are you going to go the extra mile and get them a taxi, or get them a Kleenex if they have the sniffles?' asks McDonald. Bower hesitates to summarize Toronto's restaurants as having bad service, but does find consistently good service in bigger towns. 'When I go to other cities, such as New York or Chicago, I find that the food-service professionals take their jobs extremely seriously.' McDonald says the non-professionals will be the first to leave

the restaurant industry in the wake of the recession. 'The people left standing are going to have a larger market and they're going to get the best staff, because there's a lot of staff out there now. The best managers and the best owners are going to get the best staff.'

In a city that can't commit to its own potential, the overwhelming notion that working in a restaurant is a means to an end, or a holdover career en route to something that's considered more creative or gratifying, means servers aren't usually invested in what they're doing. Rudeness feels forced and defensive and isn't due to a lack of interest or knowledge, but to a common projected insecurity about why they're bothering at all. So, wine lists remain misunderstood and poorly communicated, and the great work of chefs and their kitchens remain lost on a city that's big and hungry enough to deserve it.

Hamutal
Dotan

For the love of a good burger

You can read the manner of an animal's death from its body. The meat of an animal that is relaxed at the moment of slaughter is tender, that of a frightened animal more tough. When an animal knows or worries that it is about to die, it tenses up; this tension lingers after death, in muscle fibres that remain rigid, and in an increased number of blood clots throughout the body.

The tenderness of a piece of meat, then, is not only a symbol of luxury and a sign of quality; it's also sometimes an indication of a good death. And for those who are concerned with the welfare of the animals whose flesh they eat, it can make all the difference.

I used to be a vegetarian. Like so many others – worried for the well-being of the planet, worried for the well-being of the animals whose flesh I was consuming – I decided to forego the steaks and the stews and the shawarmas that I so loved for the sake of a greater, more important good. I studied up on the nutritional profiles of vegetarian staples, like legumes and tofu, learned what complete protein was and how to combine ingredients to get it, browsed the canon of hippie cookbooks for creative recipe ideas.

I lasted three months.

No matter what I ate, or how much, not once in that season of herbivore experimentation did I feel satisfied. I was tired, lethargic, cranky and a good bit dimmer than usual. I was convinced it would pass, that my body was simply adjusting. It didn't. And all it took was one good burger for me to revive – it was like water to a wilting flower.

Defeated, I decided to return to my carnivorous ways, but to be as mindful as I could about the meat I was eating. I developed a set of rules: it has to be free-range, it must not have been treated with antibiotics and it has to have come from relatively close by. I am, I liked to joke, eating happy meat: so long as the animal was content while it was alive, I'm more sanguine about the fact that it's now dead.

I am, of course, hardly the only person making this choice. So-called ethical meat has become one of the touchstones of our contemporary thinking about food, and a badge of honour at an increasing number of Toronto's restaurants, butchers and markets. We used to think that the only way to be moral about meat was to refrain from eating it altogether; we are now more

shades-of-grey about it – we pay closer attention to the real and important differences between various methods of animal husbandry, with regards to both animal welfare and ecological impact. Some meat, it would seem, is better than others.

The discussion around how to be a better meat eater has so far centred on two main issues: how an animal was raised and how to properly appreciate an animal once it's been slaughtered. Under the former heading come matters of agricultural practice: is a chicken cooped up or allowed to roam outdoors? Are antibiotics used prophylactically? What sorts of feed has an animal received? Under the latter come culinary considerations: movements like nose-to-tail cooking and 'less meatism,' both of which strive to make us cognizant of the fact that meat is precious and needs to be treated as such.

Hovering in the background of these conversations is the matter of the slaughter itself. We focus on the quality of an animal's life, and on preparing its meat mindfully, but we tend to skip straight past the actual moment of death. It's hardly surprising – despite some recent high-profile exposés, abattoirs aren't a very front-of-mind or appetizing subject. In part this is because they are, for all practical purposes, hidden from view, and in part because we perhaps worry about how we'll react to what we learn.

The availability of ethical meat depends on the availability of ethical slaughterhouses, however, and it turns out they are in startlingly short supply. According to most small-scale, sustainability-minded farmers, the lack of suitable slaughterhouses in southern Ontario is the single biggest limiting factor in bringing ethical meat to market.

Ideally, an animal should be slaughtered where it lives – animals are sensitive to location, and the experience of travelling away from their familiar environs is stressful. This requires travelling abattoirs, ones housed in trailers that travel from farm to farm, and in which animals are killed one at a time. Under our current system of regulations, however, it is nearly impossible to get a licence for such an operation, and though these used to be fairly common, almost none remain.

The next best alternative, the one to which many sustainable farmers have turned for decades, are small-scale abattoirs located no more than an hour or two away from where an animal lives. Much of the ethical meat available in Toronto comes from such slaughterhouses, which are located in some

smaller farming communities in southern Ontario such as Lindsay and Creemore, and though they, too, are under regulatory pressure that may prove insurmountable, there is a tremendous demand for their services. Many of these abattoirs have resting barns – that is, barns where animals stay for at least twenty-four hours after travelling and before slaughter, allowing them sufficient time to regain their calm. In stark contrast to industrial-scale abattoirs, which work with hundreds or thousands of animals at a time, animals at these abattoirs are taken onto the kill floor one by one, and slaughtered one by one. The kill floor is washed down between each slaughter, so that an animal does not pick up the scent of the blood of its predecessor and anticipate its own impending death.

Among the advantages of slaughtering animals one at a time is the ability to ensure that each one has, in fact, died. One of the biggest animal-welfare concerns surrounding industrial slaughter is that a not-trivial number of animals are not immediately killed, and thus suffer tremendous pain as they are moved into processing. (This is particularly an issue with pigs, which are scalded after slaughter.)

Another is cleanliness. Though industrial agriculture tends to emphasize the benefits of scaling up operations (primarily increases in efficiency and reductions in cost), multiplying the number of animals that are processed simultaneously also increases the likelihood that diseased or contaminated animals will make it into the food supply.

One of the greatest pressures these slaughterhouses face is from government regulation, and specifically from federal regulations that must be met if an establishment is to be allowed to ship its meat across provincial lines. Over the past few years the Ontario government has been encouraging all abattoirs, even the small ones, to adhere to those federal standards, which were crafted with the large-scale processor in mind. (They include, for instance, a stipulation that an abattoir must have a dedicated office, including a bathroom, for a federal inspector, even though said inspector may spend only a few days a year on the premises.) Making the necessary infrastructure upgrades is far beyond the budgets of smaller operations, which also face price pressure from industrial producers selling meat at lower prices; not surprisingly, the number of independent abattoirs has been dwindling for decades.

Advocates of these regulations maintain that they are the only way to ensure that our meat is safe; supporters of the

William Davies' stall in St. Lawrence Market, c. 1911.

small-scale model maintain that they don't need such monitoring because their size minimizes the risk of contamination in the first place.

Ironically, the reverse was true about a hundred years ago, when slaughterhouse regulations were first introduced in the Toronto area.

In the early nineteenth century, most animals in southern Ontario were raised and slaughtered for local consumption. By the 1850s, international demand spurred local farmers and butchers to produce and cure meat for export, and production rates began to increase. With an expanding rail network facilitating transportation, the next few decades saw substantial increases in the scale of animal farming in the region, and a corresponding industrialization of slaughterhouse and meat-packing operations.

William Davies opened Toronto's first large-scale hog-slaughtering facility in 1874. A British expat, Davies had long been producing pork products and selling them at St. Lawrence Market, and he opened his abattoir to expand his export business. By 1879 he had built another facility, and in 1891 his plant was the first in Canada to introduce artificial refrigeration. (Davies's slaughterhouse eventually grew to process so many pigs that it gave Toronto one of its nicknames: Hogtown.) In 1896 the Harris Abattoir opened: with the capacity to slaughter and process 500 head of cattle a week, it, too, was geared to the British export market.

Unlike today, a great many stockyards, abattoirs and meat-packing plants were located well inside Toronto proper. As

Harris Abattoir, November 1916.

these grew in number and size, they increasingly compromised the quality of urban life: waste disposal, foul odours and transportation in and out of the city became more and more vexing. In 1896 the Ontario government introduced the first provincial legislation governing meat inspection in urban areas, endowing local health authorities with the responsibility of monitoring meat-processing facilities. These rules were, however, inconsistently applied and enforced.

Upton Sinclair's *The Jungle*, published in 1906, caused an uproar with its graphic (though fictional) descriptions of deplorable conditions in American meat-packing houses. It prompted the U.S. government to investigate the conditions in these establishments, and was a major contributing factor in the introduction of federal regulations south and north of the border. The Canadian government was further impelled to implement federal regulation by discoveries of tuberculosis in Canadian bacon that had been shipped to Britain, and by the institution of such regulations by the Danish and Dutch governments, who were also exporting to Britain and were therefore competing with Canadian products.

The Meat and Canned Foods Act was passed by Parliament in 1907. All meat that was to be sold outside of its province of origin was henceforth subject to sanitation regulations and veterinary inspection. Only the large abattoirs were killing animals in sufficient quantity for the export market, and therefore only the large abattoirs needed to adhere to these standards. The net effect was a significant improvement in the cleanliness of meat coming out of the bigger slaughterhouses.

Today, large-scale slaughterhouses have expanded far beyond what regulators once envisioned, and it is the more modest abattoirs that are the most trusted. Provincial regulations are stringent enough to ensure that they are hygienic, and the smaller number of animals makes it easier to properly monitor each one for disease or contamination. Moreover, an additional level of monitoring exists simply because the small-scale farmers who secure the services of these abattoirs are far more interested in slaughterhouse conditions than are industrial agricultural conglomerates. Farmers who make a point of keeping their animals' welfare in mind are also likely to make a point of ensuring the abattoirs they use adhere to those same principles. Today, we can find the meat that comes from these farmers in independent butcher shops, such as the Healthy Butcher, Rowe Farms and Cumbrae's, as well as at many of the vendors at local farmers' markets. Chain grocery stores purchase their meat almost exclusively from the larger industrial meat-processing plants, such as those run by Maple Leaf Foods. The handful of abattoirs still in operation within Toronto city limits, meanwhile, are close-lipped about their practices, and no local farmer I spoke with had chosen to send animals to any of them for slaughter.

If we are going to, many of us, remain carnivores, it is incumbent upon us to give the animals whose flesh we eat as good lives, and as good deaths, as we can muster. This is, increasingly, something we can control, as the redevelopment of an engaged farmer-to-consumer relationship enables us to learn more about the meat we buy than we could have even a few years ago.

The single most important thing any of us can do is ask questions. If someone trying to sell you a steak cannot tell you where the cow it came from was raised, what it was fed and when it was killed, they aren't in a position to vouch for the animal's quality of life, or death. Find someone who can.

We are overwhelmed with a wide and growing range of labels, certification standards and injunctions that are meant to guide us towards making responsible food choices. But the simplest and best rule of thumb is to buy from someone who welcomes the inquiries, and is glad of the chance to answer as many questions as you have. It's as close as we – living in the city, unable to observe an animal's existence for ourselves – can come to knowing that that existence, and end, is as good as it can be.

Where to get good meat

The Healthy Butcher
565 Queen St. W
298 Eglinton Ave. W
416.674.2642 (all stores)
www.thehealthybutcher.com

Rowe Farms
105 Roncesvalles Ave.
416.588.4383
St. Lawrence Market (Sat only) 519.822.8794
912 Queen St. E
416.461.4383
www.rowefarms.ca

Cumbrae's
481 Church St.
416.923.5600
1636 Bayview Ave.
416.485.5620
www.cumbraes.com

Fresh from the Farm
350 Donlands Ave.
416.422.3276
www.freshfromthefarm.ca

Farmers' Markets

Friends of Riverdale Farm
201 Winchester St.
May to October
Tuesdays 3–7 p.m.

Dufferin Grove
Dufferin Grove Park,
875 Dufferin St.
Year-round
Thursdays 3–7 p.m.

Evergreen Brick Works
550 Bayview Ave.
Summer
Saturdays 8 a.m.–1 p.m.

The Stop's Green Barn
Artscape Wychwood Barns
601 Christie St.
Year-round
Saturdays 8 a.m.–1 p.m.

Jason
McBride

Food fighters: The Stop Community Food Centre and the end of the food bank

'Emergency food programs do not function in a neutral environment in which any charitable activity undertaken is automatically a net addition to the well-being of the poor.' – Janet Poppendieck, *Sweet Charity?*

In spring 2009, in the sunny new atrium of the Artscape Wychwood Barns, a panel of experts gathered in front of about 150 academics, writers, organic farmers and activists to discuss 'The Future of Food Access for Low-Income People in Ontario.' The conversation was more stormy than that bland title might suggest. Janet Poppendieck, an American sociologist and the author of *Sweet Charity?: Emergency Food and the End of Entitlement,* was the keynote speaker, and arrayed behind a long table beside her were Gail Nyberg, executive director of the Daily Bread Food Bank; Debbie Field, executive director of FoodShare Toronto; Adam Spence, executive director of the Ontario Association of Food Banks; and Nick Saul, executive director of the Stop Community Food Centre. Saul had invited Poppendieck to speak – her book's a kind of theoretical touchstone for him – and when she took the podium she graciously remarked that New York, where she lives and teaches, had much to learn from Toronto as a 'source of innovative food systems.' 'Maybe we *can* actually have humane and dignified food banks,' she said. I looked at Saul, waiting for his reaction. There was none, but food banks, dignified or not, are exactly what Saul and the Stop are working, tirelessly and systematically, to eradicate. Or, at the very least, reinvent.

Saul took off his sweater, revealing a robin's-egg-blue shirt that perfectly matched Gail Nyberg's suit jacket. Their similarities ended there, however, and the Daily Bread chief could have been forgiven for thinking the deck had been stacked against her. For one, she was on Saul's turf – the Stop owns and operates a large greenhouse, education centre and kitchen in the southernmost barn. And Saul had arranged the panel to debate the point of Poppendieck's book: that food banks, despite the apparent goodwill and generosity of those operating, volunteering for and donating to them, might actually contribute to the problems they purport to solve.

It's a provocative hypothesis, but not one that Nyberg indicated she had thought much about. At the very least, it wasn't a debate she was going to wade into this April afternoon. In the same resigned and weary tone she uses when pleading for donations on TV every Thanksgiving, she said, 'The poor will always

be with us just like food banks will always be with us.' She mentioned, almost by rote, her organization's constant lobbying for government intervention and poverty-reduction strategies.

Saul looked disappointed, even angry. 'Food banks act as if renewal will come from on high,' he said, his own voice rising. 'But social change can never happen that way.'

Since 1995, the Stop's headquarters has been a warren of offices, kitchens and multi-purpose spaces on the first floor of a drab Toronto Community Housing Corporation high-rise at Davenport and Symington. Formerly a public health unit, the space now feels less like a hospital clinic than a nursery school – it's comfortable and homey, with walls decorated with a UN-worthy number of flags, framed photographs of cheery-looking gardeners, a poster advertising Le Frigo Vert, Concordia's health food co-op: 'Still hungry for anti-capitalist food production.'

The thirty-year-old, non-profit Stop actually started as a food bank, one of the first in the country, at Kensington Market's St. Stephen's-in-the-Fields church. But almost from the beginning, and most dramatically during Saul's eleven-year tenure, the Stop's been much more. 'Community food centre' is an inadequate abstraction, but briefly put, the Stop is an anti-poverty organization whose chief tool for fighting poverty (and its corollary, building community) is food. High-quality, nutritious, sustainably grown, culturally appropriate – and delicious – food. At the Stop, food's a basic human right, regardless of income or class. The Stop's promotional litera-ture swells with comestible puns and metaphors – 'breaking bread and breaking down barriers'; 'why good food should be a matter of course'; 'recipe for trouble'; 'cooking up a dream' – and even this wordplay is evidence of food's transformative power. It can bring people together, convey hope, improve health and enrich lives – just as its absence can destroy them.

Saul – a gregarious, silver-haired forty-three-year-old who bears some resemblance to CNN's Anderson Cooper – joined the Stop in 1998. Born in Tanzania to academic parents – his father is renowned African liberation activist, author and retired professor John S. Saul – Saul was raised in both Africa and Toronto. A year in revolutionary Mozambique was forma-tive; responsible for lining up for hours to get the family's ration of bread, he watched one day as a large Bulgarian diplomat cut to the front of the line. 'Indig*nation!*' Saul says now, laughing. He later studied history at U of T, where he cap-tained the basketball team, before doing an MA in sociology at

the University of Warwick. After returning to Toronto, he
worked in Bob Rae's office in the early 1990s and was a
community organizer in Alexandra Park, one of the city's first
housing co-operatives. 'Basically, going door to door,' he
recalls, 'asking people how we could make their lives better.'

He was drawn to the Stop more out of an attraction to its
social justice ambitions than any real interest in, or knowledge
of, food. (He admits he's a lousy gardener.) When he became
executive director, the Stop had a staff of three. Today, the staff
numbers eight times that and the organization's annual operating budget has grown to $2 million. Ninety percent of the
money comes from private donations, both corporate and
individual, including heavy-hitting philanthropists like former
Alliance Atlantis CEO Michael MacMillan, who's given the
organization over a million dollars. Foundations, in particular
the Metcalf Foundation, have also been particularly generous.
Only about 10 percent of the Stop's budget is derived from the
public purse, specifically the municipal government. It's a
fragile funding formula that Saul's not entirely comfortable
with – and which requires four full-time employees, including
himself, to dig up and steward money – but he's carefully
exploring how to seek and integrate more government dollars,
well aware how proscriptive those can be.

All that money bankrolls a dizzying constellation of facilities, events and programs, which are multiplying so rapidly
the following list is already likely outdated: an 750-square-
metre community garden at Earlscourt Park; a greenhouse
and sheltered garden at the Green Barn; hands-on growing
and cooking classes for Grade 5 students across the Toronto
District School Board; perinatal nutrition training for pregnant

women; Good Food Markets, i.e., stalls that provide healthy groceries in neighbourhoods blighted by fast-food joints; civic engagement programming that encourages community members to speak out about both hunger and income issues; exclusive dinners where donors cook and dine with ex-Perigee chef Chris Brown (now the Stop's food enterprise coordinator); partnerships with local organic growers and independent grocers; a drop-in café that hands out free lunches and breakfasts; and a food bank that provides a three-day supply of food once a month. Through all of these initiatives the Stop does three things simultaneously: it brings members of the community (who are often isolated by virtue of income or language) together to share meals; it teaches these same people why high-quality, nutritious food is important; it shows them how to select, grow and prepare their own food, boosting self-reliance and self-confidence. At the same time, the Stop directly lobbies government to increase access to nutritious food, insisting, for example, that the Ontario Liberals introduce a $100 social assistance supplement earmarked for healthy food. Its Do the Math program highlights how inadequate social assistance rates have directly increased food bank use.

The bulk of these programs are targeted primarily at the low-income residents of the Stop's Davenport West catchment area (roughly Bloor to St. Clair, Dovercourt to Runnymede), a population of about 80,000. (Technically speaking, anyone can use the Stop's services, though strenuous efforts are made to ensure access for the marginalized – the median daily after-rent income for members is $5.80.) Roughly 20 percent of those residents used the Stop's services in 2008. With the opening of the Green Barn last year, however, those boundaries have expanded significantly, and, with that expansion, the Stop has pioneered a kind of two-tier programming. The Green Barn activities cater to a more affluent Wychwood Park community that can afford fancy dinners and expensive farmers'-market cheese, or a program like Supper Solutions, where participants join Stop chefs one Saturday each month, cook up five dinners in the Green Barn kitchen (using Stop ingredients) and then take those meals home. The profits of such initiatives, in turn, feed other programming at the Davenport location. This has lately been the Stop's genius – to recognize and ride the good-food wave, the increasingly popular zeal for healthy, sustainable cuisine and agriculture. As everyone from Michael Pollan to Wayne Roberts can attest, there's a food revolution afoot. The only problem is that it's a revolution driven largely by and for

the affluent and aware. One of Saul's biggest challenges is changing the cynical perception that high-quality, responsibly produced food is something only the rich can afford or enjoy.

Twice a week, the Stop prepares a free lunch in its drop-in café. On this particular Thursday, it's five minutes before noon and community chef Scott McNeil suddenly pauses over the enormous Thai chicken stir-fry he's spent hours preparing. 'I'm nervous,' he says, 'that there's not going to be enough food.' The burly, tattooed McNeil and a dozen volunteers have devoted their morning to chopping Rowe Farms chicken, mincing herbs plucked from the Stop's own garden and slicing pinky-sized radishes donated by a neighbour. The result's a surprisingly sophisticated, nutritious repast that Joy Bistro, the upscale Leslieville boîte where McNeil once worked, would be proud to serve. But about 200 hungry people – pregnant mothers, lonely seniors, new immigrants – sit on the other side of the kitchen, waiting for their food. If there isn't enough, some of them will go the entire day without a meal.

Despite McNeil's concern, the kitchen's been reasonably calm, the food prep smooth and organized. There are probably more volunteers than necessary, but a good number of them have some kitchen experience and the atmosphere's jovial and supportive. One volunteer, a charismtatic Latino in his fifties, his hair dyed golden, shows me how to properly dress the salad, scooping large clumps of romaine with his hands so that the vinaigrette coats each leaf. He whispers that he'd rather prepare lunch than serve it: 'Those people out there are very homophobic.'

And, indeed, things in the café are a bit less festive. The food's doled out briskly, each plate covered half in salad, half in stir-fry, a donated ACE Bakery roll on the side. Many people eat their meals silently and quickly. Saul has told me that things can get 'hairy'; fights break out on occasion. Some impatiently demand their food or sneak seconds. An aggressive woman, clearly mentally ill, is asked to leave. But several regulars appear as comfortable as if they were in their own kitchens. Two elderly women approach the serving counter and pay their compliments to the chef. One volunteer feeds a woman who's severely disabled. After English, Spanish is the most popular language spoken. A young Mexican woman smiles flirtatiously as she requests a vegetarian meal. There is, as it turns out, enough food. So much so that the volunteers get to eat as well, standing up in the kitchen, relieved and exhausted.

Nick Saul (with scissors), Councillor Joe Mihevc and local residents at the opening of the Stop's Green Barn.

Saul uses the word 'dignity' a lot when referring to the way the Stop helps its community. He's firmly convinced that the classic food-bank model – here's your food, good luck, see you later – not only doesn't work, but that it stigmatizes those who use them. 'It's a very difficult thing,' he argues, 'to say, "I need help with food."' When food banks were created in Canada, in the late 1970s, and then mushroomed across North America in the '80s, they were designed to provide emergency, temporary assistance. Now, they're entrenched and institutionalized. 'We all say we want to do away with food banks,' Saul says, 'but they're not going anywhere. They're here and they're problematic.' Indeed, as the Daily Bread Food Bank's most recent annual report indicates, food-bank use has only increased: visits in Toronto grew to over a million for the first time between April 2008 and April 2009.

Saul describes food banks as a 'moral release valve for government,' permitting it to appear as if it's doing something about hunger when it's really doing nothing at all. Likewise, as per Poppendieck's argument, they siphon off badly needed resources (donations, labour) that the Stop might more effectively and creatively use. What the Stop offers is an alternative where people are taught self-sufficiency instead of simply receiving handouts, where they enjoy agency and control. It's a teach-a-man-to-fish model that doesn't see itself as doing its work *on behalf* of any community; its role is chiefly to give the community the tools to agitate for itself.

Nonetheless, the Stop itself, despite Saul's criticism of food banks, is still dependent in part on Daily Bread's largesse. The country's largest food bank, Daily Bread serves as a centralized

umbrella organization that provides food to 160 member agencies, from hamper programs to full-on food banks. The Stop receives about 1,800 kilograms of donated food a week from them. And Gail Nyberg, for her part, doesn't see organizations like the Stop replacing hers anytime too soon. 'We're in a different business,' she says. 'But I do not believe that if we close our doors, which Nick has suggested at times, that all of a sudden there would be enough food and resources. That we would all grow our tomatoes in December in Toronto. That's not going to happen.'

Saul's not so naive as to believe this either. 'No fucking garden is going to solve hunger,' he says. 'It's the integrated approach: letting people in the door, supporting people where they're at, and then advocating for more just social policy. That's the stew that we have that works.'

'They're a marvellous example to others,' Michael MacMillan says. And many others, from Botswana to Brazil, have visited Toronto precisely to find out what makes the Stop tick. Closer to home, Saul's constantly being asked to speak in different cities, from Kelowna to Calgary, about how such an innovative, nimble model might be replicated in those communities. Saul and his senior staff have spent much time in recent months trying to answer this question: how does the model work exactly and what parts are transferable, scalable and replicable? They've recently drafted a document called *In Every Community, a Place for Food* that will serve as a kind of wiring diagram for a 'Stop-in-a-box.' Ever entrepreneurial, Saul hopes they can generate another revenue stream by marketing that formula (and their expertise) to other communities. Sell the sizzle *and* the steak, if you will. A chicken in every pot, a Stop in every neighbourhood. 'We could spend a lot of time talking about the inadequacies of the food-bank sector,' Saul says, 'but we don't want to get caught up in that conversation. We want to start to build these other multi-purpose food organizations that will, I hope, start to populate the province.' It's a canny way for the Stop to expand without really expanding. The key to the organization's success, for many of its staff and members, is in being neighbourhood-based – fresh-and-local, if you will – and to grow too big too quickly could undermine its impressive achievements.

'I think it's replicable,' Saul says of the Stop, 'but it won't be replicable unless the government steps in. If the provincial government stepped in and gave a million dollars to each

riding to figure out its community food centre – we're talking just an accounting error here, about $103 million – it would galvanize communities. That's what we're pushing for.'

And while government hasn't yet stepped in in this way, many food banks across the province have nonetheless already adopted some of the Stop's methods. According to Adam Spence, about a third of the province's food banks, places like Niagara Falls' Project SHARE, now serve as multi-service agencies. 'The food bank is no longer just a place where someone gets an emergency supply of food,' Spence says, 'but where folks can get the necessary support to make their way out of poverty.'

Saul's prone to infectious, almost preternatural, enthusiasm. As quickly as he or one of his staff or a board member come up with a good idea – a branded line of Stop salsa, say, made with tomatoes grown in the greenhouse – another, possibly better, idea displaces it. 'We've grown very responsibly and strategically and smartly,' Saul says, 'but now, as more ideas start to come at us, we're less in control of those ideas. And we have to seize control.'

One of the more compelling ideas came from the Sorbara Development Group, which wanted the Stop to build an organic farm on lands the developer owns at Weston Road and the 401. Saul was enthralled with the project but, one and a half feasibility studies and a staff-and-board retreat later, pulled the plug. 'To jump from the Green Barn,' he says, 'to something that would take a lot of passion, time, commitment, money, it just wasn't right. Personally, I'm a bit disappointed. But organizationally, I feel 100 percent it was the right decision.'

His disappointment didn't last, however; the organization had already moved on to other, possibly more appropriate, projects. Toronto Community Housing has approached the Stop about developing food programming at a new building down by the Rogers Centre. The Stop's urban agriculture coordinator, Kristin Wheatcroft, is trying to work with other Wychwood-area agencies like Sistering, a support organization for marginalized women, on six-month-long gardening and cooking workshops. Saul's talking to Creemore's New Farm and the west-end grocer Fiesta Farms about a partnership where Fiesta would sell New Farm organics, diverting some of the profit back to the Stop. It would seem that the Stop, for all of its success, is just getting started. 'The best parties always end up in the kitchen,' Saul says, smiling like a man who has been to many good parties. 'Food is one of those things – you break bread and talk and stuff happens.'

Shawn
Micallef

These are the restaurants of our lives

People don't just eat out for the food – they do it for the experience. Even self-confessed 'foodies' will say that food is just one of several elements that make up the dining experience; as important are service, price and atmosphere. In some circles, people go out to eat just to be seen, and some restaurants seem explicitly designed to give perfectly obvious surreptitious views of everybody else. After all, if the experience didn't matter, all restaurants would be takeout, and people who are good cooks would stay at home.

Going to a restaurant is entering into a wholly scripted event, like walking onto a stage set complete with rough dialogue and plot. And restaurants often become actual TV and movie sets – they're the kinds of places where other things can happen. These events usually include conversations and plot exposition, but sometimes they can be more dramatic: power lunches, furtive and clandestine affairs, Mother's Day brunches. One *Seinfeld* episode revolved around a restaurant where couples went specifically to break up. Restaurants are the sets where life plays out, and these interiors are a part of the real life of real cities. How they look and how they're talked about tells us a lot about that city.

When restaurants are viewed as experiences, the food (almost) doesn't matter. They become elaborate creations of architecture and interior design. There are very famous chefs whose food gets second billing to the buildings in which that food is cooked. What makes the Four Seasons restaurant famous in New York's Seagram Building: the food, or that it was designed by architects Mies van der Rohe and Phillip Johnson, and that Charles Eames and Eero Saarinen created the furniture? In Toronto, celebrity chefs Mark McEwan and Jamie Kennedy are talked about as much because of the design of some of their restaurants as for their culinary creations. (With McEwan, it's for his Bymark establishment in the TD Centre plaza – another van der Rohe building – and with Kennedy, it's for Jaime Kennedy at the Gardiner Museum.) It's form before function: C5 is up in the ROM crystal, Scaramouche has the spectacular view (of the city and the patrons) and the AGO's Frank is by Frank Gehry, and has a Frank Stella sculpture hanging in it.

Restaurant design is a major industry, and even has its own reality-TV program, *Restaurant Makeover*, which developed something of a kiss-of-death reputation in Toronto after a

series of the establishments featured in the show went out of business. In spite of its reputation, however, the show is a sign of the pop-culture importance of these spaces. Toronto's gastronomic interiors can be extremely varied, and they often boast bolder, more audacious and sometimes even ridiculous designs that other kinds of spaces and establishments could never get away with. For a few hours, restaurants transport us halfway to somewhere else, whether real or imaginary.

For all of Toronto's venerated multiculturalism, most of us experience it through food (and, often, only through food). It's possible to visit recreations of dining experiences found in most countries on earth without leaving the city limits. Apart from the crazy and audacious designs, restaurants can also get away with pastiches of various ethnic representations that, in another context, would at best be censured for not being politically correct. Restaurants are given a lot of cultural rope to play with.

Restaurant interior extremes are fun to explore – some could be featured on a show titled something like *Interiors Gone Wild*. These kinds of places are often called 'theme restaurants,' but this handle does them a disservice: they are somebody's vivid imagination brought to life. What else could have inspired a chain like the Rainforest Café? Toronto's iteration is in a corner of Yorkdale Mall, and if you're not willing to risk the food, you can just sit at the bar on an animal-print stool and wait for the periodic rainfall to pour out of the ceiling into specially designed troughs that weave their way around tables and giant fish tanks. The crocodile lying in a pond of water out front wakes up at regular intervals and roars while a smoke machine provides an appropriate jungle haze – all this, steps away from the everyday normalcy of the Banana Republic and Chapters-Indigo. Parents must hate this place, as it seems designed to ensure impassioned pleas from children asking to eat there. Pity the poor cooks who work there – nobody cares about what they're making when there's a roaring croc nearby.

More interesting, even, are the smaller or one-off fantasy-lands in the city. Canadians of a certain age (that is, people who predate Gen Y) will remember the Organ Grinder down on the Esplanade. I say Canadians, rather than Torontonians, as it was a standard item on many year-end Grade 8 class trips to Toronto. For children, the Organ Grinder – the kind of restaurant that our provincial cities could not match – repre-sented the great financial and cultural power of Toronto. An ad for the restaurant from the early 1980s described the interior

in mythological terms: 'The mighty Wurlitzer. Thousands of feet of pipes from pencil sized to piccolo to thunderous bass notes that almost shake your table. And your table is surrounded by dozens of fascinating instruments that play along magically with the invincible sound of the mighty theatre organ.' So loud you likely couldn't taste the food.

The Organ Grinder was a one-off, idiosyncratic version of the Chuck E. Cheese chain that still proliferates in North America, but with less cartoon and more Edward Gorey. Next door to where the restaurant once was, and still a going concern, is the Old Spaghetti Factory, a minor Canadian chain and another member of the how-much-crazy-stuff-can-we-put-on-the-walls genre of restaurants (like the old Whaler's Wharf on Front Street, which looked like the interior of an old sailing ship). Another ad from the early 1980s invited Esplanaders to 'step through our doors and take a nostalgic trip back in time to the Victorian era … The unique atmosphere of The Old Spaghetti Factory sets it apart from any other Toronto restaurant. Offering a wide variety of spaghetti dishes, as well as delicious veal and chicken cacciatore, the Spaghetti Factory is a diner's delight. A top favorite for business luncheon, family gathering, children's party, dinner date

or after theatre snack. The fully licenced cocktail area is full of pleasant surprises. Enjoy a drink before or after the theatre.'

This is magnificent prose. In just one paragraph, the author depicts the Old Spagetti Factory as being all things to all people, displaying the kind of versatility of function and class transcendence that only casual restaurant marketing copy can conjure, while describing food that went out of style before Brian Mulroney left office. And even though it's hard to imagine a Bay Street business meeting taking place next to a table with a booster chair, restaurants are free to claim any territory they want. In the late 1970s and early 1980s, so many pictures of Toronto restaurants in various city magazines of the day looked like they were straight out of an early episode of *Dallas*: all brass and glass with a good helping of ferns. There was a sense of drama and glamour in these pictures, a sense that Toronto was a city ready for those power meals and executive dates. It's easy to imagine a young Barbara Amiel rolling through any of these places in a Halston pantsuit.

'Verve' is not a word one would use to describe Barberian's Steakhouse and Tavern on Elm Street, which *Toronto Star* reviewer Phil Johnson described in a 1985 article as 'more than a restaurant – it is an experience.' It represents an antiquated

but quaint image of what dining out in Toronto the Good was like before the city loosened up. Though not as over-the-top as the Old Spaghetti Factory, Barberian's is certainly not subtle about the environment it is creating. 'From the rare bust of Sir John A. MacDonald to the several original works by members of the Group of Seven, the immaculately decorated century-old-plus building at 7 Elm is a step back in time,' wrote Johnson. 'Before you order, relax with a drink – while also drinking in the atmosphere – and read the back of the menu, which outlines the extensive Canadian memorabilia used to decorate the restaurant.'[1] With so much attention paid to MacDonald and the high Tory-ness and 'warm English atmosphere' of the design, it seems natural that this was the haunt of the Mike Harris folks during his reign as premier, and continues to be a political backroom-boys' hangout.

1 *The Toronto Star*, March 26, 1985.

Restaurants are a barometer of how a city perceives itself, and as Toronto transformed into a real metropolis in the 1970s, its restaurants were one of the first places this verve and sexiness were seen. Its restaurant reviewers were quick to catch on. Restaurant reviews reveal as much about the sensibility of the day as they do about the food being served: the experience is what matters, and food is just part of it. Looking through archived reviews highlights the volatility of the industry: the majority of restaurants that were written up in the *Globe and Mail*, *Toronto Star* and various city magazines a decade or more ago no longer exist. An archive search is akin to reading an endless obituary page. But though the restaurants are gone, the prose written about them remains, and it tells the story of Toronto.

The late and very missed film (and sometimes restaurant) critic Jay Scott began a 1988 *Globe and Mail* review of the now-defunct Le Bistingo restaurant at 349 Queen Street West – in the heart of what was then the fading zenith of the first Queen West arts era – in the grandest way: 'Empires topple in weeks, love affairs in an evening and restaurants deflate during a single luncheon, but not everything in the age of the ephemeral vanishes swiftly. Anne, late of Green Gables, is an octogenarian this year, and Le Bistingo has reached the age of 3, which for a trendy Toronto restaurant amounts to a mid-life crisis. In addition to being Canadian institutions of relative longevity, the red-head and the restaurant have one more thing in common: when they do change they don't change much. And when they do change, the change is invariably for the better.'[2]

2 *The Globe and Mail*, July 30, 1988.

As ephemeral as a restaurant's lifespan may be, such magnificent words aren't wasted on the inconsequential, instead used to describe something that defined a part of the Toronto scene in 1988. While Scott's words are worth mentioning simply because they turn a restaurant review into an epic Canadian story, he wasn't the only reviewer to chart Toronto's awkward transition from a WASPY colonial backwater to the cosmopolitan polyglot it is today. From a *Globe* review by Joanne Kates from the same year, and about the same Queen Street stretch: 'Arriving at the Blue Room is like descending into a suburban rec room for a fifties necking party with the lights turned down and the music turned up. But wait: it's the Eighties. On our first visit the waitress looks as if she has just participated in the electricity exhibit at the Science Centre. The hair is interesting at the Blue Room – carrot-coloured, brush cut or gel-sculpted, it makes a *statement* ... The theme is blue, as in undersea. Nothing so unhip as lobster pots and ships' wheels, but rather (tongue firmly installed in cheek) walls painted with fantasy fish.'[3]

It takes Kates a while to get to the food, which is just fine, as descriptions of Queen West hipness filtered through the *Globe*'s sensibility are quite fun. In another review from 1988, Kates wrote of the beloved and well-mythologized BamBoo on Queen: 'It is the relentlessly low-tech club-cum-restaurant that rebukes glitz-crazed Toronto, with a smile up its sleeve. I confess to having avoided BamBoo since it opened five years ago. People who are pushing 40 and sometimes forget to wear at least three items of black clothing (preferably somewhat tattered) can be forgiven for avoiding Queen Street.'[4]

Though Kates, in that particularly old-*Globe* way, can seem like a snob at times, she inadvertently gives an oblique and unique view of Toronto's culture through her reviews over the years. In 1978, she wrote of the opening of Korea House on Bloor 'where oriental fantasy takes root ... out of one wall grows a 'grass hut' roof garnished with its own jungle (some plastic, some real) ... Behind the Coke dispensing machine is a poster advertising Korean ginseng, the wonder root that heals the sick and makes young the old.'[5] Reading along with her reviews is like seeing a timeline of how Toronto struggled to come to terms with both its cultural and ethnic evolution. Zena Cherry, the *Globe*'s late society columnist, also caught Toronto's 1970s growth spurt by documenting the opening of Bangkok Garden just across the street from Barberian's, which illustrated in one block the changes taking place in Toronto's

3 *The Globe and Mail*, March 5, 1988.

4 *The Globe and Mail*, April 2, 1988.

5 *The Globe and Mail*, September 5, 1978.

food scene. Of the opening in 1982, which, by all accounts, was quite an affair, with the owners going to great lengths to find 'authentic' monks to bless the restaurant, Cherry wrote: 'After some searching, they located four monks who were able to come: Sombodilia Bodhi and Sungwal Khongchun, both from New York, and Kerian Chautes and S. Thammaratna, both from Washington ... After blessing the building the monks were taken to see the CN Tower. Included in the group was Barbara Elson's husband, Professor Nicholas W. Elson, who teaches English at York University.'[6] Collisions of new, old and exotic Toronto happened in restaurants, a setting where there was already an established language – restaurant reviews – to describe the social interaction and evolution taking place.

6 *The Globe and Mail*, August 23, 1982.

In 1980, Kates captured Toronto's late disco-era scene perfectly when reviewing Kosta's at 124 Avenue Road: 'Beautiful young men with perfect hairdo's hang off the mezzanine; maître d' is tall and slim and her crimson dress is slit to the navel. People who are young, elegant (yes, and skinny too) are table-hopping ferociously, beautifully.'[7] Five years later, the Keg at the Mansion on Jarvis got a similar treatment, though Kates was much less sympathetic to its petite bourgeoisie patrons: 'The Keg is McDonald's to the tenth degree for the up market crowd. Is this what Marie Antoinette meant when she said "Let them eat cake?" Is The Keg the edible result of a social revolution, when working folk can eat steak, and in the mansion that only 15 years ago housed Julie's, then one of the ritziest restaurants in Toronto? Furs and silk have given way to denim and 100% polyester. Is it progressive, regressive or merely tasteless that walls once covered in brocade are now paneled in paper that's trying to look like teakwood?'[8]

7 *The Globe and Mail*, August 30, 1980.

8 *The Globe and Mail*, January 12, 1985

The collision of high and middle class that Kates pokes fun at is an interesting place in Toronto today. Expensive restaurants get reviewed and talked about in the alt-weeklies and city blogs, while 'downmarket' places – essentially, smaller, independent versions of the comfortable Keg – routinely make it into the pages of the *Globe* and *Toronto Life*. As Toronto has evolved, so, too, have the rules about who gets to eat out and where. The Toronto chain Spring Rolls inhabits this new territory well. It's a place of high design (there's nothing subtle about stepping into a Spring Rolls) that explicitly welcomes everybody with its relatively cheap prices. Each restaurant in the Spring Rolls chain is designed by Toronto architect Bennett C. Lo and his firm, Dialogue 38. In 2006, *Canadian Interiors*

listed one of his restaurant designs in its 'Best of Canada' competition, and described his style, simply, as 'stylish.'

'Stylish' is a vague descriptor – it means everything and nothing. Spring Rolls restaurants are, without a doubt, stylish. One of the newest locations is at Fairview Mall, at the end of the Sheppard subway line. Rather than face the mall corridors, it's located outside, alongside the parking lot, with a view of the Bay and the modern apartment buildings south of Sheppard. Upon entering the restaurant, you immediately feel a long way from that parking lot, or the commonly held vision of what exists north of the 401 – you're transported to a strange territory that is a little bit fancy King Street, a little bit College Street and a lot of cinema. This set, like the food Spring Rolls advertises, could be called 'Pan Asian' – a place you can't fly to but, certainly, a cultural presence in Toronto. The background feels 'Asian' the way, say, a James Bond film set from the 1960s might, but it is general enough not to be narrowed to a specific country or culture. Everything is contemporary, but there are back-lit floral patterns that suggest this magical land, as well as an elaborate ceiling of parallel white lines and, in the middle of the room – like a centrepiece – two interlocking rings that change colour.

'Spring Rolls changed the Asian dining scene,' says designer/architect Lo. 'Chinatown was known as being dirty,

Spring Rolls,
Fairview Mall

Spring Rolls,
Atrium on Bay

Spring Rolls,
Atrium on Bay

Spring Rolls, Eglinton

grungy. I'm proud to be Asian, and if one day I can change people's perception of what an Asian or Chinese restaurant is, that's good.' Lo has designed each of the eight Spring Rolls restaurants since the first one opened at Yonge and Bloor in 1996. We chatted while seated in the pink-marble food court at the Atrium on Bay, outside another of his Spring Rolls iterations that is as dramatic a contrast to the Atrium's architecture as the Fairview Mall location is to its surroundings. These restaurants are indeed iterations – each subsequent location carries over elements of the previous one, but is reorganized with new designs. 'One thing Spring Rolls should be is interesting to people,' says Lo. 'Every location is different, but feels the same.' Spring Rolls has given Lo considerable freedom to push the boundaries of what has become a recognizable Toronto style that isn't rarified or precious, but open to anybody with a little money to spend. As Lo says, 'The foundation is good food, but we have to create an environment.'

It is likely too early to gauge Spring Rolls' place in the continuum of Toronto's restaurant scene. While it's a bit unfair to judge Joanne Kates's observations of the Keg restaurant's democratic appeal in 1985 as being snobbish, today such characterizations would seem inappropriate, and would either not be written or couched deeper in euphemism and code. In the way IKEA made expensively and foreign-looking furniture affordable, restaurants like Spring Rolls make expensive-seeming experiences open to more people. As Toronto continues to evolve, these are the cinematic sets where our new stories – fictional, mythic, quotidian – will unfold.

RM Vaughan **I, Rat**

Being an explanatory missive from a representative of one successful
species to another, equally prosperous, horde; written in the fond hope
of establishing a more balanced and harmonious coexistence in the
coming millennium.

I, Rat, could proceed with proper introductions but I, Rat, fear
that my true name would prove impossible to your tongue.
Imagine the sound of a sapling breaking in two under the
weight of several furious starlings, and then repeated three
times, and you will have approximated my true name.
Already, between us, a distance. No matter, my 'name,' such
as you understand names to act, as indices, tokens or charm-
sakes, is no more part of my Rathood than are the small hairs
of your forearms any marker of your own true selves. Rats do
not keep score, do not mark time, do not indulge in nostalgia.
And so, Rat, simple Rat, will do. I shall refer to you as Not Rat,
as is custom amongst my fellows to name all unlike ourselves.
No offence is intended. I am certain you are considered as
unique in shape and danger amidst your own kind as is every
shard of glass or the particular curvature of a bent nail.

What I, Rat, wish to speak of, however, is not nomencla-
ture, nor even identity, howsoever either of us comprehends
such concepts (we Rats enjoy the swallowing comfort of alike
to alike more than most, perhaps to the point of addiction –
but you know that, because you have seen us flee in common
swarm); rather, what I, Rat, wish to detail, indeed need to
communicate to you, Not Rat, is simply that the time of our
long war is near an end, and, knowing this, we must both
prepare for inevitable sacrifices in whatever armistice we can
so arrange, inasmuch as we may ever fully come to a satisfac-
tory understanding, I being Rat and you Not.

My friends (and, yes, I am so liberal as to offer the left fang
of friendship, these being especial times), can we not with
honest breath finally acknowledge that our interminable
conflict has produced nothing in the way of victory – territo-
rial, subsistence-providing, nor spiritual – for either adversary,
individually or species-wide?

Oh, there are legendary heroes on both sides, actors in
blood whose violence Rat and Not Rat can both admire. Rats
will always tell sweet tales to whelp Rats, such as the tales of
the Junction Rat, that acclaimed she who ate nine hot, pink
and screaming Not Rat babies in nine stretches of night, or of
the Garrison water Rat, a Rat of most terrible size, he who

brought down many tall Not Rat nests in one night of skilful chewing and hellfire, and was consumed in twitching fury by a net of buzzing cords. Rats will always have Title Rats on which to hang dreams.

And villains, many villains – your Not Rat corollaries to our Titled Rats, those we call the Most Hated. The Not Rat of Spadina path, a female, for one instance, she who lured countless Rats with concoctions of wine and her own leavings, only to impale each foolish Rat with a spiked stick. Her evils exist, Rats can only believe, to remind us to question the blush of our noses, our first but flawed sight, to distrust the intoxication of all flowers, gold-red or perfect black. Likewise do we sing funereal of the Not Rat of the lakelands, he of the long flat sands between the water and the Not Rats' tarry killing paths, where monsters with spinning legs break Rat bones, he who brought floods under the earth in unnatural gushes, bursting Rat lungs, who taught the Not Rats of the beach lands the arts of drowning nests, of making a sweeping flame of humble water.

And still Not Rats concoct new horrors. Death fogs and powders, malicious all the more for their sweetness, and seeds sugared with strange bile that clots the gut. To die on the back, belly fur bloodied, to die tearing out a boiling stomach, is noble neither to Rat nor Not Rat. Do Not Rats have no pity?

All over this warren that Not Rats name City and then befoul, Not Rats send Finders and Nest Breakers into Rat places, into Rat pits and caves. Finders search our darkened

hoarding places, the very runs and trails Rats first burrowed, but where now Not Rats insist on settling, to better make and waste their oiled foods. How Not Rats love to eat underground! Do Not Rats dislike the sight of their own teeth? Rats watch Not Rats share their soft, warm mush on dusty planks in sunless caverns – your noisy, bright squatting holes even Rats abhor (but food is food, to be got as can be got) – and wonder, dumbstruck. Yet, how Not Rats squeal and jump when a Rat enters, a single Rat, when a Rat traverses the very burrows Rats first dug, when a Rat takes a Rat's rightful place.

All Finders and Nest Breakers, know this: Rats smell your coming, your lower legs reek of blistering bleach and mop tails. Your inspections fool no one, neither Rat nor Not Rat. The more the Finders make their food pits clean, the more the Finders betray their own workings, become predictable in their circling. Rats wonder that you try. And Rats are faster than any eye, Not Rat eyes or the eyes that blink inside boxes.

True, some Rats forget the box eyes, some young Rats (those Rats fatted on false ease, in the great, cool, night-lit cathedrals of food Not Rats erect, where grains and fruits and flesh wait on high and low scaffolds like a bounty of bounties, maddening) and in their forgetting, these gluttonous Rats bring rains of Not Rat poisons down on their own nests, as did the Idiot Rat of Christie, as did the Careless Rat of Dupont, both brash juveniles who frolicked where they best had hid; but such Rats are as rare as sunlight in tunnels, orange flowers in winter. Rats are many, eye boxes are few.

Neither Rat nor Not Rat is without guilt. This is known, a Rat may dare say, to both factions, and, a Rat may further dare speak, is celebrated in both high and low perches. Thus, we shall leave the question of worse blame where it belongs, in the dirt between the pads of the back paws, for it will do as much good there as any place, and blame's slave, shame, will remain foreign to Rat and Not Rat alike (although Rats do not pretend otherwise).

Please pardon I, Rat, if my address wanders into the abstract, swims in the old, green wells of still and diseased waters, for digression is impossible to avoid between such contraries as Rat and Not Rat. Ours is a war of attrition and we have each unforgivable crimes committed, memories that sour our bellies.

But you, Not Rat of the City, must trust me now. You must. Do not let instinct damn us both. For we, Rats, being close to all things that grow and crawl, worm and sunflower alike, read the future of soil as you, Not Rats, read the skies for rain. And we have never been wrong. Nothing so low to ground as Rats can afford to misinterpret the very earth, the mud that sings. And know you now, Not Rat, that the mud is, of late and dangerously, very, deathly, quiet.

Soon, the mud will cease to breathe, let alone coo or chirp; tendrils will no longer call to roots, nothing will fatten in the dark warmth, turn damp and filth into green leaves. Within this Rat's lifetime, I, Rat, daresay, all growing will stop. You, Not Rat, will starve – an eventuality I, Rat, cannot in honest

whisker to much heartbreak about, except insomuch that should you, Not Rat, cease to eat, so shall Rats. Even the meat of your dead, wide middles, a mountain of rot, will not keep Rats more than three or seven birthings out of starvation's corner.

In plain, Not Rat, when the very dirt stops making grain, some too-soon hour, all we who rely on your stupidity and clumsiness, your casual disregard for sustenance, stop too, in tandem, and will die in cold burrows, fevered and fatigued. Even the eyeless crawlers, the dust worriers and mindless, hopping things, will have nothing to bite, nothing to cling to, no fur to carve their idiot tunnels across. All Rats know this to be true: when the lowliest is disregarded, all that treads above is soon obscured.

We, Rats of the City, thus sue you, Not Rats of the City, for peace. Here is Rats' truce.

First, Rats will let tender shoots grow and fatten in the few muds that still seethe. We will not take our teeth to your harvests. In trade, Not Rats will send no more Not Rats into our tunnels and pathways, will no longer scald the bowels of Rats with infected seeds or feed Rats complex moulds inside old meats, moulds that burn like salt under the eyes, only deeper.

Second, Not Rats will bother no more with their imbecile nets and boxes (lures that anyway catch only child Rats, too silly in their new blood, the first-matings mad and the tired Rats, Rats with teeth soft as black mushrooms). Not Rats will not smash our nests, and, in fair hand, Rats will let out our

droppings only in shallow, dry pits, where the grounds are already without life. As for Not Rat leavings, both that of Not Rat bowels (in which, in truth, Rats take interest only during the direst famines), but more especially of the great, rich mounds of ripe foods that Not Rats wrap in shiny pod sacks to better let the juice, that pure, gorgeous nectar, pool and swell – Rats can make no promise. We are only Rat.

Third, Rats will scratch no new paths in tall grasses or amongst fruits and bearing trees. Rats will abandon the trees altogether, leave untested their fecund barks and round sweet-meats. Let full, cooling shade calm the healing mucks in this distressed time. In turn, Not Rats will open their topmost perches, the great plateaus of pipe and tar, the mist towers, to all Rats, so we, too, may smell the clouds. You creatures who live so high from mess and spores cannot imagine the elation of the snout in high winds, our intoxication. Perhaps you did once, but it has been many birthings, cycles upon cycles of Rat birthings, since Rats smelled euphoria in the complex slush of your leavings. The endwaters of Not Rats now stink only of angry salt and fatigue.

Finally, for a time, for a time until the lint and sticks and slow mosses themselves again churn with life, in five or nine birthings, or 500 birthings if need so be, Rats will eat only what Not Rats have not stomach or teeth to gorge. But be warned: fail to make the muds slick again, and Rats will not let a single blade of wheat rise, not one berry fatten. Rats will watch the ground wither to husk-skin through a glaze of blood, Not Rat blood.

When Rats know their end, Rats die gored but fat.

Not Rats of the City must tend to that which Not Rats have fouled. Rats will be patient. Rats will be secret and simple in need, for a dozen or a dozen-times-a-dozen birthings, but steady in watchfulness for the dirt's rebirth, steady in the dark.

This is Rats' pledge.

Contorno

Amanda
Miller **Not your grandmother's pantry**

The first twenty years of my culinary life followed a meat-
starch-vegetable model. My mother began working outside
the home when I was ten, and my brother and I were assigned
nightly chores; my favourite task was making Shake'n Bake,
which I considered my masterpiece. The most exciting part of
cooking was basking in compliments as I passed a plate. I was
being a show-off, but it also made me happy that I had something to share. I learned it all from my mother. I remember her
brining cucumbers and making applesauce to last a winter of
lunches; I remember her teaching me how to level a measur-
ing cup, to battle lumpy gravy with a fork and determination,
to create 'buttermilk' by squeezing lemons into 2 percent milk.

My tastes have come a long way – from showcasing chicken
fingers to cooking by season and buying shares in a local
Community Supported Agriculture farm. Now the way I eat is
informed by a longing for something other than what's right in
front of me, and an appreciation for things close to home.

But how do you take this longing for good, local, homemade food and make it real? How do you make soup stock?
How do you roll pie crust without overworking the pastry?
What steps are essential to avoid contaminating a batch of
strawberry preserves? When is string-bean season, and once it
arrives, what should you do with the harvest? We tend to be
wooed by cherries in February and ignore fresh turnips in
June, but we can synchronize our appetites with the seasons
and become attuned to local cycles. And, more than simply
choosing local, or adopting one of the many *au courant* modes
of eating, what if we relearn the 'granny skills' our urban
kitchens have left behind?

Spring: Urban gardening

My cooking was transformed when I took an apartment with a
tiny balcony, a haven for herbs and leafy greens, with morning
sun giving way to cool afternoon shade. Urban gardens can be
cultivated in modest spaces – windowsills, fire escapes, rooftops
and patios – and require only that you get started in time.

Toronto is situated in Zone 6 on the Plant Hardiness map, a
scale based on climate factors like temperature, elevation and
precipitation. This means that plants sprouted from seed
should be started indoors in April then moved outside once
the risk of frost is over. Plant your herbs, lettuce and other

vegetables outdoors mid-May to ensure sturdy roots by July, when the intense heat can wilt less established seedlings.

Choose a spot that gets at least four hours of sun each day and has good drainage (or use terracotta containers with holes in the bottom), and avoid overcrowding. Use organic soil for anything you intend to eat, and be sure your containers are also safe – the rusty claw-foot bathtub on my balcony makes a lovely container garden, but it's glazed with leaded paint. Tomatoes, peppers, beans and peas grow well in tiny yards or large pots. Edible flowers, like organic pansies and nasturtiums, make pretty borders around bigger plants, but mint will send out runners to choke its neighbours and should be potted on its own.

Don't be surprised, or discouraged, to find yourself sharing your harvest with scavengers and bandits. Squirrels and raccoons are not easily deterred. Try shielding herbs and vegetables beneath wire coops, applying a non-toxic rodent repellent, posting fake owls on lookout or sprinkling cayenne pepper over the soil, keeping in mind the pepper can scorch young plants.

Fiesta Farms on Christie Street is an excellent source for organic seeds and soil, pots and supplies. Roncesvalles Avenue, Little Italy and Kensington Market are good destinations for seedling tomatoes, herbs, leafy greens, onions and garlic. Online, Urban Harvest stocks seedlings and heirloom seeds, and produces an annual catalogue, and Seeds of Diversity features a list of regionally available seeds, which ensures suitability for local growing. Keep track of what works, what doesn't, future projects and resources in *The Toronto Gardener's Journal* (available for purchase online), which also contains a list of seed, supply and tool sources.

Drying herbs is an excellent way to stock your pantry for fall and winter. Harvest the herbs mid- to late summer before the plants have flowered. If you have been picking sprigs all season, the plants have likely not matured enough to bloom. Cut the stalks mid-morning once the dew has dried and before the afternoon sun has grown hot enough to parch the leaves. Choose only healthy stalks, and remove and discard any brown or mouldy leaves. Shake gently to evict any insects but avoid washing the herbs as moisture will encourage mildew.

Gather single varieties into small bundles and bind them at the base of their stems with string. Remember the bundles will shrink as they dry – elastic bands also work well and contract as the herb stalks dry. Punch some small holes into a paper bag and put each bundle into its own bag, with the bound stalks protruding. Tightly tie the bag to the stalks using more string,

Web resources

www.foodshare.net/
goodfoodbox01.htm
FoodShare Good Food Box

www.foodshare.net/
kitchen01.htm
FoodShare Kitchen
- cooking classes
- community kitchens
- volunteer programs, so
  what you learn isn't just
  about serving yourself
  and laying your own
  table

www.culinarium.ca
Culinarium
- fresh produce, meat
  share, artisan share
  programs
- culinary book club, children's events, tasting
  sessions, specialized
  cooking classes (ethnic
  cuisines, breads, using
  seasonal ingredients,
  etc.)
- sourcing specialty ingredients, and schedule of
  in-season produce

www.calphalonculi-
narycenter.com
Calphalon Culinary Centre

www.thehealthy
butcher.com
Healthy Butcher newsletter
(even if you can't afford
organic cuts or enrol-
ment fees for courses,
you can locate info
online, work with what
you are able to manage
and educate yourself
through trial and error, at
least having a good
starting point)

hungryinhogtown.
typepad.com
Hungry in Hogtown
(Toronto food blog and
links to others)

www.notfarfrom
thetree.org
Not Far from the Tree
Urban fruit-gleaning
group

and hang the bag inverted in a warm, dry place. It will take the herbs two to four weeks to dry, depending on the size and lush-ness of the leaves. Once dry, remove the leaves from the stems and store in tightly sealed containers, in a cool, dry place. Keep your herbs out of direct sunlight, to discourage mould and prevent the volatile oils that give herbs their aroma from fading.

Summer: Pickling and preserving

It's easy to crave a homey pantry lined with preserved spring leeks, summer jam and pickled autumn beets, but it's another thing to actually fill the shelves. Getting started can be daunt-ing, and without some sort of plan, you can find yourself in October wondering how the harvest passed you by.

If pickling and preserving is too overwhelming to tackle on your own, enlist a crew of friends and buy in quantities large enough to make a huge batch of one thing. Divide the tasks – one person chops while another sterilizes jars and wields the rubber-tipped tongs, a third seals the lids and lines up jars on cooling racks. Or if the process of sterilizing jars and monitor-ing vacuum seals is too ambitious, start with a recipe you intend to consume within a couple of weeks (refrigerator pickles, sauerkraut or salted lemons), then move on to more complicated methods of long-term preserving.

Make a harvest schedule, watch the markets and rotate kitchens and ingredients: radishes, spring turnips and garlic scapes in June; beets, cabbage and peas in July; tomatoes, cauliflower and beans in August; root vegetables, tomatoes and leeks through autumn.

Culinarium has an excellent website to accompany its Mount Pleasant and Lawrence location, posting what's in season and sourcing local artisanal products. FoodShare main-tains a harvest schedule online. The Big Carrot, Fiesta Farms and, inconsistently, some large supermarkets showcase local produce. St. Lawrence Market and Dufferin Grove Park have year-round farmers' markets (Saturday and Thursday respec-tively), while Trinity-Bellwoods and Riverdale parks host weekly markets May to October. The Wychwood Barns also host events featuring local and artisanal growers and producers.

Summer: Jams, jellies and compotes

Local fruit is available only fleetingly, and you need to stay on your toes to catch each variety at its peak: rhubarb and

strawberries in June; cherries, currants and gooseberries in July; blackberries, blueberries and raspberries through midsummer; nectarines and peaches in August; and apples and pears from August till October.

If you pick your own berries or stop at a roadside cart in Niagara, it's tough to resist taking one of those and one of those and a quart of those, too, and suddenly you have more fruit than your household can possibly consume fresh. That's the catch: superior to the stuff that's engineered to 'ripen' aboard a truck during the long drive from California, ripe Ontario fruit stays plump and delicious only a handful of days after picking. The best way to secure a sustained supply of local fruit is to make jams, jellies, compotes and purées out of it.

Jam is contentious, each person swearing by a different technique: simmering the fruit without achieving a boil or stewing at a rolling boil till the jam becomes gooey and thick; meticulously sterilizing jars and lids versus simply inverting hot jars to create a vacuum seal. Do you add pectin, or keep it natural? And once you choose your style, there's terminology and safety tips to decipher and memorize.

Conserving fruit can be messy and time-consuming, or quick, easy and sweet. If you are loath to tackle an all-day project, try this quick method for berry jam, adapted from a long-standing family recipe:

Wash the berries and remove any stems, thorns, leaves and stones. Place the berries in a large, heavy-bottomed pot and warm at moderate heat to release the juices. Remove the pot from the stove and allow the berries to cool. Dump the berries and juice into a food mill, place a bowl beneath the strainer to catch the pulp and juice, then purée. This will extract the seeds and capture any remaining nasty bits.

Put a plate in the freezer to chill – this step is important; you will need the plate soon.

Return the pulp and juice to the pot and place over low heat. Taste one of your berries to gauge its sweetness – once the sugar is in, you can't take it out! Cherries, strawberries and blackberries require less sugar than rhubarb, gooseberries or currants. Stir in caster sugar in a quantity of slightly less than half the volume of your fruit, or to taste. Stir till the sugar is no longer gritty, then bring everything to a gentle boil.

Boil for five to ten minutes, skimming any froth that settles on the surface. Now it's time for the plate test. Remove the plate from the freezer and drop a spoonful of jam onto the cold surface. After a few seconds, press the blob with your finger – if it wrinkles, the jam is set; if it remains gooey, return the plate to the freezer, continue boiling the jam a few more minutes, then repeat the plate test.

www.thestar.com/Food/article/127141
Toronto Star roundup of local cooking classes

www.theurbanelement.ca
Urban Element – cooking programs

www.dishcooking studio.com
Dish (posted recipes and tips once classes are over)

torontogardenbook.com
The Toronto Gardener's Journal

gardening.tips.net
Gardening tips, sources, vegetable and herb garden planning

www.uharvest.ca
Urban Harvest (seeds, catalogues and local guidelines for growing)

www.seeds.ca
Seeds of Diversity (Canadian seed catalogue)

Once your jam passes the plate test, turn off the heat and ladle the jam into clean, dry jars. Cap each jar tightly with a new lid (reusing canning lids can contaminate your preserves and little nicks and dents in the metal rings will prevent a complete seal from forming). Immediately invert the hot jars to create a vacuum seal. Let the jars stand until they cool to room temperature, then turn right side up and cool completely.

Check each jar to ensure the lid has been sucked down, indicating a perfect seal. Any jars that fail to seal should be consumed within two weeks.

Autumn: Stock

Soup stock can be as simple as throwing some carrots and herbs in a pot to simmer, or as fussy as diligently skimming a pot of chicken to produce a clear broth dotted with coins of oil. Stocks can be used fresh, frozen and stored for months (remember to leave room at the top of the jar for the freezing liquid to expand), or swapped in a pantry exchange for soups, pickles or preserves.

Equip your kitchen with basic tools – easily obtained from suppliers like Tap Phong in Chinatown, Placewares at St. Lawrence Market, Nikolau on Queen West, the Cook's Place on Danforth Avenue and Consiglio's on St. Clair West – including a sieve, skimmer, cheesecloth (for binding herbs and whole pepper corns into *bouquets garnis*) and a deep, heavy-bottomed pot.

Vegetable stock: a quick method is to store up carrot tops, past-their-prime herbs, vegetable peels and zucchini ends in the freezer, then simmer it all with pepper and onion. Or begin with fresh ingredients, choosing vegetables that hold up while they cook down, that don't produce a strong smell (cauliflower, for instance) or turn the broth cloudy (potatoes are out, although their peels can add a dusky flavour that works with some soups). Once the vegetables are mushy, strain the liquid and discard the solids.

Chicken stock is simple but requires babysitting. Cover two pounds of chicken pieces with cold water, and add onions, celery, carrots and whole garlic cloves to the pot. Leeks, thyme, bay leaves and whole peppercorns are also nice additions. Chicken stock should simmer but never reach a rolling boil, or the broth will become cloudy. Occasionally skim the surface to remove the fatty foam. It is ready in about two hours. Strain through a sieve, then cool before jarring.

Fruit stock is an excellent substitute for pectin when thickening jams and compotes. Simmer whole apples, or the cores and skins, until they form a slushy broth. Strain the stock and use once cool or freeze until jam-making season.

Winter: Pastry and pies

Pastry is deceptively simple, but can be unforgiving. If you overwork the dough, you can kiss a light, flaky crust farewell. The key is learning how to handle the ingredients. Keep everything very cold (butter, bowl, fingers, tools) and your touch light and brisk.

There are three basic types – pâte brisée (short pastry – see sidebar), pâte sablée (sweetened short pastry) and buttery double-crust pastry (rolled for standard fruit pies). The latter is most challenging, while short pastry is versatile, quick and perfect for quiche, Tarte Tatin, individual tarts and savoury twists.

Putting it all together

Once you master a simple pot pie, it seems unlikely you'll decide, 'Forget this, I think I'll just switch back to frozen entrées!' But before mastery comes getting started, and this is where many of us get stalled. Cultivating a relationship with your pantry doesn't have to be about spending money to acquire skills, flashy equipment or complex recipes. Start with small, comfortable things like keeping herbs on your balcony, joining a community garden or picking up a bit too much of something at the market and making sure none goes to waste. And you might be surprised how much people enjoy talking about their special technique for preparing a roast, dealing with excess cabbage or freezing blueberries for winter when sunshine feels a lifetime away.

**Pâte brisée
(Short pastry)**

1⅓ to 1½ cups all-purpose flour (humid weather will call for the larger quantity)
½ tsp fine sea salt
4 oz (½ cup) chilled unsalted butter, cut into cubes
1 large egg
ice water (for sprinkling)

Sift the flour and sea salt into a medium-size bowl. Using your fingertips and a light touch, rub the butter into the flour until it has the texture of coarse meal. Make a small well in the centre. Lightly beat the egg, then pour into the well. Stir with a fork, gathering more flour into the egg until the dough begins to come together into a ball. If the mixture appears dry, sprinkle with ice water, about one teaspoon at a time; if it's gooey and wet, sprinkle lightly with flour, a teaspoon or two at a time. Run your hands under cold water, then dry them and dust them with a bit of flour. Turn the dough onto a floured surface and gather into a ball and pat into a disk about one-inch thick. Wrap in plastic wrap and chill thirty minutes before rolling.

The pastry can be used immediately: bake at 350°F for twenty to thirty minutes. Or the dough can be made up to one day ahead and stored in the fridge, tightly wrapped to keep it from drying out. Let stand at room temperature about fifteen minutes before rolling.

Wayne Reeves

Fermenting change:
The rise, fall and resurgence of craft beer in Toronto

As a new Junior Fellow at U of T's Massey College in the fall of 1985, I fell in with two other grad students to form the Ascended Masters. We weren't pretending to be spiritually enlightened beings; it was just a name pinched from a campus poster, a nod both to the head of Massey and our belief that the best form of 'ascension' was through a shared bottle of good beer. That belief soon led us to the new Upper Canada Brewing Company.

None of us were neophytes when it came to beer. Like many Downsview teens in the mid-1970s, my uninspiring initiation had come through Ex, Blue and Brador (the high-strength 'malt liquor' often smuggled back from Quebec in hockey bags). But an undergrad degree in B.C. acquainted me with the very different products made by Horseshoe Bay, the Prairie Inn, Spinnakers and Granville Island. Little did I know that these establishments, founded between 1982 and 1984, were the pioneers in Canada's craft-beer renaissance – the aftershock of Californian brewing tremors that had shaken up the Pacific Northwest in the 1960s and '70s.[1]

The beer renaissance hit Ontario soon after I moved back to Toronto. Jim Brickman's Brick Brewery led the way, a Christmas gift in 1984. Wellington Brewery and Upper Canada opened the following year. The former reintroduced British cask-conditioned ales to North America, while the latter represented Toronto's first modern microbrewery.

Economically, Upper Canada posed no threat to the massive operations of Toronto's other brewers – Molson, Labatt and Carling O'Keefe. Upper Canada's real challenge lay in communicating the importance of craft and character in commercial beer-making. Its beers ran counter to the Big Three's bland and indistinguishable products, which were the outcome of diversity-destroying market consolidation, lifestyle-oriented mass marketing and the pursuit of a homogenized (and pasteurized) national taste.

Upper Canada's Toronto plant is no more,[2] but its founding philosophy lives on in the twenty-five small breweries, brew pubs and contract breweries now scattered across Greater Toronto. These brewers are, in turn, part of a much older local brewing tradition dating back to the early days of York that met its end with Prohibition and the subsequent rise of the Big Three. Toronto's contemporary craft-beer culture preserves

1 Namely the 1965 revival of Anchor Brewing in San Francisco by Fritz Maytag (of washing-machine fame), and the 1976 founding of New Albion Brewery in Sonoma.

2 Sleeman shut the plant after buying Upper Canada in 1998. However, despite being swallowed by Sapporo in 2006, Sleeman still brews some UC brands in Guelph.

(and twists) traditional ingredients, styles and processes, emphasizes small-scale production and promotes taste education and celebrations. Yet while the city has seen a flood of interesting ale and lager since 1985, Toronto's craft brewers need to up their game if their beers are to gain international acclaim. This conclusion is reached after looking at how commercial brewing, beer and beer culture has changed in the city over the past two centuries – and, of course, after many a pint of beer.

Brewers, breweries and brew pubs

Greater Toronto has been home to 113 commercial brewing operations since Upper Canada's namesake, the Province of Upper Canada, was founded in 1791.[3] Henderson's, at the corner of Sherbourne and Richmond streets, was the first, holding a monopoly in the fledgling Town of York from about 1800 until 1820.[4] The 1820s and 1830s saw the rise of ravine-based brewers: Farr's on Garrison Creek, Helliwell's on the River Don, Bloor's and Severn's on Castle Frank Brook and Turner's on Taddle Creek took their brewing water and power from nearby streams. Often nestled picturesquely in the landscape, these small-scale, owner-operated establishments presented the cosy, artisanal image invoked by many of today's craft breweries.

Brewing realities in Toronto shifted considerably amid Victorian Era industrialization and population growth. Expansion in the industry accelerated from the mid-1830s to the late 1850s, with the city's nineteenth-century brewery count peaking at twenty-four in 1861. Brewing grew as a local economic force; in 1881, breweries employed 1.5 percent of Toronto's

3 'Greater Toronto,' or the GTA, comprises the City of Toronto and the regional municipalities of Halton, Peel, York and Durham. 'Brewing operations' include both breweries and brew pubs. Many of these companies, operating at a total of ninety-one sites, are profiled in Ian Bowering's *The Art and Mystery of Brewing in Ontario* (General Store Publishing House, 1988) and *In Search of the Perfect Brew: A Guide to Canada's Brewpubs and Microbreweries* (General Store Publishing House, 1990), Jamie MacKinnon's *Ontario Beer Guide* (CDG Books, 1992), Stephen Beaumont's *Great Canadian Beer Guide* (CDG Books, 1994 and 2001), the Canadian Brewerianist Society's *Toronto Brewing History Guide and Convention Programme* (2001) and Allen Winn Sneath's *Brewed in Canada: The Untold Story of Canada's 350-Year-Old Brewing Industry* (Dundurn Press, 2001).

4 After several ownership and name changes, this brewery became notable for Jane Jewell, who, upon the death of her husband in 1849, became the first woman to run a Toronto brewery. Such leadership did not materialize again until 1999, when Roxanne Diakowsky headed up Molson's new brewpub in the Air Canada Centre.

Joseph Bloor's ravine brewery, 1865. Located on Castle Frank Brook north of Bloor St. E, between Mount Pleasant Rd. and Sherbourne St., this plant operated from 1830 to 1864.

Workers at the O'Keefe brewery at Gould and Victoria streets, c. 1890. A plant was first established on this site in 1849. It operated under the O'Keefe name from 1863 to its closure in 1966.

workforce and accounted for 5.3 percent of the value of the products produced. A trend towards fewer and larger operations was well underway by the century's end. Only fourteen breweries operated in Toronto in 1901, despite the nearly four-fold increase in the city's population since 1851. Immense smoke-billowing beer factories like O'Keefe and Dominion helped define Toronto's industrial scene.

Little of this early brewing heritage survives. Contrasts in age, scale, location and contemporary function are best reflected in the remains of Helliwell's (1821–47) and the Dominion (1878–1936) breweries. Fragments of the former, which butt up against the Don Valley Parkway off Pottery Road, are now part of the Todmorden Mills Heritage Museum and Arts Centre. The Dominion's exterior survives almost fully intact, a brick behemoth embedded along Queen Street East. Though the condos and shops of Dominion Square occupy most of the complex, there's still good beer to be had at the 'Dominion on Queen' pub at the Sumach Street corner.

Detail from an illuminated resolution for the Dominion Brewery on Queen St. E, 1889. Not depicted on the far right is the Dominion Hotel, which opened in 1889 and still sports a pub. Thomas Davies, who ran both the brewery and the hotel, reportedly owned 144 taverns in late-Victorian Toronto.

While the Dominion's stolid, prosperous face evokes Victorian self-confidence, the unsettling breezes that had blown over Toronto's brewing industry in the nineteenth century became a hurricane during the Great War. The movement to control alcohol consumption, which had grown in influence through the late 1800s,[5] triumphed with the passing of the Ontario Temperance Act in 1916. Faced with a law that capped beer's alcohol level at 2.5 percent proof spirit,[6] followed by a federal order that suspended brewing altogether in 1918–19, many brewers left the industry or switched to other products. One of Cosgrove's plants became the Toronto Vinegar Works; O'Keefe's started making soft drinks. Only six breweries remained in Toronto by 1920.

Matters didn't improve after Ontario's repeal of Prohibition in 1927 and the return to full-strength beer. Strict regulations on consumption,[7] the onset of the Great Depression and consolidation within the industry all took their toll. E. P. Taylor's national brewing empire absorbed three Toronto breweries in the 1930s and eventually reduced local operations to the Carling O'Keefe plant built alongside the 401 in 1961. London-based Labatt gained a toehold in Toronto when it purchased Copland in 1946; the company opened a sprawling suburban plant on Resources Road in 1970. Montreal's Molson entered the fray in 1955 with a new suds factory on Fleet Street.

The Brewers Association of Canada justified consolidation as a response to 'new business conditions' and a total focus on the bottom line. 'Breweries,' claimed the association in 1965, 'can only stay in business by being efficient; and efficiency often demands reorganization or consolidation.' Old ways had been eclipsed by new imperatives: 'The day of the small brewery, managed almost entirely by family owners, is receding. Although members of the old brewing families still participate in the management of their businesses, they are supplemented by the new group of "professional managers," the scientists, the technicians, all the experts made necessary by the growth and increasing complexity of the business.'[8]

Toronto's brewing scene was left punch-drunk as consolidation at the national level – a phenomenon that also bedevilled the U.S., the U.K. and other countries – moved to global integration. After merging with Carling O'Keefe in 1989, Molson shut its Fleet Street plant to take advantage of capacity at its former competitor's site on Carlingview Drive. Brewing continues there despite a continental merger that created Molson Coors in 2005. Meanwhile, Labatt took a different course.

5 The Canada Temperance Act of 1878 enabled municipalities to opt in, by plebiscite, to a prohibitionary scheme. This 'local option' left part of the West Toronto Junction dry from 1904 to 2000 – one of the last areas in Ontario to ban the sale of beer, wine and spirits in licenced premises. With lots of Toronto content, Craig Heron's *Booze: A Distilled History* (Between the Lines, 2003) deftly tracks the struggle over drink and drinking in Canada.

6 This equates to just under 1.5 percent alcohol by volume, meaning that I will never complain again about today's 'lite' beers, which typically contain about 4 percent ABV.

7 Banned for nearly two decades, public drinking returned to Ontario in 1934 in licenced 'beverage rooms,' the grey successor to pre-Prohibition saloons.

8 Brewers Association of Canada, *Brewing in Canada* (1965), p. 68.

Labatt's Etobicoke brewery at Hwy. 401 and Islington Ave., July 21, 1971. Well-served by road and rail, this plant operated from 1970 to 2006.

Bruce Halstead at the County Durham brewery in Pickering, 2009. Halstead relies on family and friends to assist on brewing and bottling days.

Taken over by Belgium-based InterBrew in 1995, and now part of Anheuser-Busch InBev, the world's largest brewing company, Labatt abandoned Toronto as a brewing site in 2006.[9]

Reaction against giganticism and its products fuelled the rise of microbreweries in Toronto and elsewhere. In this alternative beer universe, size matters but attitude and approach are more important.[10] Concern for brewing flexibility, adaptability, experimentation and customer service has created a language shift: it's now all about *craft* beer, *craft* brewers and *craft* brewing.

The appearance of small brewers has created an incredibly fluid local beer industry. Since Upper Canada arrived in 1985, fifty-seven brewing companies have operated at sixty sites in Greater Toronto. In 2009, twenty-five companies run fifteen breweries, eight brew pubs and four contract breweries (tiny outfits that develop recipes and then hire other breweries to produce their beer) at twenty-three brewing sites.[11] Great Lakes, founded in 1987, now bills itself as 'Toronto's Oldest Craft Brewery.' However, no breweries have closed since 2001, when Magnotta shut its Scarborough plant and consolidated operations in Vaughan.

Brew pubs illustrate the industry's complexity. They exploded in numbers in the 1980s and early '90s, especially in the outer GTA, but three-quarters of all brew-pub locations are now gone. Most were victims of poor product quality and the vagaries of the restaurant business, but some simply adjusted their beer focus. Toronto's first, the Amsterdam Brasserie and Brewpub (1986), was succeeded by the still-thriving Amsterdam Brewing Company in 1994; two other early brew pubs, Denison's and C'est What, now have their beers contract-brewed at Cool Beer and County Durham. Current operations include the Granite Brewery and Mill Street Brew Pub (both actually licenced as full breweries with a 'tied house' restaurant, a retail store and the ability to sell beer to other pubs), Rickard's Brewhouse at the Air Canada Centre (offering standard Molson fare), Pepperwood in Burlington (which trucks some beer to a sister restaurant in Etobicoke) and Tracks in Brampton (founded in 1986, closed in 2002 and recently revived). The Granite was once a true brew pub, making and selling all of its beer on site. According to the Granite's owner, Ron Keefe, 'In the eyes of the law, we switched from a restaurant with a brewery to a brewery with a restaurant, a subtle but huge difference.'

Overall growth, as measured by the number of new establishments, slowed in the new millennium. That is, until four

new operations appeared in 2009, a growth spurt not seen in fifteen years. Little is straightforward about these upstarts. Duggan's and Cheshire Valley began as contract breweries, headed by brewers who then ran other GTA operations (Cool Beer and Pepperwood); Duggan's is now a free-standing downtown operation located on the original site of Denison's, while Cheshire Valley brews full-time at Black Oak in Etobicoke, a few blocks from Denison's current home at Cool. The 3 Brewers, strategically located two storefronts south of Yonge-Dundas Square, is part of a brew-pub chain based in northern France. Black Creek Historic Brewery, an offshoot of Mississauga's Trafalgar Brewing, makes ales using c. 1860 technology at Black Creek Pioneer Village and hopes to bottle its products soon for a wider audience.

Size and distributional scope are other ways of characterizing the range of Toronto's craft breweries. At one end are one-man operations like County Durham and Pepperwood, which sell all of their beer within the GTA. At the other end is a brewery like Mill Street, which is capable of producing the equivalent of 40,000 bottles of beer a day – enabling it, like Steam Whistle, to embark on nationwide sales far from Toronto.

Suds under scrutiny

Characterizing Toronto's beer – what's in it, the nature of its flavour, its adherence to or departure from accepted style – becomes more difficult the further back in time we go. In 1985, the Upper Canada Brewing Company was the first Canadian brewery to trumpet its conformity with the *Reinheitsgebot*, the German Beer Purity Law of 1516 that restricted beer's ingredients to barley, hops and water.[12] It's unclear if beer made commercially *in* Upper Canada measured up to this standard, though Alexander Morrice's *A Treatise on Brewing* (1810) lays out commercial recipes for twelve types of beer (among them London porter, brown stout and scurvy-grass ale) with ingredients that include coriander, capsicum and caraway seed.[13]

As Toronto's demographics, available ingredients and brewing technologies changed during the nineteenth century, so did its beers.[14] British-style ales were made by Thomas Helliwell, Jr., who purchased grain at his office on York's Market Square to complement the hops he grew beside his Don Valley malt house and brewery. Walz's began to produce lagers in Toronto in 1858, following the arrival of bottom-fermenting yeasts, Bohemian brewing processes and German

9 In Ontario, Labatt continues to brew in London and Hamilton.

10 Legally, Canadian microbreweries make less than 300,000 hectolitres annually. Federal excise duties were changed in 2006 to reflect the fact that most small brewers produce under 15,000 hectolitres each year. Tax breaks range from 60 to 90 percent for brewers of this size; cuts average 10 to 30 percent for larger microbrewers (15,000 to 300,000 HL).

11 Thirteen sites (three-quarters of the brew pubs and just under half of the breweries) are in the City of Toronto. Molson and Mill Street each run a brewery and a brew pub. Some operations have been mobile: Denison's has occupied three locations in and out of Toronto; Cameron's left the city, while Great Lakes, Cool Beer and Black Oak moved in; Amber shifted from Peel to York region; Duggan's has made beer at two Toronto sites.

12 The role of yeast in the fermentation process was unknown at the time. More recently, wheat has been permitted under German law.

13 The local influence of this British book, held by the Toronto Public Library, is unknown. Early domestic brewing also used a wide mix of fermentables, flavourings and preservatives. On August 13, 1808, the *York Gazette* offered a recipe for homemade spruce beer: 'To thirty gallons of water add 12 ounces of spruce and a gallon of molasses, mix the spruce and molasses in five gallons of water until

it becomes a lively froth, then fill it up with the remainder of the water. Thus prepared it may be brought simply to boil. Sceem it well and by the time it has coolen down to the common temperature of new milk add a pint of yeast.' By 1860, Toronto cookbooks also listed bruised ginger, dandelion tops, maple sap, sassafras roots, wintergreen and pine-buds as beer ingredients – potential grist for the new Black Creek brewery?

14 Tracking Toronto's beer consumption at this time is difficult, though national trends suggest a century of hard-liquor drinking. Beer made up only 19 percent of alcohol sales in 1871–80, while spirits amounted to 78 percent. According to Craig Heron, the long, steady shift to beer was due to it being 'a cheaper, less alcoholic and somewhat less disreputable drink favoured by working men.'

15 In *The Ontario Beer Guide: An Opinionated Guide to the Beers of Ontario* (Riverwood Publishing, 1992), Jamie MacKinnon identifies an endangered if not extinct 'Canadian ale' style, derived from British pale ale but characterized by a grainy-hunky flavour thanks to the use of Canadian six-row barley (less delicate than the English two-row variety) and limited corn adjunct. Increased use of adjuncts and decreasing hop bitterness undermined this style.

immigrants. By the late 1860s, stronger 'XX' and 'XXX' ales and porters were being advertised for sale.

Stouts, cream ales, pale ales, India pale ales, brown ales and Scotch ales were tapped over the following decades. In the 1930s and '40s, before the effects of industry consolidation were fully felt, O'Keefe produced Special Extra Hop Ale, which was 'aged in the wood' (harbinger of today's extreme oaked beers?). Copland's made a Tonic Stout from 'hops, malt and Dr. Jackson's meal.' Despite containing at least 5 percent alcohol, this beer was touted as 'A tonic beverage "in a class entirely its own," of special nutritive importance to mothers, convalescents, aged, infirm and all requiring aid to digestion and nutrition.' (This claim, made on the bottle label, is one today's Alcohol and Gaming Commission of Ontario surely would not entertain.)

Over time, barley malt was replaced with cheaper 'adjuncts' like corn and rice, which sweetened the beer and lightened its body. Pasteurization was introduced and chemical stabilizers and preservatives were added to extend shelf life. Nationally, the trend towards lighter-tasting beers began with Labatt's 50 (1950) and Blue (1951), and Molson's Golden (1954) and Canadian (1959). The Brewers Association of Canada still listed ale, lager, porter, stout and bock as Canadian beer products in 1965, though stylistic diversity and the use of quality ingredients were both under attack as the number of brewers, breweries and brands continued to decline in Toronto and across the country.[15] Fizzy, light international lagers, with little evidence of malt, hops or identifiable character, intended to appeal to all drinkers and offend none, were the order of the day by the late 1970s.

In their struggle for market share, Labatt, Carling O'Keefe and Molson introduced some dubious innovations. Under licencing agreements, Budweiser came to Canada in 1981, followed by Miller High Life, Coors and Coors Light, and then Miller Lite. 'Dry beer,' claiming to have no aftertaste, arrived in 1989; high-alcohol 'ice beer' followed in 1993. Image-based marketing drove drinkers to these beers, but critics disavowed them. In *The Beer Essentials: The* Spirit Journal *Guide to Over 650 of the World's Beers* (1997), F. Paul Pacult awarded Labatt Ice a single star with these remarks:

> Amber/gold colour, with a firm white head and good head retention; this nose is intensely yeasty, grainy, tart, and to my olfactory sense, somewhat skunky – it's nowhere near as easygoing as the Molson Ice; limp on

the palate – while the label says 'smooth,' I think a more apt term would be 'vacuous'; just another case of a quicksilver, tasteless blast of alcohol for the thoughtless masses brought to us courtesy of the megabreweries; tasting this leaves little wonder why [North America's] microbrewery population is reaching new heights every month; consumers are tired of drinking these cardboard-like beverages that someone brazenly calls beer.[16]

In their counter-attacks on mass-market beer, Upper Canada and subsequent Toronto craft brewers valued notions of tradition, style, quality ingredients and, above all, *flavour* in their products.[17] The result has been increasing diversity and choice – if not within a single brewery (as in Steam Whistle's motto, 'Do One Thing Really, Really Well'), then within the larger fraternity of local craft brewers.

In the craft-beer world, market differentiation should take place on the basis of true differences in taste rather than in the sale of many brands of essentially the same product. In Toronto, the stylistic range extends from thirst-quenching 'lawn-mower' beers (such as Cool's Stonewall Light Lager) to potent barley wines meant for sipping (like the Granite's Gin Lane Ale). One can sample most of the twenty-three major beer categories and seventy-eight substyles defined in the U.S.-based Beer Judge Certification Program.[18] The Toronto beers that populate these categories, comprising at least 188 brands in 2009,[19] contain quality ingredients that are typically sourced far from the city. Steam Whistle draws its water from springs in Caledon; Nickel Brook uses sour cherries from the Niagara Peninsula; County Durham's whole hops are grown in the Pacific Northwest; Denison's German wheat beer yeast originally came from a Bavarian prince; Old Credit buys its honey in Eastern Europe and Russia.

Style helps carve out a distinct place for craft beers in the marketplace. Doug Pengelly of Saint Andre credits Canadian drinks writer Stephen Beaumont for inspiring his Vienna lager. Beaumont told Pengelly that people often 'taste with their eyes,' and urged him to create something beyond mainstream light-straw hues, which were neither challenging nor interesting. In Pengelly's view, Saint Andre's brilliant copper-red colour is 'dark enough to be a bit different, but not too dark to be scary.'

To highlight how diverse beer can be, many of Toronto's craft brewers have assembled a menu comprised of core beers and a rotating cast of seasonal or specialty beers. According to

16 The nadir may have been reached in 2005 when Molson introduced its Sub Zero draught. Serving beer between 0 and -2 degrees Celsius renders taste and aroma moot.

17 Too often, debates about the meaning of 'craft' don't focus on the character of the beer, but on the size, ownership and professed attitude of the brewery. While everyone enjoys a David-and-Goliath story, framing distinctions solely on that basis – focusing more on politics than products – isn't very helpful. It conveniently overlooks the point that not all products produced by small brewers are equally interesting (or, for that matter, worth defending).

18 While not as engaging as the work of Michael Jackson (*The New World Guide to Beer*), Stephen Beaumont (*A Taste for Beer*) or Jamie MacKinnon (*The Great Lakes Beer Guide*), the BJCP's guidelines (www.bjcp.org/stylecenter.php) use aroma, appearance, flavour, mouthfeel, overall impression and vital statistics (original and final gravity, alcohol by volume, bitterness units and colour density) as stylistic parameters. Historical, geographical, biological and technological contexts are also sketched out.

19 Compare this to 1954, when only five brands were brewed in Toronto: Carling Red Cap Ale; Labatt's India Pale Ale (draught); and O'Keefe's Extra Old Stock Ale, Old Vienna Beer and Double Stout.

Great Lakes' Peter Bulut, Jr., the brewery makes three beers year-round, then releases Green Tea Ale, Orange Peel Ale, Pumpkin Ale and Winter Ale in successive quarters as 'something different, something unique that's available only for a short time.' Mashing up classic styles with unusual ingredients – fruit, spices and strange grains – creates the eccentric, convention-breaking world of specialty beers exemplified by C'est What's Homegrown Hemp Ale, Hazelnut Chocolate Ale, Caraway Rye Beer and Coffee Porter. This approach speaks more to passion than profits, as Mill Street's brewmaster, Joel Manning, attests: 'We do the seasonals because we love them. They are not big commercial ideas, but they are very pure beer ideas. In terms of making lots of money, they aren't very successful because they are very small batch and aren't designed for everyone. But in contributing to beer education and beer-culture development in Canada, we consider them very successful.'[20]

Introducing consumers to such new, unexpected tastes – not to mention more mainstream craft products – is uphill work. Mike Laba of Cameron's notes that his brewery relies on 'experiential marketing,' using tasting events to educate and convert one drinker at a time. Some craft brewers lead consumers away from the international lagers by offering 'starter' craft beers. Mill Street founder Steve Abrams admits that his first beer – the low-alcohol Original Organic Lager, which was packaged in minute 195-millilitre bottles – was intended as a gimmicky attention-grabber, but defends it as a useful entrée to more adventurous beers like his Black Watch Scotch Ale, Cobblestone Stout and Betelgeuse, a Belgian tripel. The net result of many of these efforts is 'slow beer'[21] – hand-crafted ales and lagers where character is everything, taste is the index of quality and the drinker is left surprised and delighted. By focusing on the integrity of the product, in

20 From an interview at greatcanadianpubs.blog spot.com/2009/04/ meet-joel-manning-mill-streets-brew.html

21 A term nicely teased out by Christopher Mark O'Brien in *Fermenting Revolution: How to Drink Beer and Save the World* (New Society, 2006).

terms of raw materials, brewing process and how the brewer engages the community, craft beer has taken root in Toronto's food culture. This point is emphasized every day at beerbistro on King Street East (the undisputed local leader in pairing food and beer, and putting beer in food)[22] and at events like the Brewers Plate, a showcase for local chefs and brewers first held in 2008 and now presented annually by Green Enterprise Toronto, Slow Food Toronto and Local Food Plus. It remains to be seen, however, if high-quality malts and hops can be produced in Southern Ontario to create a great 100-mile organic Toronto beer.

Beer culture beyond Bud

Toronto has recently seen a great leap forward in its beer culture in the many ways the city's craft brewers, beers, drinkers and drinking places intersect. 'A beer culture needs beer knowledge and beer conversation,' declared Jamie MacKinnon in *The Ontario Beer Guide* in 1992. Since then, thinking, talking and reading about beer has evolved rapidly, marked by a half-dozen books by Stephen Beaumont and others, a biweekly beer column in the *Toronto Star*, the quarterly publication of *Taps: Canada's Beer Magazine*, podcasts and guided tastings by aficionados like Mirella Amato (www.beerology.ca) and relentless promotion by the Ontario Craft Brewers, an industry marketing organization.

While many craft products are bottled for private 'off-premises' consumption, brands dispensed from kegs and casks require the drinker to venture out into the pub(lic) realm and the prospect of beer chat. Aside from take-away growlers offered by some brew pubs, the products of many brewers must be sampled on the premises: everything by Denison's, Duggan's, Pepperwood, the Granite, Cheshire Valley, the 3 Brewers and Black Creek; a few of the Amsterdam's beers; all of Mill Street's more ambitious offerings; and most of what is produced by County Durham and C'est What.

These inherently social beers require supportive drinking places.[23] While more and more pubs now stock Steam Whistle and Mill Street, beer from smaller Toronto breweries is harder to find. It's best enjoyed in the handful of pubs truly committed to taste education, and host beer festivals, beer award ceremonies and beer organizations. These places vary in focus: the Victory Café carries only Ontario craft beer on tap; Volo and beerbistro have a broader geographic tolerance, but

Scenes from a Toronto cask ale festival, 2009. Top to bottom: F&M brewer George Eagleson explains the mysteries of cask; Victory Café staff dispense it; a young crowd enjoys the result.

22 For more on this approach, see Stephen Beaumont and Brian Morin's *The beerbistro Cookbook* (Key Porter Books, 2009).

23 The quest for the perfect pint in Toronto and beyond consumes Nicholas Pashley in *Notes on a Beermat: Drinking and Why It's Necessary* (Harper-Collins Canada, 2008).

24 While the best connections are made in a pub, the internet has helped forge a community of craft beer enthusiasts and enhanced beer hunting. Surfing brewery and pub websites to find products pales in comparison to seeing what the LCBO is carrying where (a tool not offered by the Beer Store, the retail oligopoly owned and dominated by Molson, Labatt and Sleeman). Staying on top of the Toronto scene means bookmarking Troy Burtch's Great Canadian Pubs and Beer site (greatcanadianpubs.blogspot.com, with possibly all the web links you'll ever need) and browsing the discussion forums at www.bartowel.com. To see how your opinions on specific Toronto beers measure up against other drinkers, there's www.ratebeer.com and www.beeradvocate.com.

25 Fears about the impending extinction of cask led to the founding of the Campaign for Real Ale (CAMRA) in 1971. With nearly 99,000 members, it's the U.K.'s largest consumerist organization.

26 The event, held since 1995, is actually Toronto's Festival of Beer. It overwhelmed Fort York National Historic Site with 30,000 visitors in 2008 and is now based at Exhibition Place.

stock only premium products; the Rhino offers a wider range of brands to appease its Parkdale clientele. And then there's C'est What. Serving suds since 1988, it's not just Toronto's oldest craft-beer bar, it's the only one with a manifesto:

Un-diluted, single batch brewing. Each brewing batch makes one beer and is not diluted after fermentation.

All natural ingredients. The ingredients used should be easily recognized as natural and, if processed, must retain their essential character. An ingredient list must be disclosed.

Fresh. Beer tastes best fresh. Pasteurized beer will not be served at C'est What.

Our beer list is **Canadian made** only.

Despite this stern tone, C'est What knows that craft beer should be fun. The scoresheet at its 2009 Spring Festival of Craft Breweries invited the public to rank beers from 'I'd drink out of the Don River before this' to 'Liquid heaven, please take my car keys.'[24]

Nothing epitomizes craft beer's approach to culture, style, ingredients and processes more than cask-conditioned ale. Brewed in very small batches with traditional ingredients, matured by secondary fermentation in the container it's served from, and dispensed by hand pump or gravity without forced carbon dioxide or nitrogen, this is the stuff that helped fuel the craft-beer renaissance.[25] Cask is naturally low in carbonation and served at cellar temperature, revealing subtleties in aroma and taste. It's living beer, changing by the hour once tapping has introduced oxygen into the firkin. With a shelf life typically measured in days, freshness is vital and local production an asset.

As retro as beer can get, cask is arguably the hottest craft-beer trend in Toronto and across the continent. 'The brewers are expressing themselves through their cask as the most creative product they are doing,' says Paul Dickey of Cheshire Valley. Going out to sample cask underscores the conviviality of craft beer and its self-conscious focus on the experience of drinking. For cask lovers, ground zero is the annual Volo Cask Days festival. As the *Star*'s Josh Rubin put it, 'The Fort York Festival of Beer[26] might be Toronto's biggest suds-related event, but Cask Days is the best.' First held in 2005, this event is so popular that both brewers and drinkers often have to be turned away by Volo's owner, Ralph Morana. Across town, the Victory Café launched its own cask festival in 2008. 'Fresh,

local and traditional' was the slogan of the Victory's all too successful 2009 winter event – organizers ended the festival two hours early because they ran out of beer. And in the most audacious move of 2009, Great Lakes brought twenty cask beers to the megabrewer- and import-dominated Toronto's Festival of Beer.

Ongoing support also comes from the group CASK! (www.casktoronto.com), formed in 2008 to raise awareness of local cask ale, promote it to a wider audience and improve the availability, selection and quality of cask ale in Toronto. Its 2009 Cask Ale Crawl navigated beer lovers to Volo, the Rhino, the Victory, C'est What, the Granite Brewery and the Mill Street Brew Pub over the course of three days, giving them yet another opportunity to enjoy some of Toronto's best beer bars and their most beguiling ales.

The future: Flat or hopped-up?

When it comes to craft beer in Ontario, downtown Toronto is of central importance. Small brewers exist across the GTA, but within 7.5 kilometres of Toronto City Hall, you'll find almost all of the region's best drinking places, the leading beer festivals and award ceremonies, along with two breweries and four[27] brew pubs. It's where craft beer finds the most receptive taste-buds, as several brewers have found. Black Oak moved from Oakville to Etobicoke to be closer to its core market (and reduce commute times for its owner and staff). County Durham brews in Pickering but has only two draught accounts there; most of its beer is sold and consumed in downtown Toronto.

27 Or five, if you count Rickard's Brewhouse.

A beer-style primer

Beer divides broadly into ale and lager. Ale uses a top-fermenting yeast and is fermented and conditioned for shorter periods at higher temperatures, yielding a fruitier character. Lager uses a bottom-fermenting yeast and is fermented and conditioned for longer periods at cooler temperatures, resulting in a cleaner, crisper-tasting brew. Ales are typically served warmer than lagers, but are not necessarily darker in colour, stronger in alcohol or heavier in body. Many of the beer styles currently made by Toronto craft brewers are outlined below.

American amber ale: brewed with darker barley malts and ranging from light copper to light brown in colour; typically with more malt character than hop (Cameron's Auburn Ale, Old Credit Amber Ale, Trafalgar Port Side Amber).

American dark lager: brewed with roasted malts but lighter-bodied than its dunkel cousin; low malt and hop character (Cameron's Dark 266, Great Lakes Red Leaf Smooth Red Lager).

Barley wine: British in origin, a very strong (9 percent or more alcohol by volume), full-bodied, malty-sweet ale that can mature over a number of years (Granite Gin Lane Ale, Mill Street Barleywine).

Bock: a strong (6 percent or more) German lager with a lightly sweet, malt-dominated flavour, ranging in colour from deep copper to dark brown (Mill Street Helles Bock, Nickel Brook Special Edition Winter Bock, Pepperwood Maibock).

Brown ale: a British malt-accented, often nutty ale with tastes ranging from fairly sweet to dryish and earthy (Amsterdam Nut Brown, Black Oak Nut Brown Ale, Pepperwood Monkey Brown Ale).

Cream ale: a golden, light-bodied North American hybrid beer fermented with ale yeast at lager temperatures to take on a clean, crisp character (Cameron's Cream Ale, Nickel Brook Cream Ale, Trafalgar Cedar Cream Ale).

Dunkel: a German dark lager with mild sweetness and a dryish finish (Denison's Dunkel, King Dark Lager).

Fruit beer: a Belgian tradition; an ale or lager flavoured with whole fruit, fruit syrup or fruit extract (Amsterdam Framboise, Black Oak Summer Saison Marmalade Edition, Nickel Brook Green Apple Pilsner).

India pale ale (IPA): originally British, a pale ale with intense hop and high alcohol levels; American versions have citrus, resin or pine aromas and flavours (Cheshire Valley IPA, County Durham Hop Addict, Granite Hopping Mad, Duggan's No. 9 IPA).

Light American lager: very light in flavour, body and alcohol (4.2 percent or less), intended to be very refreshing and thirst-quenching (Cool's Stonewall Light Lager, Nickel Brook Pilsner).

Pale ale: a hoppy ('bitter') British ale that can be amber- or copper-coloured; lighter and clearer relative to porter and stout (Black Oak Pale Ale, Great Lakes Devil's Pale Ale, Mill Street Tankhouse Ale).

Pilsner: depending on its Czech, German or hybrid Continental roots, a blonde lager with hoppy, malty and/or floral character (King Pilsner, Old Credit Pale Pilsner, Steam Whistle Premium Pilsner).

Porter: a dark British ale that is lightly roasty and dryish (Black Creek Porter, Black Oak Nutcracker Porter, C'est What Coffee Porter).

Scottish/Scotch ale: malt-accented; Scottish variants are often caramelly or fruity and less strong, while Scotch versions are stronger in alcohol and more malty (Amsterdam Twisted Kilt Scotch Ale, Mill Street Black Watch Scotch Ale).

Standard American lager: light in flavour, body and alcohol (but heavier on all fronts relative to light American lager), intended to be refreshing and thirst-quenching (Amber Brewing Lager, Cool Beer Lager, Magnotta True North Blond Lager).

Stout: a very dark British ale; relative to porter, more intense aromas and flavours ranging from roasty and coffee-ish, to rich and creamy, to sweet and strong (Amsterdam Two-Fisted Stout, County Durham Blak Katt, Mill Street Milk Stout).

Tripel: a very strong (over 8 percent), golden Belgian ale, sometimes spiced with coriander (Mill Street Betelgeuse).

Vienna lager: originally from Austria; slightly sweet, amber-red and lightly toasty (Amsterdam Dutch Amber, Saint Andre Vienna Lager).

Wheat beer: a light-coloured ale brewed with both barley and wheat, often cloudy and with some citrus character; Bavarian yeasts give clovey, spicy and banana-like aromas and tastes, while Belgian beers are flavoured with coriander and orange peel (Denison's Weissbier, Mill Street Belgian Wit, The 3 Brewers Premium Wheat Ale).

While Toronto has all the makings of a vibrant craft-beer culture, challenges persist. Nationally, fewer of us are drinking any kind of beer, and more of what we do drink is foreign and drunk in private.[28] For Canada's megabrewers, flat sales of flagship brands mean more emphasis on pseudo-craft beers like Molson's Rickard's, discount 'buck-a-beer' brands like Labatt's Lakeport, craft brewery takeovers like Molson's buyout of Creemore Springs, and marketeers' novelties like Bud Light Lime, all of which create an illusion of choice and draw sales away from authentic small brewers. Add in the struggles to place local craft beer in either the Beer Store or most pubs, and it's not hard to see why small brewers account for just 5 percent of Ontario's $2.9-billion-a-year beer market.[29]

Much progress has been made in terms of product variety and quality since the days of Upper Canada, but Toronto is not yet a craft-beer powerhouse. We need only look at Quebec – where drinkers expect more, and brewers deliver more – to see how much further we have to go. At Volo's 2008 Cask Days, Dieu du Ciel!'s Pénombre was voted best overall beer. This black IPA came as an epiphany after I'd sampled a dozen decent-but-not-outstanding Ontario brews. Similarly, Rate-Beer's 2009 awards saw forty of the fifty best Canadian beers hail from Quebec, while only three – Denison's Weissbier and County Durham's Hop Head and Hop Addict – came from the GTA. It's not surprising that Stephen Beaumont declared, in the winter 2008–09 issue of *Taps* magazine, that Montreal was Canada's best beer-drinking city.

Moving forward poses a chicken-and-egg dilemma. Do we first need more experienced and adventurous brewers or more informed and demanding drinkers? 'Beer is a perishable product that just can't sit on the shelf till someone's ready to drink it,' notes Adrian Popowycz of Black Oak. Craft brewers won't stay in business if their beers (experimental or not) don't get drunk. But does this mean largely resorting to the comfortable middle ground of well-made 'entry-level' beers, if only to keep the business viable or to subsidize more creative efforts? Perhaps really characterful beer will remain a commercial outlier, despite the GTA's huge potential market of four million adult imbibers. Though the success of events like Volo Cask Days and the Brewers Plate points to a growing awareness and appreciation of craft brewing in Ontario, overcoming Toronto's conservative tastes will likely continue to be a slow process, one where the craft-beer yardsticks are advanced one millilitre at a time.

28 According to a 2009 StatsCan report, beer remains the most popular alcoholic beverage both in volume and economic value, but growth in wine reduced its market share from 53 percent of dollar sales in 1993 to 46 percent in 2008. On a per capita basis, beer sales declined 27 percent from 115 litres in 1976 to 84 litres in 2008. The volume of imported beer sold increased 7.2 percent in 2007–08, while sales of domestic products were virtually unchanged. Foreign products captured 12.2 percent of the beer market in Canada in 2007–08, up from 5.6 percent in 1997–98. The Brewers Association of Canada says that bars and restaurants accounted for 21.2 percent of total beer sales in 2007, down from 26 percent in 2002.

29 Dana Flavelle, 'Express Stores Hurt Small Brewers,' *Toronto Star*, July 6, 2008. The LCBO, which accounts for 20 percent of the Ontario beer market, has been far more supportive of the province's small brewers. Ontario craft beer is the fastest growing subset in the LCBO's beer category, with sales up 37 percent in 2008.

Kathryn
Borel, Jr. **The chicken and the egg**

Human brain, while still in use, is best presented unadorned.
Though occasionally I will fry and pickle my own. And when
my brain is fried and pickled, one of the few subjects I am able
to speak about coherently – better than when my brain is
unseasoned – is food.

It was a night in February, and my friend Bryony's twenty-
eighth birthday. Before I left for her party, I thought it might be
nice to eat a small handful of Dexedrine, as I was tired from a
long day of working and felt like my prefrontal cortex might
need a kick in the prefrontal cortex in order for me to provide
half-decent party conversation. I chased the Dexis with a glass
of Cava and a multivitamin, then left the house.

A group of Bryony's friends – most of whom I'd never met –
had planned a small dinner party for her at the beginning of
the night. The plan was to then mobilize to a bar that could
accommodate our gang, once the tower of Libretto pizzas had
disappeared and we'd washed it all down with BYOB booze.

It was half an hour into the dinner. There wasn't enough
room at the dining room table, so people were just standing
around with their heads tilted back, dumping pizza into their
mouths. The psychoactives had eliminated my appetite. My
hands were pizzaless and I was performing a kind of dance
move that looked like a robot doing karate when I turned to a
man with a jaw like a lantern and said, 'This sauce is too plain.'

'What?' he said, looking down the flaccid slice he'd folded
into a U.

'It needs a pinch of sugar to take away the bitterness. And
would someone have died if the chef had used fresh oregano?'

'What?' he repeated, clearly annoyed.

'And what about portobello mushrooms? You know they're
just a scam, right? They're overgrown cremini mushrooms
that farmers used to throw away. But then some marketer
came along and rebranded the big creminis "portobello,"
turning them into some kind of prestige mushroom. It
makes me furious.'

Lantern Jaw walked away from me.

When the pizza was all gone, our group walked a couple
of blocks over to Ossington Avenue. We crammed ourselves
into the Painted Lady – a bar with many paintings and many
ladies. The Dexedrine plus the eight glasses of red wine were
making me think of making bacon, so I walked up to two men

standing around a little table and said hello and told them my name and told them what I did and said some other things that were of no interest and eventually asked the more attractive one what he did.

'I used to be a chef, but now I teach cooking,' he said.

His name was Felix. Before he'd been hired as a cooking instructor, he'd been the sous at a posh restaurant on Davenport.

'I kill for chopped egg salad,' I said.

'What?'

'I would seriously kill a man for good chopped egg salad. But no one beats mine. The trick is to put a teaspoon of Dijon mustard in the mixture and a few drops of –'

'Lea & Perrins sauce,' he interrupted, grabbing me by the jaw like a kid holds a lizard when he wants to make its body go slack. 'I know. It's a classic.'

In the cab ride to my house, we pecked. We pecked at each other like slow-motion hens all over the sidewalk and down the walkway to my front door. In my bedroom we pecked and eventually began plucking. His jacket and cardigan lay in a pile at the foot of my bed, as did my one shirt. He grabbed a thigh, but the wine was wearing off and I was feeling less glazed.

'You know all chefs are sadists, right?'

I blinked to adjust to the darkness of the room. Now that he'd taken off his shirts, I could see his pasty Irish-descendant flesh in the cold night lights coming through my window. His arms were scrawny and had stupid tattoos on his small biceps.

'Sure, it makes sense. You beat and whip and truss for a living. I always forget how to truss when I'm making roast chicken, even though I've done it dozens of times.'

He lowered his voice and said, 'When you're doing up a bird, you can't let her limbs flop around untied. You have to tuck the wing tips under her back.'

'Hmm,' I hmmed.

'You have to make sure the twine is wet. Then you take the drumsticks, slide the twine underneath them both and tie those up.'

'Right, I see.' My voice had flattened to a monotone.

'You pull in the legs with the twine and bring both ends up against the body, wrapping the wings and flipping over the body. Then you pull the string up until both ends meet, hook them under the stub of where the neck used to be and tie them up into a bow.'

I was bored. He could tell, so we fell asleep.

**Romance and restaurants:
A Kathryn Borel, Jr., primer**

Best restaurant at which to become crazy and make a terrible mistake with someone you're barely attracted to:

Sneaky Dee's

Restaurant that will ruin the opportunity for you to bed your dining partner because you will be torpid from food consumption even though you wore your special lingerie underneath your outfit:

Batifole

Best patio upon which to go unnoticed when you are trying to seduce someone and that someone already has a partner but you just found out because they didn't tell you before the date:

The Harbord Room

Best restaurant for people whose oral fixation goes beyond food and into premium vodka and nargilas:

Banu

Restaurant with the best-looking sommelier:

Niagara Street Café

In the morning, I shook him awake.

'I'm having a dinner party tonight and I don't know what to cook. What would you make if you were having four people over?'

Felix ordered me to fetch some paper and a pen, and wrote down a nice recipe for mussels in cream sauce, made with green apple and braised fennel. He rolled out of bed and put his clothes on. I grabbed his wrist.

'And for the main course?' I squeezed his wrist twice, like a heartbeat, thinking the affectionate gesture would make him think about something really great.

'Why don't you make roast chicken, now that I taught you how to truss properly.'

He smacked me where men smack women when they say obvious things.

When he asked for my number, I gave it to him with two of the digits switched.

**Kathryn Borel, Jr.,'s Apple-Cornbread-Sausage
Stuffing Extravaganza**
(adapted from a recipe in *The Silver Palate Cookbook*)

4 tbsp unsalted butter
1¼ c finely chopped yellow onions
1 tart apple (Jonathan and Winesap are good), cored and chunked;
    do not peel
⅓ lb lightly seasoned bulk sausage (breakfast sausage with sage
    is best)
1 c coarsely crumbled corn bread
1 c coarsely crumbled whole-wheat bread
1 c coarsely crumbled white bread (French or homemade preferred)
¾ tsp dried thyme
½ tsp dried sage .
Salt and freshly ground black pepper, to taste
¼ c chopped fresh Italian (flat-leaf) parsley
½ c shelled pecan halves

1. Preheat the oven to 325°F.

2. Melt half of the butter in a skillet over medium heat. Add the chopped onions and cook, partially covered, until tender and lightly coloured, about 25 minutes. Then transfer the onions and butter to a big huge mixing bowl.

3. Melt the other butter in the same skillet. Slop in the apple chunks and cook over high heat until lightly coloured but not mushy. Transfer the apples and butter to the big huge mixing bowl.

4. Crumble the sausage into the skillet and cook over medium heat, making sure to stir, until lightly browned. With a slotted spoon, transfer the sausage to the mixing bowl and reserve the rendered fat.

5. Add the remaining ingredients to the ingredients in the mixing bowl and combine gently. Cool completely before stuffing the bird; refrigerate if not used promptly.

6. If you don't feel like cramming the bird full of the stuffing, spoon it into a casserole dish. Cover the casserole and set into a large pan. Pour hot water around the casserole to come halfway up the sides, Bake for 30 to 45 minutes, basting occasionally with the cooking juices from the bird or with the reserved sausage fat if necessary.

Kevin Connolly

From galangal to la bomba:
Where to find exotic ingredients in Toronto

I'm standing in a long line at Danforth Variety and Fruit
Market, mid-winter, in the East-West Indies enclave near the
eastern border of the old city limits. I found this place on one
of my daily trudges through the January slush ten years ago,
attracted by its bounty of tropical produce in those months in
Toronto when the tomatoes taste like wax and smell like fish.
I have an armful of mysterious greens called 'dasheen,' some
Scotch bonnet peppers, a bunch of long beans, limes and a
few packets of dried spices. The customer in front of me, a
large sunny woman from somewhere sunny (maybe
Trinidad), looks at me quizzically and says, 'You making
callaloo now, boy?'

Of course I have no idea what to do with the greens. I
thought I'd buy them and figure it out later. 'How do you cook
them?' I ask finally. 'Are they kinda like collards?' She laughs
and, as the line moves, enlightens me: you need fish or
chicken broth, onions, sometimes a crab, sometimes a pork
hock, thyme and paprika, a Scotch bonnet if you like it hot.
It doesn't take quite as long to cook as collards but the result
is similar – a tasty pot of mild, stewed greens sitting in a
smoky broth commonly referred to as 'pot liquor.'

'Clean them good, though,' she warns. 'Got to get the grit
out.' By the time we've checked out, we're carrying on like
old friends.

It's long been common knowledge that Toronto's enviable
experiment in diversity has also made it one of the best
cities in the world to eat. You can have Brazilian barbecue
one night, Korean barbecue the next, grab dim sum or
sushi for lunch, then meet friends for an Indian or Italian
or Greek or Ethiopian dinner. And all at a fraction of what
it costs you in most of the Western world. But if you're like
me, an increasingly obsessive home cook, that diversity of
food also represents a diversity of opportunity. If a kebab
house on the Danforth dusts its skewers with sumac and
zatar, it can only mean one thing: somewhere, and likely
somewhere nearby, there's a store that stocks those two
rather exotic spices.

It's taken me years, a lot of trial and error, and some
rather ludicrous pantomime with someone who speaks little
or no English to understand what, exactly, is packaged in

cellophane and marked only with Chinese or Korean or Cyrillic characters. But I can now say that as good a place as Toronto is to find a meal from almost any world cuisine, it's just as good for finding ingredients, if you know where to look.

When your cooking needs cross language barriers, ingredient-hunting is time-consuming. Thai food, for instance, involves specialized ingredients: Thai basil (which has a mildly licorice flavour); those little red chilies called bird's tongue, plentiful in Chinatown but never seen in a Loblaws; Chinese purple shallots (ditto); kaffir lime leaves; and a smaller, smooth-skinned, ginger-like root called galangal. When I first started cooking Thai food I couldn't find half these things. There was dried galangal but it added no more than a trace of the heady citronella smell that reigns over a bowl of green coconut curry; I finally discovered it mislabelled as 'white ginger' in two shops in the Gerrard Street Chinatown. The lime leaves were easier to find and, thankfully, freeze well. For almost a year I'd go to one shop for one ingredient, another for something else. It turned the making of a simple dinner into a two-day affair.

These days when I want to make Thai food, I go to Fu Yao supermarket on Gerrard, a few doors west of Degrassi. It's a bustling, slightly dingy place that's showing its age (the floor will never be clean), and the staff tend to get a little pissy late in the day (fourteen-hour shifts will do that to you), but the vegetables are well maintained, they stock almost every Asian sauce imaginable – nearly a dozen different styles of soy sauce, for example. They also have fresh galangal, kaffir lime leaves, Chinese shallots, Thai chilies and basil, coconut milk, rice and rice stick from Thailand, long beans, Golden Mountain Sauce (a hard-to-find Thai condiment that's like a cross between soy sauce and Worcestershire). Better still, they have them all, all the time, even in the dead of winter.

I've grown picky about my beef and chicken, but Asians will not put up with dodgy pork and I've found here the shoulder, neck and belly cuts that tend to be unavailable in regular supermarkets and cannot be replaced in certain dishes. It can be a little bit of a culture shock at first watching men in bloody overcoats go all Hannibal Lecter with the band saw on indeterminate slabs of meat, but what do you think goes on in the backroom at Sobeys? I say sack up or become a vegetarian.

The Chinese are very serious about their ginger, as it appears in almost every Chinese recipe. Ripe ginger is juicy and bright gold under the skin and exactly the colour of a pineapple, not the greying fibrous nightmare you tend to find elsewhere. And it's not even a question of age. Ginger will dry a little as it's stored, but it's always perfectly useable days and even weeks later. One thing I do stay away from at Asian markets is the garlic. White-skinned, slightly bitter and usually sold very cheap in three-pack nets, it's harvested early so it won't spoil on the trip from China.

So where do you find good garlic? Where people won't put up with bad. One such place is Masellis Supermarket on Danforth just east of Jones, which stocks local, purple-skinned garlic when in season and good bulbs from California the rest of the year. As the downtown Little Italy has slowly gentrified, most of its Italian grocers have closed or moved elsewhere.

But Masellis Brothers, as it used to be called, has been here since the 1960s in this east-end Italian/Macedonian/Greek enclave and stocks the best selection of imported Italian products I know of, from good olive oil from dozens of makers and balsamic vinegar from Modena to gourmet dried pasta and canned tuna packed in olive oil.

Even good imported Italian tomatoes aren't created equal. I've found one brand (De Cecco) where the ingredients list reads, simply, 'tomatoes.' They're not cheap (they can be four to five dollars for a thirty-two-ounce can) but they're just that little bit better, and when they're the key ingredient for an already cheap meal like a pot of pasta sauce, I say spend the extra fifty cents a portion. Since you're in the neighbourhood, it's worth stopping in at Uzel Olives and Olive Oil, a relatively new specialty store a few doors west of the Donlands subway. Uzel may not, as its Turkish owner proudly states, sell 'the best olives in the world,' but they do sell the best olives I've ever tasted. The place keeps odd hours ('I'm a wholesaler,' explains the always affable, always weary-looking owner, 'this is more of a showroom.') and I've often dropped in at quiet hours of the evening and picked up some of the dozen or so varieties of certified organic olives, available in 200 gram packages ($3.99, or $7.50 for two) or sold by weight from behind the counter. I'm not exactly sure what makes them so good – maybe the small family-owned organic producer outside Istanbul, maybe that they're produced without chemicals. The last time I was in, a

woman who was born in Kalamata (kind of a hotspot for olives) was arguing with the owner about his sign. She was mostly kidding, but he was having none of it, pointing out that unlike commercial black olives, the slightly wrinkled ebony beauties from his family farm are left to blacken 'on the tree.'

I mentioned sumac and zatar earlier, Middle Eastern spices that are so specialized most merchants give you a blank stare when you ask about them. Ground sumac is tart, earthy, citrusy and slightly bitter, a mahogany-coloured spice you sometimes see sprinkled over a kebab or a bowl of hummus at an authentic Middle Eastern restaurant. I used to be able to get it at Asia Supermarket, on Danforth near Victoria Park, but that's a carpet mall now. I've seen it occasionally at Mumtaz Groceries, the best of a string of four Afghani/Muslim stores in a strip mall on the south side of Danforth just east of the mosque at Donlands. The same shop carries dried zatar, a kind of wild thyme, and bottled pomegranate molasses, and orange and rose flower water from Iran and Lebanon (used in anything from fruit salads to baking) at a fraction of what they sell in fancy-looking gift bottles at Pusateri's. They also stock Hewitt's Natural Yogurt, a great product from a smaller local producer, again at a price appropriate to the modest, family-oriented neighbourhood of mostly Muslim immigrants.

Speaking of Little India, the resurgence of Leslieville to the south has pulled what looked like a badly slumping strip back from the brink and promises to restore it to its former glory. It doesn't hurt that Indian cuisine is back in, especially for the legion of well-heeled vegetarians buying and renovating the older but larger homes in what was once a working-class neighbourhood. As far as ingredients for East Indian cooking go, I like B.J. Supermarket, which carries most of the standard Indian ingredients: spices and spice mixes, rice of various grades and origins, atta (whole-meal wheat), flour for rotis and chapati, methi leaf (the green plant that also produces fenugreek seeds), green chilies (different from those used in Mexican or West Indian food), and red and yellow onions in ten-pound bags – no cuisine uses more onions than Indian, and any cook appreciates it when you can get good onions in bulk for forty or fifty cents a pound.

I buy my Indian spices a few blocks west, at Toronto Cash and Carry, because of the consistent freshness (as important in a dried product as in a fresh one) and because the owner

buys in bulk and packages them in various sizes. Everything is here, from black cumin and whole brown cardamom to packages of hulled black seeds, from the green cardamom pods (a big timesaver when you're making garam masala), padna, jasmine and good basmati rice sold in one- to five-pound packages, and some fresh produce in boxes out front.

You've probably deduced by now that I'm an east-ender. But the truth is that Toronto's east-west subway line traverses so many distinct neighbourhoods, you can chart the food almost by stop, from West Indian, Mexican and Philippine at Main and Victoria Park, Italian at Woodbine and Coxwell, to Afghan, Pakistani, Turkish and Iranian at Donlands, Italian and Macedonian at Pape, Greek and Asian in Riverdale, and, after the downtown core, Hungarian, Korean, Cuban, South American, Spanish, Portuguese and West Indian again as you hit Bathurst, Christie, Ossington, Dufferin, Dundas West and beyond. In the spring and summer, what I cook is usually determined by what's in season. But in the fall and winter I'll often hop on the subway, choose a stop west of me, walk home across Bloor or Danforth and let the neighbourhood grocery stores decide what I want to cook.

During one such walk I ran across Nosso Talho, on Bloor between Dovercourt and Dufferin. Like a lot of essential city grocers, it caters to more than one national cuisine. There's Portuguese bread and cheese, rustic chorizo sausage and dried fish (it happens to be from Norway, but ... whatever), and specific cuts of beef for Brazilian barbecue like pichana, a piece of sirloin that sits over the rump that's now called 'tri-tip' and all the rage with foodies. My local butcher, Royal Beef (on Danforth west of Woodbine), has been touting the tri-tip cut for decades. At Nosso Talho the piece comes with a fat cap that sears and bastes the meat as it's cooked on the rotisserie.

A few blocks east at Talho e Salsicharia de Rui Gomes the atmosphere is more specifically South American and just a little less about the meat. There's always an avocado or mango in evidence and the store carries all you'd need to make any Cuban, Portuguese or Brazilian meal. They even sell bags of washed, rinsed and julienned collard greens, which are the backbone of caldo verde, a classic soup made with sausage (chorizo or linguisa), potatoes, broth and hardy

greens (always kale or always collards, depending on who you're talking to). I've made it with both, and by far the hardest part of the job is cleaning, stemming and shredding the cumbersome greens – it's like wrestling a couple of dismantled ceiling fans.

Outside of a little Korean-style barbecue, I've yet to really delve too far into cuisine from that part of Asia. But the ingredients have much in common with Chinese and Japanese food, and all of it (I mean *all* of it) can be found at PAT Central at Bloor and Manning. It's a big store and absolutely chockablock with fresh and imported ingredients, from fresh chilies and packaged seaweed to spices and store-made kimchi and Korean takeout meals (in the refrigerator section). A foodie friend of mine who works at Whole Foods downtown swears by the fresh beef short ribs there (trimmed and sliced fairly thin and wonderfully marbled), and anyone who's been to that part of the world and has a craving for the snack food will find just about anything they miss, from packaged instant ramen – they must have fifty varieties – to Mongolian sausage or cuttlefish-flavoured potato chips. They've got combu, the big ribbon of seaweed that makes the broth for Japanese shabu shabu, every kind of rice and vinegar imaginable. Even if you're just exploring, it's a fun place to spend an hour.

If PAT Central deserves an hour, better reserve two for T&T Supermarket. The B.C.-based Asian grocery chain that moved into the GTA with three suburban stores a few years back opened its first downtown store in 2007 at the site of the old Knob Hill Farms terminal on Cherry Street, south of Commissioner's. Each store is a little different, but all have sushi, BBQ and prepared hot and cold food counters (the Cherry Street T&T also has a dim sum station), and aisles of Asian produce, sauces, condiments, spices and ingredients, organized by region (Philippines, Vietnam, South Asia, Japan, Korea, etc.). But the real boon for cooks might be the seafood counter, where you can buy live lobster and Dungeness crabs, live B.C. prawns and shellfish of all kinds (oysters and conch as well as mussels, clams, etc.) set in streams of salt water that bubble constantly into shallow open tanks.

Of course, there are at least two famous markets in the city, Kensington and the St. Lawrence Market, although one could be forgiven for wondering whether the former is quickly becoming a place to eat rather than a place to shop,

and the latter is going so upscale it's only for people who drive BMWs. The top end of Augusta is being taken over by restaurants and club spaces, while the Spanish and Polish butchers at the south end sometimes look like they're a few days away from closing their doors. Still, a few oases remain for the home cook.

Anyone who's ever taken the trouble to make an authentic Mexican dinner has probably had the experience I had when I walked into the glory that is Perola Supermarket (on Augusta, just below Baldwin). The sometime pupusa stand at the back is mostly out of commission these days, but the imported Mexican ingredients seem like a miracle when you first see them, from the wealth of fresh and dried chilies out front to the towers of canned goods and condiments inside (two dozen different hot sauces alone). Tomatilloes (which look like sticky green tomatoes with husks on them and are the basis for all green chilies and salsas), giant packages of corn and wheat tortillas from Mexico and from authentic tortillerias in places like Chicago and north Michigan – this place has it all. In the fridge, there's fresh Oaxaca cheese (like mozzarella) and queso fresco (like a slightly dry feta), along with homemade sopes (thick tortillas), Mexican crema (like crème fraîche, but much less expensive – you drizzle it over your enchilada) and a selection of Mexican sodas, absolutely delicious with flavours like mango, lime, tamarind and apple.

But the chilies alone are worth the bike ride to Perola. They're sold by weight out of old wooden boxes out front, labelled with fading felt marker. There are anchos (red ripened poblanos left to dry – kind of medium-hot, and a little raisin-sweet), chili pasilla (earthy, not so hot), guajillos (sweet and aromatically fiery), chipotles (smoked red-ripe jalapenos – which look like large, dried, squashed bugs) and chili pequins, which come with a handwritten warning: 'fiery little devils.' I have a small bag of pequins in the pantry I haven't even used in a recipe yet, but somehow I feel a little safer knowing they're there.

There are other reasons for a cook to go to Kensington, not least because it may be the only place in Ontario where you're guaranteed to find a ripe avocado – you know, because you want guacamole *this* week – but outside Perola's and the House of Spice, I know better places closer to home to find what I need than the slowly fading West Indian and vegetarian grocers that seem to be holding out against the

encroachment of nightspots like Supermarket (the club) and Ronnie's Local 069. I still love the Market – but it's less a destination for me as a cook than it used to be, and I'm worried about what will happen to it when the older generation of shopkeepers retire.

Not so the St. Lawrence Market, undergoing its own slow, creeping gentrification, but also holding up a tradition of being a great place to find the ingredients for almost any meal. The upstairs now has a boutique wine shop (aren't we half a mile from that giant Queen's Quay Liquor Barn?) and a place that sells flowers, none of them edible, but there's still the good greengrocers near the north entrance (I like Family Food Market – same stuff, better prices) and a decent butcher, Witteveen's, right there in the middle.

Then there's Scheffler's, my vote for the best delicatessen in Toronto. They'll cut you a piece of any of the hundreds of cheeses and imported charcuterie on hand, but unlike, say, at Alex Farm, which also stocks good cheese, you can actually pick your own precut piece of most of them, wrapped in plastic with a price on it. Last time I shopped at Alex Farm, I asked for 250 grams of expensive small-farm Cheshire cheese, and the attendant (who, it must be said, *weighs shit all day*) cut me a 570-gram slab, wrapped it and asked me for eighteen dollars. I told him to keep it. At Scheffler's you can point at a six-dollar piece you want, ask what it's like, and a cheese monger will happily cut you a taste off the block. They have things like whey butter and a wide selection of European cheeses, but they also stock products from small farms in Quebec and Ontario, and no one there has ever made me feel like I asked a stupid question.

It takes a few visits to figure it out, but the real finds at St. Lawrence are on the lower level. Phil's Place, right in the middle of the north wing, stocks a lot of specialty ingredients, though you often pay a premium. They usually have poblano and serrano chilies (at twice the Perola price), wild mushrooms like chanterelles and lobster mushrooms in season, heirloom and cherry tomatoes, purple and yellow carrots and golden beets, even fresh chervil, which is something you usually don't see outside a restaurant (chervil is like fine, slightly anise-tasting parsley, and a lovely addition to a simple green salad).

The place I seem to go most often is labyrinthine Domino's Foods, in the deepest corner of the north end, a

bulk food and import shop with a Mediterranean bias that is a treasure trove of packaged ingredients from around the world. They have those excellent Italian canned goods like tomatoes and tuna and the tomato paste that comes in a toothpaste tube, very good olive oil from around the world, saffron and Mexican oregano and other high-end spices at good prices, dozens of varieties of chocolate (Italian, French, German, Swiss), dried gourmet mushrooms (porcini and the like) sold by weight, combu and ponzu and Japanese soy sauces and a whole range of other things I no doubt haven't discovered yet.

I know those who swear by Lively Life, which does have an impressive array of ingredients for all kinds of cuisines: Mexican, Indian, Asian, etc. But I find the prices out of whack (there's no reason for five dried chilies to cost ten dollars, for example) and I have often taken an item home only to find the expiry date long since passed.

It's a different matter altogether at Rube's Rice Shop, one of my favourite food stores in Toronto. I bought my first bag of basmati rice from proprietor Rube Marcos, a beloved man now in his mid-eighties who started out selling peanuts at the Woodbine racetrack. No stale stock or plastic bags here – everything is top quality and scooped (by you) into three sizes of paper lunch bags, which Rube ties with an elastic before he makes change like a ball-game usher, from his pockets and the pile of coins lying on the wooden counter. He has the best rices for sushi or risotto, and Rube's is the only place I know that stocks, by weight, dried French flageolet beans (green kidney beans used for cassoulet) or la bomba, the very short-grained Spanish rice that's the basis of a classic paella. He's got four varieties of quinoa, every bean and legume imaginable, and he doesn't blink when your total order comes to eighty-eight cents. My favourite encounter with Rube has to do with those flageolet beans (which are really good with lamb and are, for dried legumes, very expensive). I bought a small bag once after asking Rube about them, then about a year later, remembered how well a recipe turned out and dropped in for another small bag. Before I uttered a word, he pointed to the sign and said, 'Good day for you to get them. The price went down.'

You've got to love the old-school guys.

The stores

Alex Farm Cheese
93 Front St. E (in St. Lawrence Market)
416.368.2415

B.J. Supermarket
1449 Gerrard St. E
416.469.3712

Danforth Variety & Fruit Market
2742 Danforth Ave.
416.690.1646

Family Food Market
93 Front St. E (in St. Lawrence Market)
416.203.1288

Fu Yao Supermarket
564–638 Gerrard St. E

House of Spice
190 Augusta Ave.
416.593.9724

Lively Life International Fine Food
93 Front St. E (in St. Lawrence Market)
416.362.1464

Masellis Brothers Grocery
909 Danforth Ave.
416.465.7901

Mumtaz Groceries
1069 Danforth Ave.
416.778.1010

Nosso Talho
1048 Bloor St. W
416.530.1941

PAT Central Market
675 Bloor St. West
416.532.2961

Perola Supermarket
247 Augusta Ave.
416.593.9728

Royal Beef
1968 Danforth Ave.
416.421.1029

Rube's Rice Shop
93 Front St. E (in St. Lawrence Market)
416.368.8734

Talho e Salsicharia de Rui Gomes
874 Bloor St. W
416.535.2886

Scheffler's Delicatessen
93 Front St. E (in St. Lawrence Market)
416.364.2806

T & T Supermarket
222 Cherry St.
416.463.8113

Toronto Cash and Carry
1405 Gerrard St. E
416.466.3599

Uzel Olives and Olive Oil
585 Jones Ave.
974 Danforth Ave.

Whole Foods Market
159 Yonge St.
416.603.4888

Witteveen Meats
93 Front St. E (in St. Lawrence Market)
416.363.6852

Rea
McNamara

Never see come see: Toronto's Trini roti

Roti is Hindi for bread. It is a thin bread served with a curried filling, a filling that's either poured onto the whole for stuffing, or served on the side for dipping. Flour, baking powder, salt and water: sift the dry, add the water and knead. All the recipes begin this way, and all the recipes will end with balls of dough rolled out as thinly as possible, cooked individually on a hot pan, to be served, when cool, with a curry. This is how my mouth opens.

In Toronto, I often eat roti in stoplight storefronts with neon palm tree signs. Sometimes I'll call ahead, but usually I'll just wait, to see what it is I never come see. The menu boards entice with doubles and aloo pie, the refrigerator cools Solo, Peardrax and Apple J, the counter offers kurma in small plastic bags. A *Share* newspaper left behind on the table is half-opened on a 'Caribana Gets Federal $$ Boost' headline and a full-page ad for small-claims matters on Islington Avenue.

In this West Indian roti shop, the islands we fly across the Atlantic for exist simultaneously with their corresponding 416/905 municipalities. These four walls serve roti wrapped in wax paper and foil, in a paper bag or on a tray. Fat and folded-up, this roti warms my two palms and dusts my fingertips in chickpea flour. The spicy, turmeric-tinged gravy swallows my tongue and maybe, just maybe, will let the stories jump out: 'lost roads, tracks, and smells and incidents.'[1]

1 This quote is from Dionne Brand's *Land to Light On* (McClelland & Stewart, 1997): 'Look, let me be specific. I have been losing roads / and tracks and rivers and little thoughts / and smells and incidents and a sense of myself / and fights I used to be passionate about / and don't remember'

Between 1973 and 1978, Caribbean migration accounted for 10 percent of the total number of Canadian immigrants. It was a peak period of landed statuses: you came up as a student or as the domestic help; you could even be the good boy or girl who married a sponsor and begot a new history. But this history carried sadness: crying binges, horrendous long-distance rates, photos and small cheques sealed in envelopes, care packages bound in cardboard and tape. All of this dialled or mailed – usually disconnected or lost – to those you left behind.

Then, the small, unlicenced roti shop was a lifeline for the homesick, the homesick that were up at five in the morning, punching a clock, desperately in need of a hot midday meal. The ancestors – labourers on the sugar and cocoa estates – sweated for it as street food, off the side of the road, from a stand. The descendents – those in their new Honest Ed's winter coats – jostled for it as fast food from a roti shop, standing in the lunch-rush lineup.

For my mom, that shop was Ram's Roti Shop. She and my dad met on a 1969 BWIA flight: the suited-up first officer from Sylvan Lake and the miniskirted stewardess from Agra Street. They married two years later, in Calgary, with only two witnesses; my mom couldn't afford to have the entire family come north, so my dad didn't invite his parents or sisters out of respect. They then went from bachelor apartment to bachelor apartment in Calgary, Montreal, Ottawa and Brampton. When they happened upon Ram's a few years later, on a visit to downtown Toronto, it was the first time my mom had had roti since she'd left St. James.

Inevitably, my two older brothers and I – we who came up in Nobleton, forty-five minutes north, just off Highway 27 – grew up on Ram's.

Ram's Roti Shop was the first: August 1967, 490 Dupont Street.

Ruby Maharaj had come to Toronto two years before with the basics – curry powder, turmeric, cumin and a pound of Sindoor powder for her prayers that, forty years on, is now half a pound. Ruby's husband, Ram – the shop's namesake – settled her and the five children in a rented space for six weeks with a German landlord who strongly discouraged West Indian cooking in the shared kitchen (curry was considered a smell then, not an aroma).

Two and a half years after Ram's started up on Dupont near Bathurst, it was 'discovered' in a 1970 *Toronto Life* food column exploring the city's unlicenced 'Two Dollar Banquets.' This food was a curiosity for the Hogtown foodie: roti (an 'ingenious meal') was described as 'fried dough bags,' and the Jamaican patties at forty cents each were 'dough stuffed with spicy hamburger.'

Mr. and Mrs. Ram (Maharaj was long ago deemed an unnecessary formality) remember a mixed Bathurst and Bloor crowd that on any given day, by Mrs. Ram's count, looked like 'one from Barbados, two from Trinidad and ten from Jamaica.' Ram's may have had cracking plaster, peeling paint and only three tables (for a total seating of ten), but the homesick were able to catch up on their cricket matches, Lord Kitchener and greater piquant nostalgia.

Today, Ram's is far from Bloor and Bathurst, hidden in a strip plaza surrounded by fields, highways and subdivisions. (The children and grandchildren ensure, however, that these subdivisions are no longer overwhelmingly Cookstown white, but Mississauga brown, red and black.) Ram's remains a

family-run institution with a devoted clientele: in the kitchen, a City Taxi calendar marks the upcoming visit of a Texan customer who yearns for Trinidadness; there's also the often-told story of a woman who, while in labour, ordered takeout for the hospital delivery.

Mrs. Ram reminds me of my grandmother – gold bangles that clink and clack with a wave of the wrist while she talks about what makes the roti she cooks here different from the roti she learned growing up, outside of San Fernando. 'The only difference – like your mom would tell you – we put the curry on the side and break the roti and dip. But because of the convenience to sell it, right? You wrap it like a sandwich,' she explains. 'If you want to see, I'll show you. Come, come now.'

I follow Mrs. Ram to the kitchen and watch. The cold cellar is full of cookie trays lined with dough balls. Her son Vijay rolls one out to pizza size, lays it on a hot pan and douses it with oil using a wooden stick with stripes of oil-soaked cloth at its end; very quickly, I hear the sizzle of the tiny bubbling pockets that turn into the slightly browned spots you see on the wrap. Meanwhile, Mrs. Ram shows me how she makes a vegetable curry: mix hot oil and cumin in a pan on high, chop onion that's turned yellow by turmeric. A bit – wait, a lot – of garlic. Five minutes later, an emptied frozen bag of peas and carrots. Cut-up cabbage, a spray of salt and another handful of cumin. By this time, Vijay has taken the roti – please don't call it a skin – off the heat and is pouring in curry, tucking it in with the roti, quickly wrapping, sliding into package, onto a tray he'll walk out to the waiting customer. There's actually no recipe for this, and whatever changed from there to here is the varying mixture of spices, the adjustments made from know-ing in your bones how large quantities of ingredients react –

sniffing the air, squeezing the lime, your forearm muscles pulsing as you churn the dough.

Roti can be sada, dosti, buss-up-shut and dhalpourie. All are flat, light and unleavened; all involve flour, baking powder, salt and water. Once the thin dough is rolled out, it's cooked on a long-handled cast-iron, steel or aluminium griddle (a *tawa*). Set the kitchen-stove dial on medium so the roti will fry quick; before you flip, baste each side in vegetable oil with a cotton-clothed brush (a *puchara*).

Sada doesn't veer far from the above directions: flatten four disks using rolling pin, resting at intervals so the dough can firm, then fry. Dosti involves the do-si-do of two pieces of dough, rolled out together. Buss-up-shut is the most climatic – it's hot and silky and torn. Two wooden spatulas slap the dough into shreds, or bare hands beat it while it's wrapped in cloth.

Dhalpourie, though, is the lightest: four balls filled with cooked yellow split peas that have been food-processed with ground turmeric and cumin, crushed garlic, Scotch bonnet (minced, stemmed and seeded) and *shado beni* (or the substitute, cilantro) puckered inside. Four balls made from flour, baking powder, salt and water, sifted then kneaded and allowed to rest before the *tawa* is hot enough.

'No one I know in my generation has been able to master dhalpourie,' my mom tells me over the phone from Nobleton. I'd rung from Dundas West to declare my impulsive intention (it was three o'clock on a Sunday afternoon) to cook dhalpourie from scratch for dinner that night. This would be the first time the roti wasn't takeout from a shop, or bought frozen in a package from Nicey's Food Mart, near Oakwood and Vaughan. She tells me that the last attempt was made in the early 1940s, on Agra Street, by Grandma. 'It was crisp like a Crix biscuit,' my mom warmly assures me. The failure looms large, assuaging maternal mishaps that bind us (cooking from scratch, a stubborn nature, shopping during the off-season).

And I fail, too, fairly early on: soon after the flour, baking powder, salt and water are combined, I knead wilfully, but the dough remains lumpy and stiff. It doesn't thumb-press right, not at the ten-minute mark, nor at fifteen or twenty, moments marked by the heel of my hand's heavier and heavier push on a cutting board too small for the stretching and folding and rotating. A recipe can't give you sweet hands, can't tell you what rhythm to knead; your eyes won't close, you'll peek at

the words, you'll forget to add a little oil for that just-right consistency. *Never see come see* sada, dosti, buss-up-shut and dhalpourie; *never see come see* an East Indian meal that's take-out in Toronto, takeout in Port of Spain.[2]

2 The *Cote ce Cote la Trinidad & Tobago Dictionary* definition of *never see come see*: 'Someone who has recently been exposed to anything new, and who overdoes it to ridiculous proportions.'

My mom always told me that if you can read, you can cook. As the oldest daughter of seven children, her family's daily chores were lined up. She cleaned, one of the four sisters cooked (the three sons did neither). So it wasn't until she married my dad (as my mom tells it) that she wanted to cook right (and maybe even prove too – distance be damned – she always had a *sweet han' fuh so*).

Our kitchen's sideboard held recipe books strewn with legal-pad sheets filled with girlfriends' recipes and different versions of chili found in and ripped out of *Canadian Living*. Editing was done in pencil or pen within the margins, and I grew up with recipes as productions – epic when Dad was home from a layover – with the meat seasoned for three hours, and just the right amount of canned substitute when something on the grocery list was forgotten at the IGA. Five or six hours of kitchen prep that'd soon disappear from four dinner plates.

But the rise and fall of this performance involved equal-parts ego and sacrifice, so I always fought to do it on my own, with a recipe. Of course, my mom would still watch while I stirred a pot, quickly catching me out if I wasn't stirring the right way or if I didn't measure out the cup by overfilling it and then using the back of a knife to shave off the excess. This went against the if-you-can-read-you-can-cook ethos! It was only later, in Mrs. Ram's kitchen, understanding her need to watch me, that I began to regret the fuss I'd made when my mother tried to show me the way her body moved into preparing the food we shared. It would always be a conflict between the recipe that was in print, doctored in loose, handwritten notes, and the recipe that was spoken, but hardly moved between us.

'So what do you want to ask me now about roti?' says my mom, looking a little bored in her pixellated Skype form.

This is where it all began: in February, while she's still in the Bahamas with my dad, on the boat he built. (Port of Spain is too far south to charter, a visit dominated by family and friends, a visit that starts as a vacation but never ends as one.) I'm in Toronto, looking at the snow outside my kitchen window, still seeking out takeout roti in the unlikely corners of town. It was the exposure to something anew – those little

places – that hadn't yet been overdone; roti was a skin, dhal-pourie was just a word.

'What makes good roti?'

'What makes good roti?'

'Yeah, like, like –'

'There's different kinds of roti – the plain roti, and then there's paratha roti and buss-up shut. I don't know – it's been such a long time. But my favourite is dhalpourie roti, which is the one with the split peas between. That's my favourite.'

She always orders shrimp roti, but slices it in half, to save for a lunch the next day. Her memories involve the Hott Shoppe, or the 1950s Rialto cinema house they'd tumble into for B-movie gunslingers. She tells me of a time when roti was cooked outdoors with a cold pot, a flat iron over a coal fire.

We're able to talk longer on the phone when my mom's back in Nobleton. She tells me how she feels more Canadian than Trini; she's been here since 1971, and has lived most of her life here rather than there. She doesn't call herself a Trini anymore, and now only goes back a week each summer – a visit that involves ensuring that all her girlfriends, mothers themselves with daughters at the University of Miami, sons with Texan PhDs, are back in Westmoorings and Maraval, too – to see Grandma, whose health is waning, which means she can no longer travel on a plane alone. Spending so much time behind the locked gates with the guard dogs can chip away at those memories of the Rialto.

The singular voice is foreign to me; my mouth opens and stories jump out. But lost roads lead you astray, and smells and incidents complicate the one story out of many.

This story is fragmented, non-linear and not necessarily my own. *Bazodee* in its messy form, a form that twists in anticipation of the *picong* stab, a stab that'll tease at the attempt to cook from scratch what's takeout in Port of Spain, takeout in Toronto. So I speak in tongues on disparate things: she who ate through Toronto's Trini roti, she who made Toronto's Trini roti and she who will translate how that happened.

Translating is easy: it's an in-between that doesn't require any speaking for yourself except to say *bazodee* and *picong* before or after the licking of lips for curried crab and dumplings. Stay in the middle for long enough, and you'll start to believe that you know this, naturally, the *cote ce cote la* – I mean, the *co-tay-see-co-tay-lah* – of words and phrases and stories.

So let me be honest then: I grew up in Nobleton, a small town forty-five minutes north of the city known for its horse farms, golf club and two Italian bakeries. So my Trinidadness has a *never see come see* complex: it's the splashing of lime sauce like gravy instead of the discreet drop on the side of the plate (because the difference between hot spicy and flavourful spicy hasn't been tasted yet). It compels me to grocery shop at Nicey's Food Mart, and revel in recognizing the cans of *calaloo*. It makes me categorically file away the details of a Trini roti shop: the centrepiece arrangement of ceramic *patchoi, julie mango*, avocado and sorrel at Island Foods' King West location, the stack of Naparima Girls' cookbooks at Ali's on Queen, the bottles of Angostura Lemon Lime Bitters cooling in the fridge of Bloor and Bathurst's Caribbean Roti Palace.

But taste is a great equalizer that slices through Toronto's neighbourhoods, the gated fences and guard dogs in Port of Spain. It is a universally agreed-upon ritual shared between clerk and customer – the order of curry in dhalpourie. The roti is thin and flaky, the curry's gravy isn't soupy like Jamaican or wet like Guyanese; you might eat it with your hands (this is Trini), or you might fork-and-knife it, even slice it in half to save a portion for lunch the next day (this is Canadian).

Then again, maybe you even embrace the maternal mishaps – to be unafraid to take shortcuts from scratch, from the supermarket aisle, from the takeout counter. Eat for your own sustenance, for your own belonging. Know in your bones the recipe that was passed on.

So, you want to make roti. Go to Nicey's Food Mart. Buy two packages of Roti Galore plain roti (without the chickpeas). When you get back home, see what ingredients you have in your cupboard: garlic cloves, Chatak's curry masala powder, one can of chickpeas, cumin seed, sunflower oil. Walk over to the No Frills and shop the aisles for the ingredients you don't have: two onions, four potatoes, a Scotch bonnet pepper, a package of Canadian stewing beef.

• When you get home, cut up the beef in one-inch pieces. Take half an onion, one pepper and a clove of garlic and chop them in the food processor. Add a dash of Maggi's, a glop of Geeta green seasoning, a drop of Angostura Bitters and the blended onion, Scotch bonnet and garlic to the beef. In a bowl, let your fingers squeeze the seasoning into the beef pieces. Put the meat in the fridge, and let sit for an hour.

• After the hour is up, take the beef out of the fridge. Sprinkle a bit of curry powder on it, set aside. Mix three heaping tablespoonfuls of the curry powder with 1/2 cup of cold water.

• Cover the entire bottom of a pot with the sunflower oil, heat it on high. When the oil is hot, take one peeled garlic clove and let it sizzle brown on both sides in the oil before removing.

• Add the curry mixture to the hot oil. It's going to boil like mad, so turn the heat way low. Worry a little that it might burn – the last thing you want to do is let it burn. Let it simmer for two minutes. Add a little water, stir constantly.

• Add the drained chickpeas to the pot, toss in all of the crushed cumin seed as well a few pinches of the cumin powder (the recipe encourages you to be 'generous'). Stir the chickpeas so they're completely coated by the curry/cumin mixture. Add the meat right after, turn it as well.

• Let the mixture simmer for the next two and a half hours. Stir periodically. Add water as needed to keep the gravy consistent. Be patient.

• After the two and half hours on simmer, fork the beef and bite into it. The flesh is tender, and you're ready to take those four potatoes, which you've peeled and halved and quartered, into the pot. Give the potatoes twenty to thirty minutes to get soft.

• Take the one package of the Roti Galore plain roti skins. Microwave each individual skin for forty-five seconds on high on a microwave-safe plate. When it's done, the roti will feel warm and soft. Take the plate over to the pot, and dollop two spoonfuls of the curry onto the roti. Wrap the roti like a burrito – one hand over, the other hand over, and then folded at the bottom to keep it all in.

• Take a photo.

• Eat! You can eat it with your hands – it's the real Trini way, as the oils from your fingers will actually do the food good. Or be Canadian and go at it with a fork and knife, with a little lime hot sauce on the side that you can dip each biteful into. You'll have leftovers, and the leftovers will probably be even better.

To give credit where credit is due: the curry is a modified version of my auntie Althea's recipe.

Damian
Rogers

Ontario Food Terminal: Behind the curtain

The Ontario Food Terminal is a strange, mysterious and intimidating place to the outsider, and, unless you work in the produce industry, you, my friend, are an outsider. The gated and guarded terminal is not open to the general public and it doesn't throw open its doors to the general media either; to gain access to the homely horseshoe-shaped government facility, you need to prove you have business there with someone on the inside. I spent three days there on assignment with a Florida-based produce trade magazine under the wing of a woman who has worked for years to cultivate relationships with those on the inside; when I went back by myself, I was blocked by security the minute I naively used the word 'press' like it was a backstage pass. Eventually I convinced the guard I had a legitimate appointment.

Once you learn that an average of 5.1 *million* pounds of fruit, vegetables and related foodstuffs move through here on any given day, you begin to understand why they don't want random people wandering around poking at the avocados. Because this is a business built around a perishable product, everyone who works at the terminal – the growers, the suppliers, the transporters, the wholesalers, the brokers and the retailers – are playing a perpetual game of Beat the Clock.

From the crack of dawn, the floors are flooded with throngs of shop owners from all over the city competing for the best goods while day workers hustle to unload boxes of fresh produce off trucks as soon as they dock. If while walking along the pedestrian walkway you sleepily drift out of the safety zone and into the main artery that links the long chain of companies, you might be run down by a motorized cart speeding from one temperature-controlled unit to another. This is not a racket for late risers: for many here, the day gets going well before sunrise and the bulk of the action is over by 9 a.m. By early afternoon the halls are nearly evacuated.

The primary purpose of the terminal is to get food from the fields onto market shelves, through a dizzying network of deal makers. Nearly every tomato and potato, every banana, starfruit and Iranian fig that you see at your corner store or mid-sized market has filtered through the Ontario Food Terminal. Due to the volume they work with, the

national grocery chains – like Loblaws, Walmart and Metro – buy the bulk of their produce directly from their own suppliers. Still, even the chains will call up wholesalers at the terminal when one of their orders comes up short – if the Boston lettuce shows up too wilted for their standards, for example – to fill in the gaps. But really, it's the mom-and-pop shops – from the humblest veggie stall in Parkdale to the impossibly posh Pusateri's in Rosedale – that drive the market in the morning.

Although modern forces have certainly had an effect on the way the terminal works since it was established on a forty-acre tract of choice real estate off the Queensway in Etobicoke in 1954 – emails play a larger role, there's a greater demand for organic and locally grown product, there have been extensive renovations to improve labour safety – you get the sense that, at the heart of things, not much has changed in the last six decades. It's still a heavily male-dominated industry – there aren't many women on the floor, and the ones I met were all born or married into the business – and each company depends entirely on maintaining close, long-term relationships with their customers for success. It's bustling, but there's a lot of closeness, even intimacy, here, too.

There's a farmers' market connected to the terminal that is newer to the scene, but many of the established wholesale and broker companies here are family-owned-and-run businesses forged two and three generations ago by mostly Italian, Jewish and Dutch immigrants. Immigration continues to play a vital role, particularly in Toronto, where the city's multicultural identity is reflected directly in the items available on the market floor. One example is the Indian bitter melon – a crazy-looking, dark green, gnarled, tubular fruit I'd never seen before. When I asked Dorjee Namgyal at the Italian-owned Veg-Pak Produce Ltd. what it was, he explained that it's prized in many Asian communities as a blood purifier. Namgyal – who speaks five languages, which allows him to connect to a broad customer base and makes it possible for Veg-Pak to stay in touch with emerging product demands – tells me the melon 'has picked up in volume 70 percent in five years.' He recommends throwing it into stir-fries.

The produce industry, actually, is surprisingly influenced by what could be called food fashion. I saw crates and crates of POM-brand pomegranate juice, and some of the buyers spoke reverently about the success of that particular

marketing campaign in persuading people of the benefits of the tart fruit's antioxidant properties. People are hungry, literally, for food that is supercharged with healthy goodness. Novelty is also a major factor; another recent hit has been the mangosteen, a tropical fruit that had suffered under an import ban in the U.S. until a couple years ago. Although sometimes the rush to offer the latest of the latest yields some dodgy results – did anyone really need to engineer the looks-like-an-apple-but-tastes-like-a-grape 'grapple' hybrid? Everyone I talked to thought it was a stupid product, but apparently it's selling.

These trends make a difference in such a volatile business. Some companies down at the terminal distinguish themselves by focusing on a specific strength, while others strive to have a little bit of everything. But all are quick to acknowledge that it's a speculative industry. Most of the wholesalers are also involved in multiple areas of the business – they are often also growers, shippers, importers and exporters. 'We're gamblers,' says Lorrie Goldfarb, president of Morris Brown & Sons Company Ltd., who calls himself 'the Tomato Guy.' So many variable elements threaten their bottom line every day: the weather, the price of oil, the fluctuating dollar. Considering the degree of stress this can create, the atmosphere at the market is pretty warm and friendly – once you break into the inner circle, that is. People like to tell almost-off-colour jokes or family stories, many of which follow a similar trajectory: somebody's father or grandfather built an international importing empire after starting out with nothing but ten dollars and a fruit cart.

And as these terminal-based businesses have grown over the years, so have their needs. There have been occasional rumours about moving the facility out of the city and into the suburbs, where there would be more room for expansion – as it is, most of the more successful wholesalers do a great deal of their business off-site, as the 80,000-square-foot cold storage space isn't large enough to accommodate all of the tenants. Taking the terminal out of the city would also open up a big chunk of land that would be attractive to developers. Still, according to Ian MacKenzie, executive vice-president of the Ontario Produce Marketing Association, this kind of move is unlikely, since the City of Toronto has done studies that highlight the economic benefits of the jobs provided by the terminal. It turns out that many of those transient workers that make my trade-

magazine friend nervous would not be able to find work elsewhere in the area. 'I don't see it moving in the short term,' MacKenzie says.

And although the wholesalers spend a lot of time at their various warehouses and repacking facilities, the community remains deeply rooted in this blockish grey building. 'About 80 percent of my business comes out of my facility, ten minutes from here,' Goldfarb says. 'I'm here for presence. People want to see me – I'm the Tomato Guy. This is where the personality is, this is where the action is.'

Charles Z. Levkoe
& Airin Stephens

From school meal programs to food citizenship: Doing food at George Harvey Collegiate Institute

It's 8 a.m. on Friday at George Harvey Collegiate Institute in downtown Toronto's northwest end, and although classes don't begin for another hour, students are already bustling through the halls. In a large classroom on the second floor, Vince McCormack, the school's Child and Youth Worker, is artfully scripting the morning menu and helping the student cooks with last-minute preparations for the daily breakfast. Volunteers are taking their places to greet fellow students as they begin to file into the room. Newspapers are spread out across tables, while three novice musicians fill the room with their latest composition. The tables fill quickly, and students munch away at freshly cooked pancakes, French toast, juices and smoothies while chatting about everything from the latest political issues to pop-culture news.

While the early-morning commotion is a regular occurrence at George Harvey, it also highlights the reality that increasing numbers of students are coming to school with empty stomachs. But GHCI is serving much more than just a morning meal. As a response to the growing problem of hunger in Toronto, the school's teachers, staff and students have developed a unique set of food programs that include the Jump Start breakfast program, the Stone Soup after-school community cooking group, a vegetable garden shared with the on-site daycare, and curriculum connections to academic subject areas. These initiatives also open the door to engaging with the wider neighbourhood, giving students an opportunity to build new skills, to get to know their community and to begin to find solutions to the larger systemic challenges of poverty and food insecurity. By integrating these school-based food programs, GHCI is moving beyond simply providing food to hungry students by nurturing a new generation of food citizens.

One hungry student is too many

There is no doubt too many students come to school hungry. Over 25 percent of Toronto children report that they don't eat lunch. For the other 75 percent, cafeteria options have limited healthy food items, offering cheap food that is highly processed and filled with fat, salt and sugar. In Canada, studies have shown that over 60 percent of boys and almost 70 percent

of girls aged nine to thirteen consume well below the recommended minimum number of servings of vegetable and fruit. Furthermore, almost 30 percent of their calories come from junk food.

Hunger is more than simply an ache in the belly. Lack of, or poor quality, food for children and teenagers at important developmental stages can have a serious impact on their health and their ability to learn. Health Canada studies have shown that inadequate nourishment can result in behaviour problems; difficulty concentrating, solving problems and remembering information; and increased sickness and absenteeism. Short-term health impacts can range from iron-deficiency anemia to tooth decay; over the longer term there is the risk of chronic diseases such as type-2 diabetes, obesity and cardiovascular disease. While there are debates around the direct causal effects of these ailments, there have been measurable impacts around social inequality.

Schools are a natural battleground in the fight against youth hunger and an ideal setting for building a healthier and more sustainable food system. Unlike consumer-based food initiatives such as farmers' markets and food-box schemes, which have been shown to privilege wealthy eaters, school-based programs can reach a broader population at a crucial time in their physical and psychological development. A recent study commissioned by the U.S.-based Sodexo Foundation[1] showed that school breakfast programs were highly effective in providing children with a stronger basis for learning in school and leading healthier lives both emotionally and physically. Serving a nutritious breakfast to students significantly improved interpersonal and cognitive abilities, enabling them to be more alert and to improve their skills in reading and math. More importantly, teachers and parents witnessed a decrease in behavioural problems and fewer illnesses related to hunger.

The first school breakfast program in Toronto can be traced back to Contact Alternative School in the downtown core, which started its meal program in the late 1970s. Since then, it has been joined by an estimated 500 programs across the city that serve over 90,000 students a day, in about 65 percent of Toronto's schools. While partly funded through a collection of provincial, municipal and private grants, meal programs are often organized and run by teachers on their own time, with the help of willing parents and community volunteers. These programs are an important grassroots,

1 L. Brown, W. Beardslee and D. Prothrow-Stith. November 2008. *Impact of School Breakfast on Children's Health and Learning: An Analysis of the Scientific Research.* Commissioned by the Sodexo Foundation. (www.sodexofoundation.org/hunger_us/Images/Impact%20of%20School%20Breakfast%20Study_tcm150-212606.pdf)

'At first I didn't like coming outside but when I saw how the plants grew they were like my babies and I wanted to take care of them.'

'In the garden we had to figure out how many seeds we needed by calculating the number in each row and the total amount of rows in a raised bed – and holy, I was doing math!'

'I could be out here all day – it makes me feel more alive.'

'When we brought in the tomatoes, carrots and the pumpkin that they grew, the smiles on daycare kids' faces were so huge … It made me feel so good about helping out.'

'It was my favourite day at school when our Leadership class came out and picked tomatoes, basil and eggplant and then we actually used them to cook in my Food and Nutrition course.'

'Food tastes so different when you get to pick it off the plant and then eat it … I sometimes sneak out in between classes and eat a cherry tomato.'

'In just one day I could be helping write a funding proposal for the food program in an English class, work outside in the gardens in Leadership, cook the food in Food and Nutrition and then write a speech in my Public Speaking class about food security.'

school-community response to difficult circumstances, but they also illuminate wider challenges, including a failure to develop more permanent solutions to address the root causes of poverty and hunger. School budgets and staff time are stretched, making these programs unsustainable in the long term, especially as the problem continues to grow. But, as the case of GHCI illustrates, school food programs have the potential to meet short-term needs, while at the same time building longer-term solutions.

Planting the seeds at George Harvey Collegiate

George Harvey Collegiate Institute, at Keele and Eglinton, is in the heart of one of Toronto's most culturally and economically mixed neighbourhoods. The school's community is over-representative of the city's diverse population, with more than fifty different languages spoken. GHCI has struggled with some of the lowest graduation rates in the Toronto District School Board and has had a hard time finding ways to support the growing needs of its student population. Some of the school's leaders turned to food programming as a way to engage students and encourage learning beyond the classroom. Since 2000, under the headstrong determination of Vince McCormack, the school has taken localized initiatives and widened them to include the broader school community and the neighbourhood, attempting to address wider structural inequalities that underlie the need for these programs in the first place.

The approach began with one simple program. During its first year, 2001, the Jump Start breakfast program (just three days a week at first) served over 1,500 breakfasts; it has since increased the number of meals served each year, reaching over 13,000 in the 2008–09 school year and drawing explicit attention to the community's growing need. Some school meal programs target particular groups and demand proof of economic status, but Jump Start does not discriminate. The program is open to all students, ensuring healthy food is available to everyone regardless of need. As a result, it has become a hub for social networking and occasionally a space for catching up on homework and interacting with teachers. The food served at the breakfasts comes from a variety of sources, including neighbourhood grocery stores for staple items and bulk orders from local farms for apples and other select in-season produce. By promoting nutrition through diverse

menu options as well as consciously designing and promoting a welcoming space, the Jump Start volunteers have worked to reduce the negative stigma attached to most meal programs.

The community food garden was conceived in 2005 by the school's student Green Team, interested teachers and the on-site daycare staff at the George Harvey Child Care Centre. The site selected for the garden was on the south end of the school's property, an area mostly covered by concrete; the small fenced-in area was piled up with neighbourhood trash and a preferred spot for late-night drug use. After the area was cleaned up, soil samples deemed the ground suitable for planting. Kushboo, a Grade 11 biology student who joined other classmates to construct the garden, boasts, 'Building the raised beds and learning about the soil and plants really made our textbook come to life.' In 2007, GHCI received a grant through Toronto Public Health and FoodShare to develop a more permanent design and involve the broader school community. Under the supervision of Ed Scherer, the lead teacher of the garden initiative, students in science, Student Success, geography, English and phys. ed. began to spend time in the garden as part of their coursework. They quickly took ownership of the garden beyond simply academic work and made connections to their own cultural and social back-grounds. Natalie, a participant in the Student Success program, brought in her family's okra seeds to share. 'I like being out in the garden planting seeds and watering. I even

Raised beds in the GHCI food garden being prepared for winter by planting garlic bulbs covered with straw and winter rye as a cover crop for green manure.

like weeding,' she explains. 'I love going home and telling my mom about what I am doing and hearing her stories of growing food in Trinidad.' Natalie is only one example of how the garden has provided a way for students to be physically active and to build skills as they learn to grow their own food and experience how the broader food system works.

Cross-pollination

The success of the Jump Start program has been demonstrated by its ability to feed students' bodies as well as their minds. While teachers oversee the program, students take responsibility for the day-to-day activities. Max, a student volunteer with Jump Start, learned a number of life skills in his three years with the program: for instance, he had to work with a team of student cooks to meet tight timelines to prepare large amounts of food for the morning rush. And the program has spread beyond serving breakfast to engage other parts of the school; the co-op department, for example, often asks Jump Start volunteers to cater and participate in special breakfasts student leaders have with the local business community. Family Studies classes have become involved in planning daily menus, and the music department now requires final presentations be performed during the breakfast program – this not only provides enthusiastic diners with live music, it is also a way for students to play for their peers, build up confidence and create links within the school.

Joel, a community member who participated in the Jump Start program as a GHCI student, still returns to volunteer four years after graduating. He talks about gaining leadership skills and hands-on experience, which helped him get his Food Handlers' training and certification. 'I really like volunteering,' explains Joel. 'It is a way to meet friends and to give back to the school and my community.' Joel also credits Jump Start with getting him hired as a chef in a Toronto restaurant.

The school garden has also brought together different groups in the school, including public health workers and the parents and staff in the George Harvey Child Care Centre, who tend the garden over the summer. Championed by daycare co-coordinator Colin Hercules, the daycare staff has become involved in all levels of garden planning and implementation. They participate in regular meetings and have developed programming that engages the toddlers in hands-on learning. In spring 2008, the daycare grew seedlings, and in the summer the children made daily trips to the garden to water and weed, at the same time creating curriculum around healthy eating and growing food. A daycare parent commented that she was both surprised and impressed that her daughter was eating fresh vegetables directly from the garden. She was also grateful for the extra produce she could bring home in the summer to supplement her family's food. In the fall, garden produce is used in the Jump Start program and in Family Studies classes. One of the more recent goals of the garden is to plant a greater variety of seeds to reflect the school's diverse cultural composition.

The food programs have sparked new opportunities beyond GHCI. In 2008, the school began hosting weekly workshops called Stone Soup Mondays, where top Toronto chefs come to the school to prepare restaurant-quality meals alongside students. Workers from Toronto Public Health have integrated Jump Start and the school garden into programming offering nutrition workshops for students. Earl, an early Stone Soup participant and now a student leader in the program, points to his exposure to professional chefs, culinary techniques and nutritional education as a key motivator for other aspects of his life. 'I actually cook at home now for my family and I am applying to collage for a culinary arts program,' he explains. By bringing together individuals from both inside and outside the school, GHCI is becoming a community hub, engaging difficult issues beyond the local neighbourhood.

Cultivating food citizenship

While these programs make a big impact on the school community, their next challenge is to 'scale up' and effect change at a more systemic level to address growing social and economic inequalities and food-related health concerns, and to increase connections to the natural and built environment. Toronto's two English public school boards do what they can for the 90,000 students who rely on breakfast, snack and lunch programs to make it through the day, but they are increasingly underfunded and ill-equipped. Attempting to navigate the complicated political landscape to make change can be overwhelming since there is no common approach to food issues within the different levels of government and Canada has nothing resembling a school food policy. Instead, communities must rely on a patchwork of parents, teachers, students, public services and charities to respond to local needs.

Starting with the next generation of youth, GHCI is teaching far more than nutrition and growing and cooking food; it's cultivating food citizenship – engaging in behaviours that support the development of a food system where everyone is equally able to obtain a safe, culturally acceptable and nutritionally adequate diet. Beyond a focus on hunger, access and availability, food citizenship also recognizes that a truly sustainable food system must be democratic and maximize community self-reliance, environmental responsibility and social justice. Joan Seignoret, GHCI's Family Studies teacher, notes that an increased number of students involved in the school's food programs are learning to advocate for themselves and realizing their responsibilities within the community.

A group of satisfied growers at a GHCI community planting day.

Over the past five years, students such as Kushboo have gone to City Hall to make deputations to Toronto Public Health requesting systemic and stable funding be made available to school-based programs like Jump Start. Kushboo has learned to speak at municipal meetings about the importance of these types of programs in her community, and her peers see her as a leader in the school. 'It feels good knowing the work we are doing here at GHCI can be used to support other programs across the city in other schools,' says Kushboo. Student leaders from GHCI have also been involved in a pilot youth food-security initiative with two other Toronto high schools, Marc Garneau Collegiate Institute and Parkdale Collegiate. Initiated by FoodShare's Field to Table Schools program, the council meets to discuss food issues in Toronto as well as how to budget funds earmarked for each school's food programs.

While the food programming at GHCI represents a unique model, it is joined by other schools in Toronto addressing similar challenges with their own innovative approaches. Further, a number of non-profit organizations have been helping to 'scale up' these successes; FoodShare's Field to Table Schools program has been involved in teacher training, school workshops and assisting with funding opportunities to support existing programs. Other key organizations supporting school food programs across the city include Evergreen's Learning Grounds Program, Toronto Partners for Student Nutrition, the Toronto Foundation for Student Success and Green Thumbs Growing Kids. Many of these organizations have also been involved in the promotion of municipal, provincial and federal policies that would support children's access to healthy food at home and at school.

While school food programs are a vital first step, to have broader impact and long-term success they must become more creative in their delivery and more coordinated within the school and the neighbourhood and with system-wide efforts. George Harvey presents a working model for the expansion of these programs through its long-term vision and ability to involve individuals and organizations within the school and beyond. This approach can provide internal sustainability and at the same time challenge governments to notice and take action. GHCI hopes its story will serve as an invitation for a broader dialogue and open a space for other schools to share their experiences around food-related initiatives and cultivating food citizenship.

Chris Hardwicke

Reviving St. Andrew's Market

St. Andrew's Playground is easy to miss among the new condos and old industrial buildings of the King-Spadina neighbourhood. The small city park is partially hidden by the public-works building that presents a blank facade across the northern edge of the park. The opaque building reveals little about its current function or intriguing past. The playground and works building both sit on the site of the former St. Andrew's Market, an indoor public amenity that once rivalled St. Lawrence Market.

Recently, local groups have reanimated the park with a new open-air market. The Historic St. Andrew's MyMarket is bringing fresh local produce to the neighbourhood for the first time in seventy-two years. This seasonal market was created by the self-organization and sheer public will of citizens who are taking a renewed interest in the public life of our city. The City should support this grassroots effort and reinvest in the neighbourhood by recreating St. Andrew's Market Hall. The time is ripe to convert the public-works building to a new indoor market and centre for the community.

What makes a great city? I believe it is an interest on the part of its government and citizens in creating a sense of belonging in its public places. Great cities are defined by public places that encourage creative expression, cultural diversity and social connections. These public places should encourage us to become engaged in our communities and take stewardship of our neighbourhoods. We often criticize the ugliness of modern cities, but it's more than their physical shape that gives

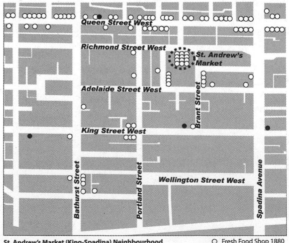

St. Andrew's Market (King-Spadina) Neighbourhood
Comparison of Fresh Food Supply 1880 & 2009

○ Fresh Food Shop 1880
● Fresh Food Shop 2009

them life; people also give life to our civic spaces. Public life is essential to urban identity, and its roots lie in food.

Food has played a key role in shaping our civic spaces. The Roman Forum and the Athenian Agora are early examples of great public places that were originally food markets. Many Toronto neighbourhoods – Roncesvalles, Chinatown, Little India and the Danforth among them – are defined by their food culture and street festivals. St. Lawrence Market, Kensington Market, Dufferin Grove Park and the many new local markets that crop up every year have rapidly become the centre of their neighbourhoods. Markets are the heart and soul of civic life, places where people share food and stories, places that are alive with social and economic activity.

One hundred and fifty years ago, Toronto was well-served by three public market buildings: St. Lawrence, St. Patrick and St. Andrew's. In 1861, a population of only 45,000 people supported these three markets. Today, only St. Lawrence remains a functioning indoor market. Though a resurgence in healthy eating, organic and local foods has seen a growth in the number and popularity of farmers' markets, our city of three million is served by only one market building.

Toronto is growing and intensifying, but investments in parks and community facilities in all areas of the city are not keeping pace. The King-Spadina neighbourhood is an example of an area of recent growth with little investment in public amenities. The neighbourhood has come a long way since its days as one of the city's main manufacturing and industrial areas, transformed over time into a diverse community with a mix of residential, business and institutional buildings and a thriving restaurant and entertainment district. In only twenty years, the population of the neighbourhood has grown from 1,000 to 10,000, and it is still growing. Despite this rapid growth, the area has seen no new parks, community centres or other public amenities. And while the neighbourhood is well-known for its entertainment and dining scene, no new grocery stores have been built in the area.

The first regular market in Toronto was established in 1803 by special proclamation of Lieutenant-Governor Peter Hunter on the site of the present St. Lawrence Market. The St. Lawrence Market we now know was established in 1836 and has served its community well for over 150 years. St. Lawrence Market was soon joined by a second, smaller market called St. Patrick's Market, situated on the north side of Queen Street, between McCaul and John. Though St. Patrick's Market was intended to

St. Lawrence Market, between 1885 and 1895.

Chris Hardwicke   247

L: Derelict St. Andrew's Market building, 1921.

R: Derelict St. Andrew's Market building prior to demolition, 1932.

serve the western end of the city, it was quickly surpassed by the new St. Andrew's Market, originally known as the West City Market or Western Market, which was located on a uniquely shaped city block bounded by Richmond Street to the north, Adelaide to the south, Maud to the west and Brant to the east, on newly available tracts of former Military Reserve lands set aside in 1837.

The Western Market was used as an open-air seasonal market until the late 1850s. As the neighbourhood grew into a centre for industrial production and workers' housing, the City decided to create a permanent market building on the site. A wooden building was built, with stalls for vendors and wooden planking so vendors could avoid standing in mud all day. The new building was named St. Andrew's Market after the ward it occupied, and the market functioned as the centre of its neighbourhood. St. John's Church held its first meetings and Sunday school in St. Andrew's Market, and the market hall was used for public meetings as well as market functions. However, in 1860, only ten years after its founding, fire destroyed the building.

After the fire, the market continued as an open-air market for thirteen years, while the City debated rebuilding. Over that period, local butchers established their shops in stores surrounding the open market square, while seasonal local produce was sold at the open-air market. The butchers often slaughtered their own animals, and dealt in beef, pork, mutton and poultry, as well as in salted meats such as ham and bacon. Also on offer were butter, eggs, lard and all kinds of vegetables in season.

By 1873, the City had succumbed to public pressure and revived the market by building a much grander St. Andrew's Hall and Market. The new building was constructed in French Renaissance style using white brick, following a design by architect William Irving. Much more than a simple market building, the new structure was a centre for its community. The complex included stalls for fresh produce, over thirty butcher

stalls, a police station and a second-floor public hall. The Toronto Library's second branch, the Western Branch, was established in the building in 1884, offering free library service to the western end of the city. The public hall was quickly put to use for community events, including church services, concerts, benefits for injured workers and temperance meetings.

The second revival of the St. Andrew's Market was short-lived. Many shopkeepers were reluctant to relocate to the market and pay the new market fees. The City reacted by restricting butchers from operating within a certain distance of the market square, thus forcing them to become market tenants. These restrictions further diminished the success of the market and, in the early 1880s, the southern portion of the block was turned into a public park that brought new life to the square.

The last attempt to regenerate St. Andrew's Market came in 1889, when the City built an impressive Romanesque Revival addition on the northwest corner of the square. The new addition was intended to rival St. Lawrence Market and attract more activity by creating more market stalls. In 1896, St. Andrew's Market was used as a meteorological observatory for cloud observations in conjunction with the University of Toronto. The roofs of the School of Practical Science and St. Andrew's Market and the observatory were used to triangulate cloud heights, velocities and directions. In 1909, the public park was redeveloped into the first city playground dedicated to supervised children's play. Renamed St. Andrew's Playground, it offered tennis courts, a wading pool and a large green area for games organized by City staff.

Despite the 1889 addition, the market stalls were largely empty by 1900, although the hall continued to be occupied by the police station and the library branch. Over the same period, the neighbourhood transformed from predominantly residential to industrial, and the declining population took its toll on the market. The City voted to demolish the market buildings in 1912, planning to use the site for its new waterworks building. Delayed by the war, the market buildings were not demolished until 1932, when the present art-deco public-works building designed by architect J. J. Woolnough was built on the northern half of the block, leaving the southern half to St. Andrew's Playground.

Today, the public-works building remains on the site, along with a small parking lot at the western end of the block, facing Maud Street. The newly renovated St. Andrew's Playground is well used by the neighbourhood, as it is one of only

St. Lawrence Market, interior, 1919.

Existing public-works building.

Revived community centre with outdoor market.

Existing public-works building behind St. Andrew's Playground.

Proposed outdoor public market connected to the building.

four small parks in King-Spadina. The pressure on these parks has steadily intensified over the past decade and will continue to increase as the residential population grows. As the majority of the new residences in the neighbourhood are condominiums or loft conversions with little open or private amenity space, there is a great need not only for parks, but for multi-use public space and community meeting places. Developing additional traditional park space will be a challenge for the City in King-Spadina, as land supply is scarce and costly.

In response to the need for social connection and access to healthy food, a local citizens' group formed in early 2009 to revive St. Andrew's Market. Working with Councillor Adam Vaughan, they secured permission to start a seasonal farmers' market in the parking lot adjacent to St. Andrew's Playground. The small market has been well-attended every Saturday morning since its first day on June 6, 2009.

The new St. Andrew's Historic MyMarket has planted a seed for the potential redevelopment of the whole block. The new seasonal market, with its tents and trucks, is humble in comparison to the St. Andrew's Market of the late 1860s. At its peak, the St. Andrew's Market complex housed a diverse range of social activities and services as well as an all-year indoor market, which was the centre of a far less populated neighbourhood. The present day public-works building currently underserves its community, housing functions that could be located in any industrial building.

Following the successful models of the Artscape Wychwood Barns and the Brick Works, the public-works building should be renovated and retrofitted to house an indoor farmers' market, community services, a social innovation centre and artists' housing. The parking lot could be redesigned to create a public plaza that could facilitate an expanded outdoor seasonal market. The existing public-works building already houses a Montessori school. Other community services such as community kitchens and daycare could also be included in the program.

The King-Spadina neighbourhood has been struggling to build a centre for its neighbourhood for over 150 years. If the relatively low-density neighbourhoods surrounding the Wychwood Barns and the Brick Works can sustain new community centres, then it is time for the city to transform its old public-works building and work with the community to rebuild St. Andrew's Market and continue the revitalization of the neighbourhood.

Chris Ramsaroop
& Katie Wolk

Can we achieve racial equality in the food security movement?

The food security movement has gained popularity in recent years. More and more people are eating locally and in season, there are more farmers' markets (twenty-nine in Toronto so far[1]), many young people are volunteering on organic farms and planting their own gardens and there is a growing interest in learning forgotten skills such as dehydrating, canning and freezing. These initiatives are fantastic; they clean the air, educate people about food sources, encourage physical exercise and provide an opportunity for consumers and farmers to meet. Lacking in this progressive environmental food movement, however, are critical issues of racial justice. As consumers and food security activists, we need to ask ourselves: Who is able to buy and sell at farmers' markets? Who is able to grow organic produce? What are the systemic barriers keeping people from marginalized communities out of the progress of the food security movement? What is keeping the food security movement from progressing? A discussion about who is producing local food is lacking in the movement. Racialized migrant workers are working in unsafe and exploitative conditions.

One of the first obstacles facing the food security movement is white privilege. Many food security organizations acknowledge that racism exists within the food movement, and several hold anti-racism workshops, which focus on the barriers that keep people in racialized communities underprivileged, for staff, volunteers and members of the community. On the surface, it appears that people are taking action to ensure that everyone has equal access to food, but, upon closer inspection, the structures of the organizations themselves seem to be problematic. Hiring culturally and ethnically diverse staff members is a step in the right direction, but the executive directors of many of these environmental organizations are white. This can lead to diversity issues being left out of the boardroom, and racialized people being 'on the table and not at it.'[2]

Another example of how the food movement excludes racialized communities is apparent at farmers' markets. The majority of Toronto's farmers' markets are in the downtown core, in the area bordered by Roncesvalles and Bayview avenues, and City Hall and St. Clair Avenue. While the population of this area is diverse, those who attend the markets often

1 Toronto Farmers' Market Network. List of Markets. tfmn.ca/?page_id=2 (accessed June 15, 2009).

2 Rachel Slocum. 'Anti-racist Practice and the Work of Community Food Organizations.' Department of Sociology and Anthropology, Saint Cloud State University, 2006. www.rslocum.com//slocum_Antipode_2006.pdf

are not. It is easy to ensure people have access to local and organic food when they have time to grow it themselves, or have enough money to buy it. However, we are not doing enough to improve the affordability and accessibility of organic foods – an integral part of the definition of food security. Farmers' markets provide an opposition to the larger food system for a relatively small proportion of Torontonians, but they are not a feasible alternative for everyone. What's more, they put consumers in direct connection to only a unique type of small-scale farmer. While many food security organizations promote patronizing farmers' markets, growing organic veggies in backyards and buying local, organic, free range and fair trade, few are talking about the current food system or working towards building a sustainable alternative. The current model divides communities and contributes to the separation of the haves from the have-nots. We do not talk enough about the privilege of food security.

Finally, the conditions found in our farming industry have also become an obstacle to achieving racial equity in our food security movement. Canada, like many other countries, is in the midst of a farm crisis: small farms are losing money, while agribusinesses see increasing profits. In 2004, the realized net farm income from markets, excluding government subsidies, was negative-$10,000 per farm in Canada.[3] Many farmers have to hold down other jobs to supplement their income. According to the National Farmers Union, 2009 will mark the twenty-fifth year of a continuous farm income crisis. On average, the net farm income from markets is approximately $1.45 per acre of Canadian cropland per year. Agribusiness transnationals, who supply fertilizer and chemicals, make $386 per acre – 266 times the farmer's share.[4]

While there has been ample discussion of the death of the family farm and the rise of agribusiness, this debate rarely addresses the experiences of migrant agricultural workers, who often endure unjust working and living conditions on farms of all sizes. Instead of focusing on the size and output of farms, we should shift the discussion to the structure of government migrant-worker programs, the absence of labour protection for those workers, the power imbalance between them and their employers, and the racialization of agriculture labour.

The farm workers involved in Canada's agricultural industry are often hidden from consumers. The majority of these workers are in Canada temporarily through the government's Seasonal Agricultural Workers Program. SAWP started in 1966

3 National Farmers Union. 'The Farm Crisis and Corporate Profits.' November 30, 2005. www.nfu.ca/briefs/2005/corporate_profits.pdf (accessed June 15, 2009).

4 National Farmers Union. 'Canada's Farm and Food Sectors, Competition and Competitiveness, and a Path Out of the Net Farm Income Swamp.' A report prepared for the House of Commons Standing Committee on Agriculture. June 11, 2009. www.nfu.ca/briefs/2009/competition%20compe titiveness%20standing%20committee%20brief%20SEVEN.pdf (accessed July 26, 2009).

as a government-to-government agreement between Jamaica and Canada. Farmers lobbied the federal government that the importation of migrant labour was needed to address labour shortages during harvest season. In collaboration with Canadian employers, the two governments agreed to the importation of Caribbean migrants, who would work in Ontario fields for up to eight months a year. The following year, Trinidad and Barbados agreed to join sawp and, in 1976, the government of Mexico and some represented by the Organization of Eastern Caribbean States – Montserrat, Grenada, St. Lucia, St. Vincent and the Grenadines, Dominica, Antigua and St. Kitts – entered into agreements with Canada. Today there are over 20,000 migrant workers from these countries working on Canadian fields in every province except Newfoundland.

Recently a new federal initiative previously called the Low-Skilled Foreign Worker Program, and now called the Pilot Project for Occupations Requiring Lower Levels of Formal Training (National Occupation Classification C and D), also an employer-driven program, expanded the number of migrant workers arriving from new source countries such as Thailand and Guatemala. While sawp employs workers for up to eight months, the new program employs workers for up to two years. The new program also allows private recruiters to bring workers from their home countries and find them work in Canada. Many workers have recounted that they were recruited with promises of permanent residency in Canada, jobs with security and benefits and the ability to provide a stable income for their families. Upon arrival, however, they find that they are tied to one employer, paid lower wages than promised, have no chance to apply for permanent residency and often end up working and living in conditions that are less than desirable.

The low-skilled program operates under the broader provisions of the Temporary Foreign Worker Program (tfwp), whose acronym has come to represent the different classifications of migrant workers who work in Canada under these employer-driven programs. Recently, the federal government made a significant policy change in their temporary-foreign-worker policy, allowing employers to re-apply for work permits for low-skilled labourers while they are still in the country, instead of requiring them to return to their home country for a period of four months, as was formerly the case. This significant shift has the potential to create a permanent and perpetual class of migrant workers who can live in Canada and work for a specific employer, while simultaneously being

denied rights to citizenship and permanent residency.

Justicia for Migrant Workers (J4MW) is a non-profit organization that strives to promote the rights of migrant farm workers and farm workers without status. In discussions with J4MW, workers have compared the conditions they experience in Canada to slavery and indentureship. It is common for workers to say that they are treated like animals, or that they work and live under conditions no Canadian would accept. Workers employed in SAWP and the Pilot Project for Occupations Requiring Lower Levels of Formal Training are barred from applying for permanent residency, irrespective of the number of years they have worked in Canada. Other conditions commonly cited include:

- Working twelve to fifteen hours a day without overtime, holiday pay or breaks
- Use of dangerous chemicals with no safety equipment, protection or training
- Being crammed into substandard housing with leaking sewage and inadequate washroom facilities
- Overt racism from townspeople, sometimes resulting in physical altercations
- Acute pay discrimination between migrant and non-migrant workforces
- Unfair deductions such as EI and other services to which they have little or no access
- Inadequate health attention and services
- Exclusion from basic human rights and labour legislation
- Being prohibited from collective bargaining and joining unions
- Inadequate representation in policymaking and contract disputes
- Inability to claim residency or obtain educational opportunities for children despite years of employment and paying taxes in Canada
- Lack of appeal process when employers repatriate workers to home country
- Depression
- Barriers to essential services due to language and location
- Lack of basic ESL training
- Gender discrimination (i.e., few opportunities for female workers; women are heavily controlled and disciplined in various ways by employers)[5]

5 List retrieved from Justicia for Migrant Workers website, justicia4 migrantworkers.org (accessed August 31, 2009).

These conditions will persist as long as the food system separates consumers from producers. The invisibility of these producers and the dearth of information about their working and living conditions has been reflected in food policies and rhetorical commitments to ethical food practices, which do not acknowledge the difficult conditions under which food is produced in Canada. Existing policies give implicit approval of the conditions within Canada's agricultural industry and have characterized our industry as one that is dependent on temporary and marginalized farm labour.

On April 2, 2009, immigration raids occurred across southwestern Ontario, and hundreds of undocumented workers and temporary foreign workers were arrested, detained and, eventually, deported. The majority of these workers were arrested at Cericola Farms, a carrot farm and chicken-processing facility in Bradford, just north of Toronto. Subsequent to this raid, dozens of migrant workers were picked up in locations across Ontario. Media reports depicted these workers as criminals who had taken advantage of Canada's immigration system.

J4MW organizers were on the frontlines dealing with the aftermath of these raids, and they watched as a counternarrative emerged. They learned, through first-hand accounts, that many of the detainees had paid thousands of dollars to work in Canada, particularly under the Low-Skilled Foreign Worker Program, so they could earn enough money to pay off their debts and support their families. Chanachai's story is just one example:

> I had to mortgage my farmland to get the 60,000 baht, the money I paid in order to come to Canada. [This] had a negative effect on me. I am paying 3 percent interest for the debt. Even when I started working in Canada, for the first one or two months, my boss deducted about $1,000 from me. It might be airfare, I am not quite sure. The money I earned from working is sent home to pay for my debts and interest. I perceived my situation as being better, for example, compared to my sister, who paid 250,000 baht to come [to Canada] and is now working at a chicken farm. I did not mean to run. I was scared that I wouldn't be able to stay and work in Canada anymore. That's why I ran. The reason I was scared is because there are responsibilities and obligations back home such as paying for my children's tuition fees. My children are depending on me for the

money. One day when I was working, all the workers were told to get into lines because the immigration is coming. The police checked each worker's profile. I was supposed to work at the fish factory instead of the chicken farm I was working at, that's why the police cuffed me and sent me to this place where I and others who also got arrested stayed. I stayed at the place for about a month and a half.

In these interviews, many workers said recruiters had held their passports and would return them only if they paid a minimum of $1,200 on top of the $10,000 they had initially paid to come to Canada. Finally, many of those who had ended up at Cericola were workers who had run from exploitative workplaces and found whatever work they could to survive. These workers were paid anywhere from $6.50 to $9.50 per hour depending on the availability of work, and whether they are employed continuously under the SAWP or TFWP. However, many of the arrested migrant workers were making $7.50 per hour. The absence of continuous work gives many workers no choice but to search for other work, even though their conditions of employment specify that they can only work at the farm specified on their work permit.

This immigration raid was only one in a series that took place in spring 2009. Criminalizing migrants and undocumented workers has become standard fare, and the exploitative and abusive workplace conditions that many endure persist without penalties or prosecution. J4MW has documented raids at numerous farms across Ontario – in the first half of the year, there were at least six reported workplace raids.

The story of Marcos, as reported to J4MW, represents how migrant workers become 'criminal' in the eye of policymakers, politicians and the general public. Marcos came to Canada from Mexico under the TFWP. He was employed at a large organic mushroom facility in the Greater Toronto Area, and had been promised a two-year contract there. He was depending on the money to pay for his children's education costs. Marcos took pride in his work; while the work was difficult and dangerous, he never complained, working to the best of his ability despite substandard working and living conditions. Seven months into his contract, he and dozens of other workers were called to a meeting by the employer. At this meeting he was told that his employment was being terminated, and

that he was not only fired from his job, but that he was to be evicted from his housing and deported back to Mexico. How could an employer hold such power? Why was he not allowed to seek work elsewhere? And why could he not stay at his residence until he found other work? Marcos was shocked and angry. This happened a few days before Christmas. Devastated by his employer's decision, he tried to make the best of a desperate situation. With several of his co-workers, he evaluated his options. He could not afford to go home, and he had not made the money he needed to fulfill his financial obligations. Marcos also had aspirations of living in Canada and bringing his family over, too.

He decided he would not return home, and would instead try to find whatever work he could. In the middle of a recession, his options were few and far between. Finally, he found regular, under-the-table work in Leamington, about forty-five minutes south-east of Windsor. Working under the table was his only option, as the restrictions on his work permit denied him the labour mobility to seek employment. While the situation was not ideal, Marcos was content that he could send money home to his family. He tried to a build a new life in these unfamiliar surroundings.

One morning at around 9 a.m., police and immigration officials surrounded the greenhouse where Marcos was working. Officials entered the facility and began to corner workers, demanding identification. Fearing the consequences of an arrest, Marcos attempted to leave the work premises. Police cornered him. He surrendered and went willingly with immigration officials. After several hours in custody, he was brought to the local jail and held there for several weeks. He was released under an irregularly high bond because he was a temporary foreign worker working at an unauthorized work site, where his movements were highly curtailed. A few weeks after his release, Marcos was deported to Mexico, with little if any chance of ever coming to Canada again.

Countless testimonies such as this represent the common experiences of migrant workers, a reality omitted from 'buy local' food campaigns. The discussion of fair labour standards is often absent in local food strategies. The conversation turns to absolute silence when we bring up the racialization of the globalized and expendable labour force that is exploited to ensure the existence of our local agricultural economies. In the U.S., scholars such as Robert Bullard, the Edmund Asa Ware Distinguished Professor of Sociology at Clark Atlanta

University, have defined 'environmental racism' as the power imbalance between racialized communities and institutional, structural and systemic practices of discrimination in relationship to environmental practices. Environmental racism is defined as 'any policy, practice or directive that differentially affects or disadvantages (whether intentionally or unintentionally) individuals, groups or communities based on race or colour.'[6]

Food production can be seen with this lens. Canadian policies and legislation differentially affect migrant workers due to: (1) the power imbalance that exists between them and their employers; (2) the fact that provincial labour laws provide limited employment rights and that there is virtually no enforcement; (3) the absence of meaningful health and safety regulations, which leads to high rates of pesticide and chemical exposure; and (4) the fact that workers are employed under a federally operated, employer-driven immigration scheme where workers are fearful of exerting their rights due to threats of deportation and permanent disbarment from working in Canada again. Migrant workers are disadvantaged by their working, living and immigration status in Canada; they are experiencing environmental racism.

Governments and local food organizations must enact policies that address the precarious situations facing many migrant workers. The basis for change and action can be found in the experiences of these women and men. Issues of food security, sustainability and environmental protection cannot be divorced from the struggle for decent wages, safe working conditions and humane immigration policies. However, to get to this point, we need to shift the direction of the current dialogue away from consumer-driven ethics to a framework that is inclusive of all stakeholders in the production of food. Sadly, the voices of migrant workers and their advocates have not been included in food policy discussions.

A campaign developed by a local environmental group highlights this point. In supporting a 'buy local' agricultural policy, this leading environmental organization spearheaded a publicity stunt to raise awareness about the importance of buying Ontario-grown apples. In its media action, the organization, in conjunction with farmers and community members, delivered 2,000 locally grown apples to city councillors. According to their press release, each apple represented one Torontonian who had signed a petition calling on the City to avoid jet-lagged food and buy local food first when it

6 R. D. Bullard, 'Environmental Justice: It's More than Just Waste Facility Sitting.' *Social Sciences Quarterly*, 77(3), 1996, pp. 493–499

purchases food for its daycares, shelters and seniors' homes. Each apple sends a clear message to City Hall, said the petition: buy local food first and help the environment, help local farmers and help preserve precious agricultural land in the Greenbelt and surrounding area.

After receiving this release, J4MW inquired about the absence of discussion pertaining to working conditions from the organization's list of reasons to buy local. J4MW has had close working relationships with apple pickers in many parts of the province, and has witnessed health and safety violations, workers' compensation issues, employment standards violations and many other rights abuses. In response to J4MW's inquiry, the representative noted that if the City supported their campaign (it was adopted on October 30, 2008), labour standards for all agricultural workers would improve. However, by not addressing the root causes of the abuses, an absence of proactive legislation, lax enforcement and precarious immigration status conditions will persist.

In our experience, trickle-down policies are not effective. The complex realities experienced by migrant workers must not be essentialized. To make a change, we need a holistic framework that includes not only environmental protection, but also a legislative commitment to prosecuting exploiters and protecting precarious workers rather than persecuting them. One worker responded to wages and deductions by stating that

> right now the wages is piecework we doing right now ...
> I don't know what piece work is but I getting robbed ...
> They telling you get eighteen dollars a bin. We don't
> know how much apples in a bin ... They taking money
> out for bruising if it get a little touch they taking out ...
> we lose 1 percent ... Piece rate is really screwing we
> over.

Living conditions were described by one group of pickers this way:

> First of all the bunkhouses very terrible, water problems, basement problems, sometimes with stove and sometimes heat shutting off. Sometimes hydro shutting off. We don't have dryer, one suit of cloth and stuff ... The water in the pipe coming like chocolate, you can't cook ... Water comes brown most of the time ...

Recently, temporary foreign workers have started to strategize about how to organize across industries. The discussions were

initiated by a coalition of organizations including J4MW, Workers Action Centre, Caregivers Action Centre, No One Is Illegal and several labour unions and community organizations that want to change the direction of the current debate on migrant workers in Canada. It was necessary to link struggles in order to counter divide-and-rule policies implemented by the provincial and federal governments. These migrant workers want to develop a worker-centred approach to addressing their concerns. In taking this campaign to the next level, they are challenging policymakers, environmentalists, politicians, academics, activists, consumers and producers to formulate a real food security initiative that extends beyond local food initiatives (i.e., 100-mile-diet radius strategies) and ethical and organic proponents.

To be successful, their challenge must also lead to the incorporation of the demands of workers, including a right to permanent residency; a right to equal access to all social entitlements (health care, old-age security, EI, pension); a right to a fair appeal process against repatriation and deportation; a right to be employed without paying fees for work; and a right to full protection under all provincial labour laws. This will involve reforming employment standards, occupational health and safety and workers' compensation laws and provincial labour relations acts to reflect the realities of all migrant workers.

The coalition held a historic rally and public event in St. Jamestown in July 2009. The rally featured music, poetry and speeches by migrant workers from across the country. Hundreds attended and celebrated their right to resist exploitation. They demanded a vision of what a humane, people-centred immigration system would look like. The coalition continues to organize to ensure that the voices of migrant workers are not excluded from the current debate. In describing why migrant workers need to engage in collective action, a farm worker remarked:

> I believe all the farm workers [and migrant workers must] come together – Trinis, Jamaicans, Bajans – and we have a protest … It would make an impact if there was no farm workers. The work would be more hard for the Canadians because the Canadians not going to work in the coldness … No one would get up three in the morning to pick apples or pick tobacco to make eight dollars an hour. Our hands swell or burn. This

is why we do it, we have no choice [to stand up for our rights].

While this essay has proposed ways to address the exploitation of migrant workers, we want to conclude with a vision that we should be striving towards. The environmental justice movement best articulates the vision we believe has the potential to dismantle the systemic barriers that exist not only for racialized communities, but for all marginalized communities. As Andil Gosine and Cheryl Teelucksingh observe in their critical examination, *Environmental Justice in Canada*:

> ... [Environmental justice] connects a range of social movements, including anti-racism movements, Aboriginal rights and sovereignty movements, labour union movements, and the mainstream environmental movements. Proponents see this movement 'as a movement to address a wide range of social and environmental problems and seeks to eliminate harmful practices such as land use, housing, industrial planning and health care.'[7]

7 Andil Gosine and Cheryl Teelucksingh, *Environmental Justice and Racism in Canada: An Introduction*. (Emond Montgomery Publishers, 2008), p. 11.

Justicia for Migrant Workers views environmental justice as a tool to link food production and food security with the experiences of migrant workers so we can better understand how our food is produced, the conditions that exist for those who produce it and how we can address current injustices so that they are not repeated in the future. In Canada, environmental justice is a burgeoning research field that champions the redefinition of traditional environmentalism to include the voices of communities most impacted by environmental degradation, and to ensure that those communities most impacted are at the forefront of any struggle for justice. Traditionally, whether in the food movement, the environmental movement or the labour movement, racialized workers have been at the proverbial back of the bus. Experts and mainstream activists have spoken for these workers without providing the space where workers can speak for themselves, and from which they can direct policies that best reflect their experiences.

The food security movement can learn a lot from the writings and activism of people who have been attempting to redefine the discourse on issues related to food security, the environment and racialized and indigenous communities. Proponents of sustainable living and food security need to come to terms with the fact that 'buy local' strategies enable

healthy living for a few at the expense of the racialized work-force that produces their food. These existing inequities are not a by-product of the system; they are a central tenet in food production across Canada. Simply put, it's no coincidence that racialized workers are imported and exploited to put food on our table.

In our desire for healthy sustainable living, it's critical for all of us to break the cycle of invisibility. One easy way to begin this process of deciphering food production is to undertake this exercise: The next time you turn on the TV or listen to the radio and see a commercial promoting locally grown food, ask yourself, your family, friends and co-workers who is missing from these commercials. Who actually harvests our local produce? What conditions exist for them? Why did they come to Canada to harvest our local fruits and vegetables? What are their experiences, and how are they differently treated by our laws and policies? Then consult the website of an organization such as J4MW to juxtapose the commercial with what is missing.

Finally, the next time you are at a farmers' market, ask those who are selling their produce about the working conditions at their farms. Furthermore, ask your locally elected representative why agricultural workers are excluded from basic laws that exist for other workers, and why our immigration laws discriminate against migrant workers. Until there is meaningful change in the policies and practices of our institutions, and our elected officials, the employers and the recruiters are held accountable for these injustices, the familiar chorus of 'Good Things Grow in Ontario' will be 'Good Things Grow in Sweatshops in Ontario.'

Chris
Nuttall-Smith

Scrambling for eggs

I spent five years of my childhood on a hobby farm. We had
half a dozen Shropshire sheep, as well as turkeys, ducks, an
unrideable pony named Fancy and, most of the time, twelve
or fifteen chickens. My favourite day each spring was when
my father and I would go to Buckerfield's, the local farm store,
with its smell of saddle leather and wood chips and pelletized
grain, and fill a cardboard box with day-old chicks that
cheeped and skittered on matchstick legs as I groped for
them under the heat lamps. As those chicks became hens
and began to range freely around our pasture, my dad
obsessed about how extraordinary the resulting eggs were:
how the whites were firm and mellow, and how their rich,
golden yolks, which stood up high when you cracked them
into a pan, tasted like cut grass and butter and the sun. He
always supervised as my sister and I ate them; he insisted that
we eat the yolks whole, in one bite. I'm not sure if he was more
worried about the dirty dishes – he hated scrubbing dried
yolk from egg cups – or that we might waste even a drop of
something quite so good.

Our flock produced more eggs than we could eat, and I
got $1.25 per dozen for the extras, mostly from the teachers at
my elementary school. This was highly illegal, I realize now.
My teachers must have realized it, too, because they always
seemed a little too happy to see me when I had a carton of
eggs in hand.

My father always liked life on our farm more than my
mother did. When I turned twelve, we moved to a big house in
a baldly aspirational suburb that she had deemed suitably
removed from the agricultural belt. That was the end of our
hobby-farm experiment, and of our chickens, and it was the
end of the good eggs for a while.

'Have you got any of S—'s…?' My voice trails off before I can
finish the sentence.

I've made sure to pull off my sunglasses so the woman at
the cash register can see that I'm not a snitch. She knows
exactly what I'm looking for. It's early spring in Kensington
Market. The afternoon sunlight floats in under the little store's
awning, playing over tables of organic sweet potatoes and
long-haul organic greens. Above the checkout, a psychedelic
painting implores shoppers to 'Surrender to the Melody of
Cahos.' I stare up at it for a minute, trying to puzzle it out as

the cashier runs off to where she keeps the stash. She rings me through – five dollars for the dozen – and I step gratefully back outside, relieved to be done with my little chore.

The eggs are a mix of sizes and shapes, from medium and round to huge and elongated, and though most are plain brown, or brown with darker speckles, there are three light bluish ones, too, cheery-looking in their cardboard divots, like windows to a clearing sky. And the taste? They taste like the eggs I grew up on. They taste like eggs are supposed to. It seems strange to me that this so often feels like a lot to ask.

I've been collecting illegal egg suppliers lately. There's the young, lanky back-to-the-lander from near Lake Simcoe (he looks a lot like Shaggy from *Scooby-Doo*) who delivers his full-flavoured, ochre-yolked eggs and bags of undocumented capons to some of the city's best-regarded restaurants. There's the sixth-generation meat and produce grower, organic for the last couple years, who sells his pastured eggs at a busy Saturday farmers' market in town. There's the tomato queen a couple hours east of the city who delivers cartons of eggs – her farm's governing ethos is peace and love; if her chickens could speak they'd probably sound like Joan Baez – to her green-box subscribers.

S—, who supplies the store in Kensington Market, keeps black and white Polish hens ('They have these marvellous hairdos, just big pompoms on top of their heads,' she says), downy white Chanteclers and Ameraucanas, which lay those blue eggs.

And there's also my book-publicist friend, who gets some of the best eggs going at a rendezvous every second Saturday in a parking lot on the northern edge of town. The eggs he gets are nearly as rich, dark-yolked and fully flavoured through winter as they are in spring, summer and early fall because his farmer freezes buckets of compost to keep her flock in greens and potato peelings throughout the indoor months. For the past five weeks or so, those eggs, cooked for three minutes and flecked with kosher salt and cracked pepper, have felt like the most comforting things on earth.

Good eggs come from chickens that run around on grass and scratch for bugs and seeds and weeds. Or, at very minimum, from chickens that eat something greener than commercial layer feed. Good eggs are fresh – no more than two or three days old, about the maximum time it takes for the whites to

slacken and sour a bit with that slightly sulphurous note that's so often found in their supermarket incarnations.

Almost without exception, good eggs in Ontario are either sold at the front gates of little farms or they are sold illegally. Any farmer who has more than 100 laying hens or the intention of selling eggs beyond the farm gate – to a restaurant, at farmers' markets, into grocery stores, for example – has to buy quota through the Egg Farmers of Ontario, the province's egg-supply management board. Quota costs between $160 and $170 per bird, which makes sense (in a perverse way) if you're an industrial-style, bottom-line-focused sort of producer; as the general manager at Egg Farmers of Ontario recently told me, the system works well for 'efficient' farmers.

In strictly industrial-production terms, my pastured egg suppliers are among the least efficient farmers in North America. They roll their flocks manually around their fields in ungainly wood-and-wire-mesh 'chicken tractors,' or herd them between electra-fenced fields from day to day. They have to train the birds to come indoors at dusk; since nature and the seasons, and not veterinary science, dictate pastured chickens' laying cycles, they often lay less frequently than their factory-farmed cousins. And my suppliers just don't do economies of scale. Their flocks range from sixty to 130 birds. By the Egg Farmers of Ontario's accounting, the typical legal layer flock in Ontario counts 21,000 birds (although some number in the hundreds of thousands) and holds just north of $3.4 million worth of quota, give or take.

Which is why the Egg Farmers of Ontario can get so titchy about little people like my tomato queen and Shaggy and the farmers' market seller and S— and my book-publicist friend's parking-lot connection. They produce good eggs. (*Fresh* good eggs, too; they often sell out the same day they're laid, whereas quota eggs almost never make it to store shelves before they're five to seven days old.) Not only that, they sell their eggs where they're not supposed to sell them – in places that are convenient to people who live in cities. If a lot of consumers started buying fresh, good eggs in places that are convenient, the Egg Farmers of Ontario's monopoly wouldn't be a monopoly anymore, and all of those quota millions quite suddenly wouldn't be worth a thing.

I spoke with Harry Pelissero the other week. Pelissero is the general manager of Egg Farmers of Ontario. He doesn't pull a lot of punches in the battle against the growing threat.

Tactic one: you wouldn't actually want pastured eggs if you knew how hard freedom is for a chicken. 'Birds left to their own device will in fact huddle in greater density than we allow for in our code of practice,' Pelissero alleges. They smother each other, in other words – a phenomenon neither I nor my suppliers have yet to witness in actual free-range birds. 'And hens are very cannibalistic,' he continued. 'They will pick on the weakest ones, and I've seen that.' This part is true to some extent. Hens do peck other hens. What Pelissero neglected to mention, however, is that this happens nowhere more frequently, or more brutally, than in commercial egg and poultry operations. Pastured hens have lots of other things to peck at, like grass and grasshoppers and dirt.

Pelissero's second argument was agri-food's version of an orange alert. Non-quota eggs might kill you, he told me. A little context here: eggs that are sold through the quota system are 'graded' before they get to retail. Grading's greatest benefit is that it commodifies eggs for commercial and retail industries: grading sorts eggs into like-sized groups, so they can be sold by the tractor-trailer load. But a secondary benefit of grading is that the eggs are also washed, refrigerated and scanned with a strong light to ensure they're not cracked or otherwise imperfect. This is all very useful, though the way Pelissero describes it, it's as if running water and refrigerators and bright lights – the backlight inspection technique is still referred to as 'candling' – are way beyond the technological abilities of mere independent farmers. Without the Egg Farmers of Ontario, every egg is its own little Hot Zone, ready and eager to poison and kill.

At one point during our conversation Pelissero says, 'Ungraded eggs cannot go into the retail chain! And you understand why, don't you? Can you say Maple Leaf?'

He's referring to Maple Leaf Foods, whose listeriosis-tainted luncheon meats killed at least twenty people in the summer of 2008 and sickened hundreds more. Never mind that Maple Leaf was and is and will continue to be one of the most heavily inspected and regulated (and, like the Egg Farmers of Ontario, *centralized*) food operations on the continent. Never mind that ungraded hens' eggs are perfectly legal when sold at the farm gate or that, provided they're clean and fresh and crack-free – they meet the same basic standards store-bought eggs do, in other words – there is no evidence that they pose any more of a health risk than quota eggs. (In fact, thanks to the natural diets of pastured chickens, they have

more good nutrients like Omega 3s, and less cholesterol and bad fat.) When I called Ontario's health ministry to see if it had any record of health problems associated with ungraded hens' eggs, the best it could produce was a handful of garden-variety food-poisoning cases that may or may not have been linked. The ministry's numbers for *graded* eggs, though equally inconclusive, were far higher.

'You're bringing up the spectre of listeriosis and Maple Leaf Foods?' I asked Pelissero. I couldn't help but sound incredulous. 'I don't understand the link.' Our conversation ended fairly quickly after that.

I asked one of my suppliers, the guy who sells at the farmers' market in Toronto, why he does it. It wouldn't take much for a health inspector or an Egg Farmers of Ontario staffer to find him and shut him down. His answer surprised me. He said he secretly wants to get caught. He said he would welcome getting caught – he's articulate and thoughtful, and has the financial resources, he told me, to put up a winning fight. 'The egg farmers don't matter politically anymore,' he told me. 'They have this monopoly only because the provincial government still says they can. All you need is one good person to expose the system for what it really is.'

I'm not convinced that lone martyrs are always a good addition to debates about public health – even when, as in the case of ungraded eggs, the public-health question is an illegitimate one at best. Michael Schmidt, the rebel Ontario raw-milk producer, has done a far better job of exposing the quackery in much of the raw-milk movement – one of his key backers argues that unpasteurized milk cures autism and cancer – than advancing the cause of legal access to his product. (It's worth noting, too, that unlike the grading of eggs, pasteurization didn't spring from the brains of a power-hungry agricultural lobby; it became law because before pasteurization, people died every year from drinking milk.)

But whether good eggs someday become legal or not seems almost beside the point. Because if you shop at farmers' markets or in places like Kensington Market – if you shop in the sorts of places where people who want pastured eggs would typically shop, in other words – good eggs are getting easier and easier to find. You can find them through community-shared agriculture providers, and through many, if not most, of the city's more discerning chefs. (You think that

soft-poached yolk sitting atop the lentil and heritage testina salad you ordered at the restaurant that bills itself as 'fresh and local' came from No Frills? Think again.) Failing all that, you can find good eggs legally by driving down country roads outside of town and watching for the signs. If you see chickens running around on grass, you're probably in a good place.

Dolce

Bert
Archer

Giving food a second chance: Leftovers and gas

I'm sitting in a big truck with Blayne Walker. He's been driving trucks like this for eight years, but this one for only three days. It's new – just donated to Second Harvest by the Morrison Foundation. The back is partially refrigerated. He's a little rig-proud, and everywhere we stop this morning, people comment on how shiny it is. We're on the way into town from Second Harvest headquarters, a couple of bus stops away from the Downsview subway station, on Lodestar Road. Blayne's telling me a story about two other passengers he had in my seat a little while ago. It seems he has quite a few ride-alongs: students doing volunteer work, sponsors seeing where their money's going and others who are just curious, like me. On the particular day Blayne is talking about, his two passengers were of the curious variety: food magnate Wallace McCain (McCain Foods, Maple Leaf Foods) and his personal assistant wanted to see how Second Harvest does what it does. Mr. McCain, about seventy-seven at the time, was full of questions.

'Do you always pick up this much meat?' he asked, after Blayne picked up about 200 pounds of almost but not quite bad meat from the Loblaws at Bathurst and St. Clair, to be redistributed that day and the next to one of the 250 food banks and soup kitchens and other social agencies around the city; Second Harvest redistributes about 2,700 tonnes of food every year.

'Yes,' Blayne said.

Mr. McCain seemed impressed. 'Do you guys work with Longo's?'

Blayne had been telling me that they'd been trying to get more grocery stores to donate food. Metro didn't give them anything. And Loblaws, though generous, left the donations up to their individual store managers, who in turn left it up to their department managers, who were sometimes quite forth-coming, and other times not so much. After all, every pound of food they donate means a pound of food they over-ordered, and with competition from Walmart getting ever stiffer, they were less and less likely to want to make a big deal of how much of their employer's money they were wasting. Whole Foods donates, but as I was to see in a few minutes, that was a mixed blessing. They seem to treat their donation boxes as garbage. I pick up one and among the apricots I find a pizza crust and a used latex glove. I pick up another and find the kiwis packed underneath the melons, and therefore crushed. Blayne sighs and we chuck the stuff.

The back door of this men's shelter in the east end is always open to Second Harvest deliveries.

But most donors are more conscientious, so new grocery-store clients, with their panoply of produce, proteins and long-lasting and easy-to-stack processed foods, were a real boon to Second Harvest.

'No,' Blayne said.

McCain pulled out his phone. 'I know Tony,' he said, referring to chain CEO Anthony Longo, dialling. A minute or so later, Longo's was a donor.

And a good one, too, according to Blayne. Instead of the random discarded items in boxes they (gratefully) accept from other retail donors, Longo's gives them well-packed and stacked skidloads. 'Very generous,' Blayne says.

I relate this little story only partially because I like telling stories about billionaires in whose seats I've recently sat. I tell it mostly to illustrate an obvious but nonetheless compelling point. Big things get done when big people drop little words in big ears. And the reason I wish to illustrate this is that dealing with food waste needs a few more words in a few more ears. But talking about food waste is like talking about toilet paper. People prefer not to, because it forces thoughts of goo and muck and grossness. In fact, to talk about toilet paper at all, we have to call it toilet tissue, or toilet rolls, or TP or bathroom tissue. So maybe coming up with a new phrase for 'food waste' might be a good first step to getting more of those words into ears.

It's been about three minutes since I wrote that last sentence, and I haven't been able to come up with anything even a little bit better. How about you think about it and we'll get back to it? Write it in the margin here if you think of something, or you know you'll forget it.

Among environmental issues, that which we will soon no longer be calling food waste ranks somewhere behind fossil fuels, livestock waste and rice paddies, and only a little ahead of termites,[1] but unlike all that, food waste is easy. Toronto started its green-bin program in 2006, and by 2008, 128,000 tonnes of what the city helpfully refers to as SSO (for Source Separated Organics) were being collected per year, an average of more than 250 kilograms per single-family household, which they figure captures about 70 percent of the total.[2] Pretty good. The City also picks up waste from 20,000 small businesses, or about one-fifth of the total number of businesses in the city.

Next stop is the high-rises, which is going to be tough. As far as Councillor Gord Perks knows – and he knows pretty far when it comes to these things – Toronto is the only city

1 According to an authoritative and comprehensive 1993 study (Reedburgh, Whalen and Alperin) on what's called the methane budget, rice paddies emit about 100 teragrams (million tonnes) of methane a year, livestock 80, food waste in landfills 40, and termites 20.

2 As I was writing this, the *Toronto Star* came out with all sorts of stories about just what happens to our organic waste. It's the subject of a lawsuit Toronto's head garbage man (Geoff Rathbone, see below) is aiming at the *Star* just now, so it may be better not to get into too many details. But the latest I read said this: the City estimates that 30 percent of our household waste is organic. The city currently picks up about 16.2 percent of our total waste from green bins. That means the city would be picking up 54 percent of our organic waste. The *Star* has also written about 'unfinished compost dumped in a gravel pit; rotten bags of organic waste sent to a Quebec landfill; and the stockpiling of organic waste because the companies contracted to compost it faced serious restrictions from the provincial environment ministry.' Another story quoted City employees who alleged they routinely mix green bin organics with regular garbage headed for the Michigan landfill, an allegation the City denies. Councillors Denzil Minnan-Wong and Brian Ashton are apparently hot on Rathbone and Miller's respective tails about all this, so we'll have to wait to see how it all plays out.

anywhere on the verge of picking up ssos from high-rise residential buildings. The City did a pilot program last year, testing 4,330 units in twenty-eight buildings. They were able to get people to put out an average of one kilogram a week per unit, or a little less than a quarter of what single-family dwellings were managing a few years into the process. Once again, not bad. The City figures that once the high-rise collection is running across the city, it'll be able to collect about 30,000 more tonnes of food waste than it does now. Geoff Rathbone, the guy in charge of all this up on the twenty-ninth floor of City Hall (his title's General Manager of Solid Waste Management), estimates that when the system tops out in a couple of years, the city will be collecting 170,000 tonnes of food waste a year, diverting it from landfills and, by 2011 or so, feeding much of it into anaerobic digesters, reducing the mass into high-quality fertilizer and sellable methane gas in five-megawatt batches (enough to power about 3,000 homes). Not bad at all.

But it's also not good. For several reasons. The biggest, though not our fault, is that Toronto is one of the only places on the continent doing this. Though there is a clutch of other Canadian cities in the same league, there are almost none anywhere in the States. I was talking to Jonathan Bloom, who is writing a book on the subject in Durham, North Carolina (the working title is *American Wasteland*), and he can think of only a couple of places – San Francisco and Davis, California. And when I ask him if he thinks that might change, and how, the first thing out of his mouth is a pretty fair indication of why nothing's going on in his country. 'There's always going to be resistance when this sort of thing is forced on individuals,' he says when I talk about municipal governments instituting the sort of incentivized program we've got here. 'I don't know if in the long term that's the best idea.' He thinks governments should enable composting in urban areas (which they mostly haven't done yet, either) so people can decide for themselves. The idea that government can provide a useful kick-start doesn't seem to occur to even this food-waste activist. Governments should follow, he suggests, rather than lead. And people say the only difference between Canadians and Americans is the size of our penises.

But something that *is* our fault is what proportion that 128,000 tonnes we're now picking up is of the total estimated food waste Toronto produces, which is about 2.5 million tonnes, according to Dave Ireland. He's leading a project to set up an anaerobic digester at the Toronto Zoo, where he works.

He's become a self-made expert on the subject since his wife started running a food home-delivery business called Mama Earth Organics. 'The amount of food they got rid of on a weekly basis appalled me,' he says, making it clear that it's not his wife's profligacy, but the basic nature of the food business that concerns him. 'They can't give it away. If it's bruised and brown, they can't even give it to the homeless, so it becomes organic waste.' And no one's picking it up, though Ireland estimates there's the equivalent of twenty-five to thirty households' worth of waste just at his wife's small business.

But as appalled as Ireland is at the logistics that complicate the pickup of waste from Mama Earth Organics, it's small potatoes. The real waste comes from some of those big girls. Only four or five of the twenty-two tenants at the huge Ontario Food Terminal donate useable food to Second Harvest; tonnes and tonnes of lettuces and mangoes, avocados and cherries, berries and beets – no one knows how much in total – get picked up every day and trucked by private waste contractors 100 kilometres to the nearest landfill. And hundreds of thousands of tonnes more are shipped out from the major food processors on the city's outskirts, operations too big for the city to claim as clients (they'll only pick up from small businesses), at least according to Rathbone, at least in the forseeable future.

Like many conundrums, the answer to this one is probably going to be capitalistic. And as Norman Lear might say, there ain't nothing wrong with that. I've mentioned anaerobic digesters a couple of times, but it strikes me I haven't said what they are. This may be because I'm not sure, just like I don't know how microwaves work, or what makes all the pretty pictures and words pop up on my laptop screen when I type the magic words into my google machine. But the basics are that they turn biomatter into fertilizer, methane and water. The water's not good for much at the moment, but the other two things are potential commercial products. Chemical-free fertilizer is a hot commodity, and methane is also known as natural gas. At the moment, no one in Toronto is making enough of either of these things to make anybody any money, and with no ambitions beyond the five-megawatt digesters they're planning on building in the next few years, including that one at the zoo, the City, at least, probably won't.

But other people, like Ryan Little, are thinking a little further down the line. He's the vp of a company called

StormFisher Biogas, one of the bidders on that Toronto Zoo digester project, and he figures food waste is a squandered resource – squandered mostly because the companies with the waste are not yet thinking of it as another saleable thing they produce, like those people in North Africa and Arabia a century ago who would just abandon their wells when the water got fouled up with that noxious black stuff.

Little hopes his company might be well-placed to be the next Standard Oil of California, the folks who found oil in Bahrain. Chances are, they've got a better shot at being latter-day Ignacy Łukasiewiczes; he was the guy who was able to modify Nova Scotian Abe Gesner's method for refining kerosene from coal and apply it to what was then called rock oil. What they hope to do is to convince large companies – Mr. McCain's Maple Leaf, for example, is the biggest food waster in the Toronto area, he says – to hire them on to manage their waste and turn it into methane and high-grade fertilizer. At the moment, these companies are paying about $120 a tonne to get it hauled away to landfills. Companies like StormFisher are currently underbidding, offering to do it for them for, say, $60 a tonne, and then they sell the anaerobically produced by-products. He figures that at some point, though possibly not for twenty years or more, companies are going to realize they're paying someone to do something they could be charging them for, and that's when things will really take off.

But until then, he's happy to do house calls at potential client facilities, offering them free waste audits and letting them know what his company does and how signing with them could cut their waste-disposal costs in half. He finds, in fact, that these companies often have no idea how much waste they're producing; some companies' own estimates are off by as much as a factor of ten. 'We went into one mid-sized food processor where they literally said they didn't have any waste,' he says. 'We found 3,000 tonnes a year.' That's 12,000 houses' worth of waste. That's more houses than there are in the Annex, the south Annex, Cabbagetown, Dufferin Grove, Kensington-Chinatown, Trinity-Bellwoods and the Junction combined. That's one mid-sized food processor that didn't even notice the waste.

Which makes you think. Anyway, it makes me think. It makes me think those little bins we put out are a sort of green herring. They don't matter. Like those plastic bags we've been expending so much righteous juice over, which account for less than

1 percent of the landfill, when the effluvia of construction and renovations, which we mostly like, accounts for 25 percent. Looked at one way, it's a little silly, possibly even stupid, and if you were pessimistic, you could see it as a way to let off a little enviro-steam that might be better used to push for the stuff that really matters, the stuff we never think about, like those kitchen renos and those commercial bakeries.

But that's only if you think of it in terms of tonnage. There's also something to be said for the notion that if we can do something, and it doesn't screw us up into pretzels of inconvenience, we probably should, no matter how small the payoff.

So we can keep the green bins, and be pleased about people like Laura Reinsborough and her Not Far from the Tree project, which is starting to harvest some of the 1.5 million pounds of fruits and nuts that fall from downtown trees every year. We should ask the stores we buy our food in if they contribute to Second Harvest, and suggest we might look elsewhere if they don't, and if we work downtown, consider helping out Second Harvest's Hunger Squad, which sends volunteers out on foot during lunch hour in the financial district to pick up leftover boardroom catering and deliver it to nearby social agencies (melissad@secondharvest.ca). We could even pick up some Depression-era recipes that make meals out of bits of food we usually waste. Or you could call up Claudio Aprile, chef at Colborne Lane and Origin, and ask him about what he does with food waste, and he'll give you a recipe like this one in the sidebar.

Thought of a better word for food waste yet? I like second-hand food myself, now that I've thought about it a bit more, but I can see how some might be put off by the regurgitative associations. We could archly refer to it as our bounty's excess, if we were that sort of person. Used food? Previously loved protein? Vitamins on the verge of destruction? No, obviously I can't think of one. So, best of luck with that. Let me know what you come up with.

Potato-skin soup
The flavours of pub potato skins in a soup

First, drop the skins from ten potatoes in a chicken stock made from the leavings of yesterday's roast chicken and cook for three to four hours at a slow simmer.

For the dumplings, mix the cooked potato flesh with a Beemster or other old cheddar, along with green onions, bacon, crème fraîche or sour cream. Roll into dumpling wrappers you can buy in Chinatown, seal with egg yolk (which you can reserve from other recipes calling for egg whites) and poach them.

Strain the broth, add the dumplings and serve.

Sasha
Chapman
The constant gardener

In the aureate light of the harvest sun, the neighbourhoods clustered around Toronto's Christie Pits Park feel predominantly Mediterranean. Wasps buzz around family wine presses; the musty smell of rotting grapes permeates the air. Different immigrants have transplanted the ways of the old country with varying degrees of success: Roma tomatoes and purple-streaked Sicilian eggplants grow just fine in the patchwork gardens that line the alleyways, but only occasionally do you catch a glimpse of fig leaves waving their broad, leafy digits over a neighbour's fence.

About five or six years ago, I visited a friend on Delaware Avenue and wandered into the garden of his father, Shoukry Roweis, a retired University of Toronto professor of urban planning. Behind a modest semi, Roweis has spent two decades cultivating his small garden, which is fringed with persimmon trees. I left that day captivated by his silver-barked fig tree. It looked just like the trees you see in the Mediterranean: as gnarled and twisted as an arboreal Quasimodo. And the fruit! Roweis boasted it could yield two or three hundred figs – some big enough to fill your hand.

Roweis, who was born in Cairo, left Egypt in 1966 at the age of thirty-one. He has longed for the taste of sun-warmed fruit, plucked straight from the tree on a hot summer's day, ever since. The fragrant fruit he remembers was far softer – almost overripe – than any figs he could buy at a supermarket in Toronto. The flavour of a tree-picked fig is delicate and fragrant; the texture of the pink flesh lush and sensual. 'Some people find music a powerful evocation,' he muses, 'but for me, it's taste and smell.' After decades of bad figs, Roweis embarked on his own grow operation. Little did he know it would become all-consuming – a project twenty years in the making.

The fruit itself was only part of the appeal. As knotted and intricate as human history, fig trees have stood as sentinels in Mediterranean gardens since the dawn of civilization. They may have been our first teachers in the garden: a few years ago, *Science* published an article suggesting the fig tree was the first fruit tree to be domesticated, after two botanists and an archaeologist discovered the remains of nine 11,400-year-old figs in the ruins of a burned building near Jericho, in the West Bank. (The ancient figs bore no fertile seeds, so the researchers concluded they could only have been propagated by human hands.) In theory, at least, most figs can root very

easily: if a branch or leaf falls on fertile ground in just the right way, it will plant itself without any help from us. But Toronto's gardens are not as fertile as Jericho's; our climate isn't nearly as hospitable. Planting even the hardiest cultivar here requires considerable zeal.

Two decades ago, Roweis started, as most Toronto fig-growers do, with potted trees that he could wheel indoors at the first sign of frost. But the pots were too small and the basement where Roweis stored them in wintertime had low ceilings. Between the pots and the thirty-two fluorescent bulbs hanging above them (even dormant trees need to photosynthesize), he couldn't grow a tree more than five or six feet tall. The crop was never more than desultory. He began tinkering with the growing model.

Roweis trained as an architect in Egypt and as an urban planner at MIT; he's a natural scientist and problem-solver. To walk down the street with him can take time – something always piques his curiosity: city workers, perhaps, digging holes for new telephone poles. He never does anything by

halves: when his daughter-in-law expressed interest in learning how to make tabbouleh, he gave her a two-hour lesson, complete with a CD-ROM of downloaded Arabic fonts and a short treatise on linguistic and culinary variations among Middle Eastern nations.

Roweis wanted to find a way to grow a fig tree outside. First, he built a greenhouse out of clear plastic tarp and put a heater in it to keep the tree warm. Without proper insulation, the tree died. He abandoned the temporary greenhouse and instead experimented with an electric heating coil at the bottom of his pots to keep the roots warm, insulating each tree in a tall cone of layered bubble wrap. 'They looked awesome, militarily speaking,' he recalls. Especially when a cold north wind picked them up and sent them flying around the neighbourhood.

He came to realize he needed to find a way to put the tree in the earth and keep it there forever. 'In the Middle East,' he says, 'the fig is a noble tree, not just a producer of delicious fruit. It's second only to the olive. And of course the story of Adam and Eve is well-known ...' A fig tree in a pot can't put down real roots. It can't be what it is in the Mediterranean – a cornerstone of the community, a powerful symbol of what was and will be.

Roweis isn't the first Toronto immigrant to plant a fig tree in the ground. Some of his Italian and Portuguese neighbours devised their own method decades ago. After collecting the last of their figs, and before the ground freezes, they bind the branches to make the tree compact. Then they dig a trench next to the tree, and around the roots. Slowly, they tip the tree into the trench, with the main root still in the ground, until the tree is laid to rest. Then they cover it with dead leaves, shroud it in plastic and bury it alive. Four or five months later, when the danger of a deep-freeze is past, the tree is excavated and propped up on some sort of crutch. In this way, some families manage to keep their fig trees alive for several generations.

Roweis never considered burial an option. 'The principle behind this is sound,' he says thoughtfully, as if addressing a lecture hall of students, 'but it's humiliation for the tree.' Growing more insistent, he adds, 'I would never be able to bring myself to do this. It gets very ugly when you see it happening. Like slaughtering an animal.'

Finally, he hit upon a solution that would root his fig tree in the ground and preserve its dignity. He bought a five-year-old Italian cultivar, with a main trunk as thick as a child's arm, from a neighbour. He began by digging four feet into the

ground, all the way down to the water table. Then he lined the hole with a circular wall of roofing rubber to protect the roots from competition. (A massive chestnut dominates the other end of the garden.) In May, when the young leaves were growing and the first crop of figs was budding, he planted the tree. Above ground, the fig shelter is a semi-permanent structure that changes with the seasons. In summer, Roweis leaves the walls open – all that remain are four tall metal posts and a slanted roof of corrugated plastic. Remembering the high winds that wrought mischief on his bubble-wrapped torpedoes, Roweis has reinforced the posts with heavy-gauge cables that are pegged to the ground.

The tree thrived that first summer and yielded a good crop – or so thought the squirrels. (Roweis eventually made

green mesh curtains that he Velcroed onto the posts to protect the fruit during harvest season.)

When the mercury dipped into the single digits, Roweis and his wife carefully prepared the fig for winter. They put an electric heater next to the tree and boarded up the four sides of the shelter, attaching walls of plywood and several inches of Styrofoam for insulation. Though the tree was no longer visible, he monitored the temperatures inside and outside the hut with heat sensors that sent information back to a control panel in Roweis' basement. During that first winter, Roweis checked the panel frequently. Unwilling to leave anything to chance, he kept backup heaters at the ready in his garden shed. The only way into the fig bunker during the winter months was through an emergency trap door.

In late February and March, he poked his head inside, looking anxiously for the first signs of life. Success. Everything was as it should've been. The tree budded and blossomed, eventually yielding a healthy fig crop that fall. One year, the tree started budding prematurely, long before it was safe to take off the walls. Roweis decided the ambient temperature inside the fig house was too warm – it was sending the wrong signal to the tree. So he installed a cooling system to keep the tree from budding early, something his wife has never forgotten: at the time, their house didn't have air conditioning.

After five years of tinkering, Roweis seemed to have cracked the fig code. The harvests were good. The tree was happy. Then, suddenly, the figs began souring on the branches before they were ripe. Heartbroken, Roweis began hypothesizing – was the tree under attack? He began researching fungicides, emailing California, sending samples of the tree to labs

at the University of Guelph for testing. Everyone told him to give up. 'When you tell them you are growing a tree in Toronto,' he says, 'they laugh at you – even in email.' Even if the fungicides were the answer, suggested the experts, he wouldn't be able to buy them because they're a controlled substance only available to licenced industrial growers. Fine, he said. He enrolled in a five-day licencing course and drove out to Georgetown to write the exam.

But the hard-won fungicides didn't help. The fruit continued to sour. Desperate, Roweis began to consider another possibility: the roots might be rotting. Over the years, he had noticed the neighbourhood's water table rising. So he retrenched – literally. He installed weeping tile around the tree and buried a barrel to collect water when the table rose too high. He installed a sump pump to slowly suck the water out, and black piping to carry it to a drain by the house. His hunch had been right. Almost immediately, the tree improved. When I last visited the tree, it was thriving: new nodes were growing everywhere, and small green figs were ballooning from the muscular branches and trunks, sheltered by the tree's new green leaves. (Sadly, those 'false' figs are inedible and fall off in June before the real crop begins to grow.)

Roweis tells me the tree is healthier and happier than it's been in years. 'This year we took a little risk.' He and his wife took the walls off in the first week of April. 'Because I'm always thinking about the tree – it wants to be liberated, of course.'

Still, the innovator's impulse is hard to give up: Roweis has now set his sights on grafting. He is waiting impatiently for the first branch (a black Italian variety grafted from a neighbour's tree two years ago) to fruit. In the summer, he grafted more contributions from his fellow fig growers in the neighbourhood – two branches from Chile, one from Portugal. Just as in Egypt, the tree has become a cornerstone of Roweis' community, and his fig-growing friends, who settle for pots and burials, drop by to admire it in the fall.

'The fruit is absolutely beautiful to look at and, needless to say, absolutely delicious.' Roweis considers it a point of honour to eat the pale green figs fresh and unadorned, all the better to appreciate their delicacy. 'There are really no celebrations or fanfare,' says Roweis. 'Just figs!' When he's eaten his fill, he gives them away to neighbours – he couldn't imagine beginning to tire of them. Christie Pits may not be Mediterranean in climate, but after years of trying, Roweis has made his garden just as hospitable.

Brendan Cormier

Bringing food to the street:
Strategies for ubiquitous food markets in Toronto

What if there were a fresh produce stand where you wanted it when you wanted it? What if shopping for fresh food in the city were a spontaneous act rather than a planned one? And what if many of the city's major street corners, subway entrances and public spaces were decorated with the sights and smells of fresh fruits and vegetables?

Toronto is on the cusp of a potential food-market revolution; interest in fresh organic and locally grown foods has expanded in the last decade, and the number of farmers' markets in the city has grown rapidly – from a handful ten years ago to twenty-nine at the time of writing. Two new markets hit the streets in the summer season of 2009, and ten markets were started up between 2007 and 2009 alone. Regardless of this growth, shopping at local markets remains a marginal act in light of the overwhelming ubiquity, convenience and relative cheapness of supermarkets. Is there a way to overcome this convenience price gap so fresh-food vending in the city can become more prevalent? Can Toronto harness the inherent qualities of open-air markets – their flexibility and mobility – to become a city of ubiquitous public food markets?

Agenda

What are the advantages of having more food vendors in the city? From a public-health point of view, making local, fresh and healthy foods more readily and conveniently available just makes sense, provided that the system is properly regulated for health standards. By putting fresh foods on the streets, at the intersections of our daily routines, we become more inclined to buy those foods instead of the junk, processed and take-away foods that are so readily available.

An expanded market system would also help to diversify the retail food industry – a notoriously concentrated industry – and would support local farmers while also creating new vending jobs.[1]

There's also a third perspective – one that, as an urban designer, I have a specific interest in – and that's the impact a system like this would have on public space.

Since the first conception of cities, and lasting up until the nineteenth century, the marketplace held a crucial position in the social, civic, economic and political life of cities and their

1 According to an Agriculture and Agri-Food Canada study titled 'Components of the Agriculture and Agri-Food System: Food Distribution (Retail, Wholesale and Foodservice)', the market share of the top five retail food firms in Canada hovers around 60 percent. This is less than some European nations – in Sweden the number is around 90 percent – but still quite high. www4.agr.gc.ca/AAFC-AAC/display-afficher.do?id=1205781159471&lang=eng

citizens. While its primary function was the exchange of goods, the market was also a main meeting place for people, a place to get news and gossip, listen to political speeches, watch sports and spectacles and demonstrate beliefs and opinions. With major religious and political institutions almost always close by, the market was also a crossroads for people coming from and going to these various institutions. This intricate layering of programming created a dynamic and vibrant public situation rarely seen in other parts of the city.

Although the layout of most modern cities has changed dramatically since then, the open-air markets that have endured remain critical incubators of interesting and unique public happenings and encounters. In an urban North American context, where the quality of public space – and its perceived decline – is a major urban-planning issue, supporting a program of open-air markets could be a powerful tool in defending and increasing the quality of public space in our cities.

Against the ubiquity of supermarkets

With few exceptions, the atmosphere in supermarkets is the antithesis of the vibrancy and diversity of the traditional marketplace. While some argue that supermarkets are ersatz public spaces, where shoppers run into acquaintances, flirt, people-watch and generally feel a connection to their community, the fact remains that they are privately owned buildings under corporate control. To their credit, many supermarket chains have attempted to create a market-like feel in some of their large-format stores, reintegrating services like the baker and the butcher, offering activities like cooking classes and demonstrations, and adding cafés, florists and wine shops into their buildings. However, the basic problem of context is inescapable: these stores are often set back on sprawling lots and surrounded by parking, the land they sit on located in big-box-zoned commercial areas that are inaccessible to many. The kind of community-led programming and use that defines public spaces just isn't encouraged within their walls.

This is not to discredit supermarkets unconditionally. The innovations and efficiencies introduced by the supermarket system – logistics, networks of distribution centres, just-in-time delivery – have proven an effective way to feed our increasingly growing cities while lowering food-spoilage rates. However, this shouldn't stop us from looking for alternatives

that mix healthy food shopping with vibrant public spaces. Might there even be a way to incorporate the efficiencies of the supermarket into an open-air market system?

Strategies for expanding market vending

1. The farmer doesn't have to be the vendor

Renewed interest in open-air markets in North America revolves around the concept of the farmers' market. The main justification for reviving the market concept seems to be the desire for a stronger sense of community and connection to food and the region it comes from, a connection achieved through a short verbal and cash transaction with the producer. This goal of bringing farmers in contact with consumers – however laudable – may have to be re-prioritized to bring more small-scale food vending to the city. Already, farmers' market advocates experience difficulty in convincing enough farmers to travel into the city to sell at the markets. Participating in a farmers' market means organizing the time, staff, equipment and vehicles to attend the market, and gambling with weather and customer attendance from week to week. Farmers with existing business relationships with wholesalers are unlikely to want to take on the added risk and effort of participating in a farmers' market.

One possible remedy is to encourage independent or farmer-hired vendors to do most of the vending at the markets. Vendors would be able to devote more time and attention to customer needs and trends, marketing and promotion activities, and would act as the go-between between customer and grower. The spirit of the farmers' market[2] would be sustained, since the products would still be local and the vendors independent, but responsibilities would be more evenly distributed.

2 A comprehensive examination on barriers to local food vending and farmers' markets can be found in a report put together by the Canadian Institute for Environmental Law and Policy and written by Maureen Carter-Whitney called 'Bringing Local Food Home: Legal, Regulatory and Institutional Barriers to Local Food,' published in December 2008.

2. Bringing it to the crossroads

Open-air markets have the ability to revitalize public spaces, but they aren't public-space miracle workers. They need to be located in places that already carry the potential to become dynamic public spaces. Placing a market on the periphery – in a parking lot, set back in a park or away from busy intersections – severely limits the number of incidental customers it can serve and restricts market shopping to a planned activity.

To get more people shopping at open-air markets, it's vital that they become more visible, located at the crossroads of our daily routines.

This calls for a program that will map out new city spaces suitable for outdoor food vending. Since the City is responsible for licencing any kind of outdoor vending, it must play the leading role in this endeavour, encouraging food vending at strategic locations. These spaces can vary in size – some might only accommodate one stand, while others might house a full-fledged market of anywhere from twenty to 100 stands. It is common practice in many cities around the world – for instance, in Montreal, Mexico City and Rome – to see medium-sized markets selling everything from produce to flowers and crafts located at the entrances of metro stations. Allowing just one or two fresh produce stands outside of each subway station would increase the visibility and convenience of fresh foods in the city. While these spaces might not boast the conviviality of a full-fledged market, they would certainly make subway entrances more interesting places.

The City should also consider licencing mobile units that service major events. In Mexico City, whenever there is a bullfight or soccer match, a cluster of market and food stands pop up to feed hungry spectators. These same vendors then move to Chapultepec Park to feed Sunday strollers. Mobile units in Toronto could do the same thing outside of hockey arenas, theatres, etc. Here the focus would be on healthy prepared and take-away foods.

The next challenge would be to find adequate spaces that can house larger markets. This can be tricky, since these spaces have to be large enough to house a temporary event, while central enough to attract a large number of visitors. Here again, the market's mobility is an asset. While the area of permanently empty space in the city is limited, there are a substantial number of temporarily vacant spaces – often spaces awaiting development – that could be used for market purposes. When such a space is ready to be developed, the market could simply move to its next location. Berlin has the quintessential example of this type of public-space use, having long followed a policy of in-between uses (*Zwischen-nutzung*) as a method for keeping vacant spaces vital and used. Makeshift beach clubs, skate parks, graffiti galleries and driving ranges in temporary spaces dot the city and create a sense of fluidity.

3. *The City steps up*

A few years ago a group called Multistory Complex started to make noise about the lack of diverse and healthy take-away foods being sold on the streets of Toronto. The ubiquity of hot-dog vendors in the city – partly caused by bureaucratic red tape that made it impossible to sell anything else – was a poor reflection of the city's actual culinary diversity and did nothing to support healthy eating habits. Fortunately, with enough political pressure, the City stepped up to introduce a pilot project, Toronto a la Cart, which allows vendors to sell different kinds of prepared healthy foods. Chicken biryani, samosas and souvlaki can now be enjoyed from vending carts scattered around the city.

If Toronto wants to see an expansion of markets and fresh food vending on its streets, the City will have to step up again, providing the administration and regulation of vending activities. Market sites will have to be monitored, licences will have to be issued, studies will have to be prepared – not to sully efforts at open-air vending, but to nurture and foster them. In Holland – a country with a vibrant network of open-air markets – it is written into each civic constitution that the city government must provide the administration and guidance for market operations. Every municipal government has a department devoted to regulating markets, which negotiates between the demands of several actors, most notably the vendors' union. In Toronto, grassroots efforts for farmers' markets can go only so far. At some point the City will have to play an increasing role.

4. *Use the technology*

Large retailers rely more and more on information-communication technologies to keep tabs on supply and demand, technologies that give them huge competitive advantages over smaller retailers. While market vendors will always be limited by season and proximity, they can be flexible in the kinds and quantities of stock they carry.

A variety of possibilities are just waiting to be tested. Vendors could keep text-message mailing lists of devout customers, sending them up-to-the-minute updates on new harvests, sales times and locations, creating veritable 'flash corn mobs' – spontaneous convergences of vendors and customers in public space. Conversely, customers could use

this same technology to notify vendors of events requiring an apple stand or a watermelon hookup. Facebook groups could form an easy platform for customers and vendors to communicate and share opinions and information. Mobile phones with GPS functionality could help customers track their favourite vendors in the city at any given time – an iPhone app that does just that begs to be developed. Information-communication technology is cheaper and more accessible than ever before, ripe to be exploited by food vendors, farmers and customers who want to become better connected and networked.

5. *The new regionalism*

Many city regions are currently experiencing a diversification of food tastes and desires, coupled with new small-scale regional production techniques. Steef Buijs, an Amsterdam-based urban planner who has worked on food issues since the 1960s, has noted that the world of food production is splitting between staple foods and specialty foods. While staple food production will most likely continue to concentrate and expand using industrial farming techniques, an increasing demand for specialty foods can be accommodated regionally, and even within city limits, in the form of urban agriculture such as rooftop gardens. Architects and planners are discovering new ways to incorporate farming into urban areas. German architects have demonstrated how abandoned concrete-slab apartments can be turned into vertical mushroom farms. Dutch architect Winy Maas from the firm MVRDV has shown how previously unimaginable configurations of production can be housed in dense urban structures – most notably in his vertical pig farm. The more this demand becomes specific and local, the greater the incentive to grow locally.

This potential increase in small-scale local and urban production has new implications for food markets. More local food production means an increased capacity for farmers' markets, which could lead to new relationships between vendors and producers in the city. Whereas larger retailers require substantial resources to gather and store their stock in regional distribution centres, small producers could store their own stock in on-site warehouses, where vendors would pick up their goods on the day of sale. No longer dependent on one gigantic centralized food terminal, vendors could navigate city streets on their way to various events, picking up supplies

from a series of producers. Of course, this is dependent on the level of concentration of urban food producers. Another option would be to create smaller distribution and collection nodes for producers and vendors, similar to how FoodShare acts as its own distribution centre for its Good Food Box program. Such nodes could also act as co-ops, where vendors and producers could communicate to each other through consumer feedback and supply-and-demand analysis. With increasing demand for local food production, Toronto's food-scape could find ways to reorient itself towards a networked structure of small-scale mobile food vendors and food producers that would make market vending and local food production synergistic and competitively advantageous acts.

Changing attitudes: Finding a new balance in food retail

The growing popularity of farmers' markets in Toronto is an encouraging sign; not only do people want to eat healthier and support local farmers, they're also searching for more engaging and lively public experiences in their food-shopping routines. These changes can spur the expansion of market-vending practices in the city. It might seem like a daunting task, especially to those familiar with the commanding position large food retailers have in the sector, but open-air vending and food markets are flexible and mobile, two assets that can give them a competitive advantage over supermarkets. The last and most vital shift needed to accommodate this change lies with consumers. We have grown up as a society of stock-up shoppers – we go to the supermarket twice a month, often by car, to buy enough food to last us as long as possible. Part of the reason supermarkets are so successful is that they offer one-stop shopping. If we were to shift even slightly from a society of stock-up shopping to a society of top-up shopping, we would greatly increase the viability of small grocers and outdoor vendors.

A civic culture of food can be changed more easily than we think. It just needs to take place on the street.

Wayne
Roberts

How Toronto found its food groove

The Toronto food movement is one of the tastiest broths in the world, a mixture concocted from one part Toronto, one part food and one part movement. I've helped stir this dish for almost twenty years, both as chair of the Coalition for a Green Economy during the 1990s and as manager of the Toronto Food Policy Council since 2000, and am still amazed at how the recipe links the pleasures of good food and a happy table with environmental protection, public health, social justice, good jobs and all-round people power.

Today's food movement grew up alongside the anti-globalization movements of the past twenty years, so thinking and acting locally are crucial to it. Food issues have helped many people rediscover their sense of place, and rethink how crucial place is – not just for the foods we eat, but for the people we become. So let me begin with the terroir that nourished the local food movement.

The Toronto food movement was not born with a gourmet spoon in its mouth. Nothing about me or the city would have led someone to predict either of us would ever succeed in food. Like many World War II veterans, my parents seized the opportunity of a Veteran's Land Grant to buy half an acre of land on the outskirts of the city for $200 – the idea was that vets would have enough land to grow their own food and put a roof over their heads when the expected post-war depression descended. I grew up in this warm, friendly, humble and hopeful neighbourhood of vets. Like everyone else on the block, I ate bacon and eggs with white toast and milk for breakfast, ham and sliced cheese on white bread with Campbell's Soup for lunch, and one of seven dinners served on the same day of each week – from roast beef on Sunday to beans and wieners on Tuesday and macaroni and cheese on Thursday, all usually served with a side salad of iceberg lettuce and tomato and a dessert of canned fruit that was sometimes in Jell-O.

I don't recall ever eating without lots of yakking and goofing around. I knew lots about mealtime, but little about food. I didn't taste garlic until I went to university, never tried yogurt or a bagel until I moved downtown for grad school, never ate fish without batter and chips until my thirties, rarely had wine with dinner until my fifties, It's the social warmth around food that I still most enjoy to this day. I'll do practically anything to avoid eating alone, and never pick a restaurant where relishing the food might take precedence over having

a hoot. I'm in the foodie contingent that sees food as primarily a social, rather than a gourmet or nutritional, experience. To the extent that my upbringing was typical of that of other Torontonians of my generation, it's safe to say the Toronto food movement did not arise, as it has in so many areas of the world, as a battle to save a rich and pre-existing food culture from Americanized mediocrity. No one has ever thought that 'Toronto the Good' referred to good food in restaurants. For many, many years, Toronto had no restaurant or café culture. Going out to eat was a social, not a dining, experience. Restaurant hangouts in my neighbourhood, usually referred to as slop shops, were places friends goofed around in while nursing pop and fries – just enough to cover the table charge. Cans of Campbell's Soup and boxes of Kellogg's cereals were on show behind the counter where short-order cooks worked. There was only one place, Little Bo Peep, where a high school student would take a date for a burger (hold the onion) and fries, or a family would go out for a roast beef sandwich smothered with mashed potatoes, canned peas and gravy.

Family restaurants were rare because a typical family had a stay-at-home wife who saved more money for the family by doing the cooking and cleaning than she would earn working outside the home. To gain perspective on the total absence of resistance to the meteoric rise of fast-food chains during the 1970s, we must concede that in Toronto, as in many North American locations, junk-food joints actually raised the bar on food, as well as washroom quality. It's humbling to acknowledge that the crux of the modern case against fast-food chains is based on the link to chronic disease; few think of kicking junk food because of repulsive cooking, taste, atmosphere, ethics, isolation from public life of the street, or any rationale that might grow out of a pre-existing and public food culture.

Notwithstanding the absence of vibrant food traditions, Toronto has always had a lot going for it. First, the city won the geographical sweepstakes. Toronto is surrounded on one side by an inland sea that once supported an important freshwater fishery that could've been the envy of the world if we hadn't been so nonchalant about polluting it with agricultural and industrial runoff – a process that happened without much discussion of the consequent loss of wild foods and lean protein. Toronto is surrounded on its other sides by the largest stretch of Class 1 farmland in the country. Rain, sun and moderate temperatures are as plentiful as fertile land.

The remaining area of good land is so big that the remnants of it saved from urban sprawl in 2005 – with belated legislation adopted mainly to protect endangered ecosystems, not precious foodlands – are still enough to qualify as the largest protected greenbelt in the world.

Toronto also has location. It's closer to more U.S. cities than any U.S. city, except perhaps Pittsburgh. As a result, many U.S. corporations have placed their auto and food branch plants in the area; food and beverage processing in the Greater Toronto Area is second in size in North America only to Chicago. Plentiful jobs, especially entry-level positions, were a magnet for many immigrants who came to Toronto after the 1960s. Thanks to them, Toronto is now the most varied multicultural city in the world, with a range of Chinatowns and Little Italies, a flourishing Little India and Greektown, and countless centres of emerging excellence in Caribbean, Tibetan, Ethiopian, Brazilian and other cuisines. California has its Silicon Valley, and Ontario has a Culinary Valley.

Toronto is also blessed with valleys carved out by creeks flowing into Lake Ontario. It's been said that these valleys define the city as much as canals define Venice. Valleys hardwired the city to avoid the worst fate of North American cities: the segregated inner city, surrounded by rings of suburbs to which any group with options escaped. Thanks to valleys, which prevented sprawl based on concentric circles, Toronto is rich in mixed neighbourhoods. Most low-income residents live along a U that stretches the length and width of the city; as a result, lower-income neighbourhoods are often cheek by jowl with a variety of prosperous areas, as is the case with Regent Park and Cabbagetown, for example, or St. James Town and Rosedale. As a result, embittered politics that pit haves against have-nots don't root themselves in city wards, because no politician can win an election on the basis of one social grouping. Nor are Toronto food deserts – vast areas with only convenience or liquor stores but no decent food stores – anywhere as common as they are in the U.S.

Thanks to mixed neighbourhoods, where people bump into different kinds of people on an everyday basis, much as if they were in a small town, the poor are less likely to be marginalized, excluded or vilified as 'the other.' Toronto has long enjoyed a consensus, which transcends left and right, that the 'city that works' must be proactive to avoid the fate of U.S. cities, which have rotted at their core, polarized by racism and grinding impoverishment. Shortly after food banks came to

Toronto during the early 1980s, Liberal mayor Art Eggleton gave start-up funding to FoodShare, now the largest city-based food security organization in North America, in a bid to prevent dependence on food charity from becoming embedded in the city. With the same goal, the public health department initiated the Toronto Food Policy Council in 1991, now the most influential food council in the world. When that didn't end hunger, the newly amalgamated Toronto unanimously adopted a Food and Hunger Action Plan and Toronto Food Charter in 2001 that inspires urban food activists around the world. Not that Toronto couldn't do better, but few cities – Havana in Cuba and Belo Horizonte in Brazil are probably the best known – do.

Torontonians have also been open to ways of thinking about food that find no space in other cities. Ironically, that openness may descend from its 'Toronto the Good' past. The allegedly uptight city, which imposed severe limits on booze in restaurants until the 1970s and a non-commercial Sunday until the 1990s, was fuelled by a long-standing alliance that brought together trade-union radicals – who valued a common day off for all workers on Sunday, and a clear class-conscious brain not befuddled by alcohol for the rest of the week – with Red Tories (conservatives with a strong social conscience) and social Liberals, a base broad and cohesive enough to sustain the Toronto *Daily Star*, long Canada's leading daily and a consistent voice for progressive views. Most of Toronto's standout progressive policies – city-run non-profit childcare centres and homes for the aged, well-funded public transit, publicly owned electrical and water utilities, city-managed farmers' markets, free and low-cost recreation centres, for example – express this tradition, which goes well beyond the typical city agenda of parks, potholes and police.

After the 1970s – when the city became a centre of self-consciously Canadian intellectual and cultural life, and the city's civic activities were increasingly propelled by an astonishing multiplicity of citizen groups and non-government organizations – the old progressive consensus was enriched by a wide range of public intellectuals and writers from alternative publications like *NOW* and *Eye Weekly*, music and book publishers surviving in coach houses and other non-commercial spaces and a lively public culture on view at a long list of street festivals, parades, restaurant and club districts. Toronto, in short, has a huge number of progressive citizens, voters and activists.

Part of the robustness of this working relationship among progressives came from a showdown against Modernist planning and architecture during the 1970s. Throughout the 1950s and 1960s, Toronto's skyline came under the domination of Modernists who thought steel, cement and glass high-rises expressed the unlimited potential of high-tech homo sapiens; indeed, Toronto has one of the highest proportions of high-rises, particularly in the suburbs, of any North American city. During the 1970s, a grassroots rebellion, led by such giants as Jane Jacobs, John Sewell and David Crombie, beat back the notion of cities dominated by towers and expressways, and created a permanent safe space for a cross-cutting set of ideas around respect for human scale, appropriate technology, decent treatment of marginalized people and government accountability to ordinary people – as it turns out, the common ground beneath sustainable agriculture and community food security.

Food movements are almost by definition profoundly cross-cutting. They attract people who are into science and people who aren't, people on the left, right and centre, people linked to formal religion and highly personal spirituality, vegetarians and carnivores, health-food nuts and slow-fooders, peakniks who think we're running out of oil and people who've never heard that cheap food was based on cheap oil, recent immigrants and fourth-generation Canadians. By and large, they all take issue with Modernism and Brutalism, most sharply expressed during the last twenty years by genetic engineering, factory-farm livestock methods and globalized trade in bulk food commodities – the *bêtes noires* of the food movement. Today's foodies got a major leg up when they inherited a successful public culture pitted against Modernists and Brutalists that's been the hallmark of public discourse since the 1970s.

This brings us to the second ingredient in Toronto's food movement: food. I have a special affection for the style and content of food advocacy because I came to food politics as I was coming out of my middle-age crisis – my tame alternative to a Harley-Davidson? – after some thirty years of intense activism around student, labour, peace, anti-nuclear and socialist issues. The earthy realities of food have an impact on politics that's different from the politics that flows from age, gender and class discrimination, for example – politics that flow from human constructs, not biological needs or environmental imperatives. Food brings its own unique

taste to the Toronto food-movement broth, a taste that would be entirely different if it were a Toronto student, labour or anti-nuclear broth.

I think the special taste of a food movement comes from empowerment. The direct and unmediated connection between humans and food means food is more amenable to direct action by individuals or groups than any sector of the economy. At any given time, people can choose to give up sugar in their coffee, go for soy milk instead of cream, skip meat for one day a week, pay a little more for fair-trade chocolate and so on. The directness of food breeds what horizontal fair trader Michael Sacco of Toronto's ChocoSol calls 'actionism,' autonomous and self-directed activity in support of a concrete choice that is distinct from the activism of demanding action from another entity – i.e., government. The tendency in the food sector is to join demonstration projects as often as demonstration protests.

Empowerment is also expressed in the desire of most food enthusiasts for 'authentic' food experiences, which engage the eater as a participant, not just as a passive consumer. Being a health-minded eater also empowers people to become producers of their own health, rather than consumers of medical cures. In general, food calls on people to become 'pro-sumers,' to use the term Alvin Toffler coined in his 1970 book, *Future Shock*. Many decades after the book was written, lines between producers and consumers are being blurred, most flamboyantly in new media, but also in food, where backyard and container gardeners, foragers and serious cooks are doing to food production what blogs have done to news and comment. By inviting people to work in the body politic with the power they have rather than focus their politics on power someone else has, food inspirations tend to generate calm, good cheer and roll-up-your sleeves actionism, qualities often considered rare in the left.

So, what does this mean for the future of Toronto's food movement?

By sheer accident, I tripped onto one aspect of the answer in the fall of 2008, while I was wandering around the annual fall harvest celebration at the Brick Works, the fabulous new farmers' market organized by the non-profit Evergreen Foundation. An old friend, solar-greenhouse veggie-grower David Cohlmeyer, waved excitedly for me to come over and pointed to an elderly man with unruly grey hair who, Cohlmeyer told me in a hushed voice, had a family link to the owners of

Scaramouche, one of Toronto's most respected restaurants, and was a strong supporter of local and artisanal food producers. 'Run after him and ask him to tell you what he just told me,' Cohlmeyer said. I did as directed, introducing myself to Moie Wasserman and asking him to repeat what he'd just told Cohlmeyer. Well, he said, he'd lived in California for many years, and long enjoyed the annual Berkeley event Alice Waters puts on at Chez Panisse (one of California's most revered food havens). She brings in the best local farmers and food producers, and they take over the street with their displays. 'But they can never do anything like this,' he said, pointing to all the people feasting on samples while talking to organizers behind various displays at the Brick Works. 'To have farmers, producers, slow-food people, all these people, as well as government agencies and non-profits, all working together, you only have that here in Toronto.'

That's one, very positive side of the movement: the ability of people in some 100 configurations in the mobile food web, spanning the passions and obsessions of academics, gourmets, anti-poverty activists, gardeners, composters, seed collectors, vegetarians, restaurant critics, raw foodists, localistas, greens, economic developers, fair traders, creatives, you name it, to work easily and causally with each other in a loose solidarity (or should I say soilidarity?). University of Toronto sociologist Harriet Friedmann wrote most insightfully about this aspect of the Toronto 'community of food practice,' as well as about its pragmatism and continued openness to new ways of doing and thinking about things, in 'Scaling up: Bringing Public Institutions and Food Corporations into the Project for a Local, Sustainable Food System in Ontario.'[1]

1 *Agriculture and Human Values*, 2007, 24: pp. 389–98.

But there are two sides to that free-flowing dialectic. As is true with so many aspects of food, too much of a good thing can be a bad thing. Easy and porous relations are one thing; centrifugal force is another. The Toronto food movement can keep it together despite distinctions that might prove to be antagonisms elsewhere – this can be seen in the co-operative relationship between foodies who love fine and authentic food and social activists who mainly worry about hunger, to give just one positive example. Nevertheless, the Toronto food movement lacks a centre that holds, an organization with the moral authority to say, 'We all need to get behind this breakthrough opportunity and put our regular work on hold so we can lift the entire movement up a notch.'

It's notable that there exist no groups with the sole objective of raising public education and alarm over certain trends, or mobilizing consumer or citizen protest against government inaction on the local and sustainable food file. Neither that kind of thinking nor that kind of leadership is on the minds of many people in the food movement. In the absence of such leadership, we allow decision-making power to veer towards government agencies and foundations that fund special projects and fail to develop leadership that responds to the needs of a broader movement.

I worry about this shortcoming as Toronto heads towards the tipping point of systemic change in the food system. We are now safely out of the margins of public discourse. Food topics are covered on a regular basis in all the media. Food organizations are growing like topsy. Farmers' markets are popping up all over the place. Organic sales continue to climb faster than most other food segments. Local food is hot. The most conventional food producers – Unilever and Kraft, for example – are going out of their way to market to people who value local and real and fairly traded food. These are all indicators that we've successfully moved from the marginal avant-garde to the early adopters and are now heading to a place where those inspired by the food movement can rock the food world, both in the stores and in government service (which is, at present, far behind the stores in responsiveness).

Making the most of this imminent opportunity should be at the forefront of serious movement builders' minds – we need to find mechanisms that work centripetally, that unify diverse people and bring them together behind breakthrough causes. As I write this, I'm hopeful that a food strategy currently in early stages of development under the leadership of Toronto Medical Officer of Health Dr. David McKeown – a project I'm privileged to be working on, and that will see food experts from many walks of life coming together in a working group that will advise on a comprehensive food strategy for the twenty-first-century city – may serve to crystallize that function.[2] If that does not come to pass, another similar force must be invented. Toronto has so much to offer; I hope we can offer a model for getting to the tipping point, too.

2 Toronto Public Health (2008). 'Proposal for Development of a Toronto Food Strategy.' Staff report to the Toronto Board of Health. June 2, 2008. The working group will meet during the winter and spring of 2010, and a draft report from the group will invite citizen engagement and comment towards shaping a final report, which is expected to be tabled with City Council in late 2010 or early 2011.

The FoodTOpians

David Alexander is Executive Director of the Toronto Vegetarian Association, where he works with dedicated donors, staff and volunteers to build a healthier, greener, more food-savvy city.

Bert Archer is a columnist with *Toronto Life* and the *Globe and Mail* and has written for Coach House about Toronto's vaporous place in the popular imagination, as well as green-ness and waste water. He appears monthly on *The Michael Coren Show*, mostly, it seems, to talk about burkas and homosexuals. He lives in Toronto with a dog, a cat, a fiancé and very little extra food.

Horticulturist **Steven Biggs** regularly writes for *Country Guide, Edible Toronto* and *Small Farm Canada* magazines, specializing in stories related to food, agriculture and gardening.

Kathryn Borel, Jr.'s first book, *Corked*, has just been released by John Wiley and Sons. It is a memoir about wine, France, her father, death, jokes and existential dread. For Kathryn's non-pornographic output, please visit www.kathrynborel.com.

Jamie Bradburn is a contributing editor at Torontoist (www.Torontoist.com), where he spends most of his time writing about Toronto's past. He has a near-fatal addiction to curry.

Andrew Braithwaite, a Canadian magazine journalist, first arrived in Toronto in 2004. In 2008 he relocated to Paris with his wife and immediately developed an expensive Chablis habit. His two favourite non-alcoholic foods are pomegranates and pistachio ice cream.

Ilona Burkot completed her dietetic internship at SickKids Hospital in Toronto and works as a dietitian in paediatrics, obstetrics and the Neonatal Intensive Care Unit at William Osler Health System. Passionate about good food, she enjoys cooking for family and friends. She has not encountered a vegetable she dislikes.

Laura Burr is a registered dietitian who graduated with her Master's in Nutritional Science from McGill University. She works at SickKids Hospital in Toronto. She has a passion for cooking and enjoys sharing meals and recipes with family and friends.

Kate Carraway is a staff writer at *Eye Weekly* in Toronto, and a freelance lifestyle and culture writer.

Liz Clayton is a photographer and culture writer living in Brooklyn, New York. Her nine years in Toronto included downing more than a few double-doubles in times of need. She blogs about the international coffee scene at twitchy.org.

Sasha Chapman is an award-winning food columnist for *Toronto Life* magazine and a frequent contributor to Canada's major newspapers and magazines. She and her daughters eat like queens on summer walks in the city, snacking on mulberries, blackberries and wild concord grapes. Her husband prefers the figs from the Middle Eastern grocers on Lawrence Avenue East.

Kevin Connolly is a Toronto poet and editor, and a former cooking columnist and food editor at *Eye Weekly*.

Brendan Cormier is a Toronto-based urban designer and planner. After working and studying in Jamaica, Germany and Holland, and inspired by the different public food markets and food cultures he encountered there, he developed a special interest in the overlapping subject areas of food distribution, public space and municipal policy. His thesis paper focused on the critical success factors of the open-air markets in Rotterdam.

Pamela Cuthbert is a Toronto food writer who knows how to grow some foods from seed and how to cook from scratch. But to be food-secure, she needs more land, better skills – and maybe another era. Publication credits include *Macleans*, the *Toronto Star*, *Saveur*, *The Economist*, *Time Out* and more.

Hamutal Dotan is the associate editor of Torontoist, in addition to being a free-lance writer and editor. Though her most frequent subjects are City Hall, urban policy and Toronto lore, she sometimes takes breaks from these to develop recipes. Her favourite cure for writer's block is making jam.

In defiance of Bernard Shaw's dictum, **Mark Fram** both teaches and does: as architect, geographer, designer, essayist, photographer, what have you. A veteran accomplice of Coach House, inordinately fond of print, he dwells amidst a volu-minous collection of books, and yes he is aware of that last bit's redundancy. Raised in North York on former farmland, he immigrated to Toronto to relieve his hay fever, and remains there – that is, here.

Katarina Gligorijevic is a Toronto-based writer and cocktail enthusiast. She spends her days working with REEL CANADA, a travelling festival of Canadian film for students, and her nights working on a novel about communicating with pears. Her favourite cocktails are the Attention, Sazerac and, of course, the Toronto.

As an associate at Sweeny Sterling Finlayson & Co Architects Inc., **Chris Hardwicke** researches, designs, teaches, gives advice, makes policies and writes about places and cities. His visionary urban projects have been exhibited and published widely, including in the books *uTOpia*, *GreenTOpia* and *H$_T$O* from Coach House Books.

Karen Hines is a writer, director and performer. She is the author of *The Pochsy Plays* and *Hello ... Hello*, both published by Coach House Books. She was a child waitress.

Sarah B. Hood handles baking and confectionary while her sweetie, Jonathan, a pro cook, does mains. This is her third uTOpia essay; she writes about food for the *National Post*, *Canadian Business*, *Hosting* (the magazine of the Ontario Restaurant, Hotel & Motel Association) and her own EatLocallyBlogGlobally.com. She teaches writing at George Brown College and edits sections of online maga-zine Suite101.com.

Lorraine Johnson writes about the environmental, social, political and practical imperatives of gardening. Her book *City Farmer: Adventures in Feeding Ourselves* will be published in spring 2010 by Greystone Books. She lives in Toronto with three chickens and two cats.

Jane Lac is a registered dietitian in pediatric clinical practice. She holds a degree in Nutrition and Food from Ryerson University and is working at the Hospital for Sick Children. Jane is passionate about travelling and trying different cuisines, dragonboat racing and snowboarding.

Iara Lessa is associate professor in the School of Social Work, and research associate of the Centre for Studies in Food Security, Ryerson University.

John Lorinc writes about urban affairs, energy and the environment for a range of publications, including *Spacing*, the *Globe and Mail* and the *New York Times*. He is the author of *The New City* (Penguin, 2006) and has contributed to every volume of the uTOpia series. He prefers roasted potatoes with his schnitzel.

Charles Z. Levkoe has spent the past decade working on rural and urban food initiatives in Toronto, across Ontario and throughout the Maritimes. He is currently completing his doctoral studies in geography, working within the Canadian food movement on strategic questions around food sovereignty. Charles can be found growing garlic, kale, beans and tomatoes with his daughter as part of the Frankel Lambert Community Garden in Toronto.

Joshna Maharaj is a busy chef with big ideas! With a simple but thoughtful approach to food and cooking, Joshna has embraced her new position as chef at Food Studio in the ROM with excitement and enthusiasm. With recipes that are diverse, wholesome and delicious, her approach to food is accessible and uncomplicated. Joshna is also a member of Slow Food, and is constantly engaged in ideas about a truly sustainable food system and culture. With a love of people and an insatiable curiosity, dedication to good food and food justice fuel her work with the pursuit of great taste.

Peter Maynard lives in Toronto.

Jason McBride is a freelance writer and editor who regularly contributes to *Toronto Life*, the *Globe and Mail*, *The Believer* and other publications. He's been a vegetarian for twenty years.

Rea McNamara has written about runway shows, dub poets, hood vintage, black rockers, architectural salvage and new-media moguls for *Eye Weekly* (for which she is a style columnist), the *National Post* and other publications. A 2008 Canadian Film Centre Media Lab resident, she also engages in arts-based community development, often conceptualizing neighbourhood-building art programs for the non-profit organization Art Starts. She lives in Toronto.

Shawn Micallef is a senior editor at *Spacing* magazine and co-founder of *[murmur]*, the location-based mobile-phone documentary project. He writes about cities, culture, buildings, art and whatever is interesting in books, blogs, magazines and newspapers. *Stroll*, his collection of psychogeographic walks through Toronto, will be published by Coach House Books in 2010.

Amanda Miller is a freelance writer and editor who lives and works in Toronto. Now and then, she leaves the city for other places, but always finds her way back. She moonlights as a baker and is working on a book about cake and how it is harnessed to love.

Chris Nuttall-Smith is a writer and critic based in Toronto. His work has appeared in *Toronto Life*, the *Globe and Mail*, *Report on Business* magazine, *New York*, *Esquire* and *Cooking Light*. He lives with his wife, Carol, their son, Cormac, and a two-legged dog named Chopsticks.

Darren O'Donnell is a novelist, essayist, playwright, director, designer, performer and artistic director of Mammalian Diving Reflex. The *Chicago Reader* called his first novel, *Your Secrets Sleep with Me*, 'a bible for the dispossessed, a prophecy so full of hope it's crushing.' His book *Social Acupuncture: A Guide to Suicide Performance and Utopia* was published in spring 2006 and prompted the *Globe and Mail* to declare, 'O'Donnell writes like a sugar-addled genius at 300k/h.' His work has been presented in Lahore, Mumbai, New York, Los Angeles, Melbourne, Oslo, Trondheim, Sydney, Bologna, Milan, Derry, Dublin, Terni, Portland, Calgary, Ottawa, Montreal, Vancouver and Victoria. He lives in Toronto.

Chris Ramsaroop is an organizer with Justicia for Migrant Workers, www.justicia4migrantworkers.org. Previous to J4MW, Chris was an organizer with both the United Farm Workers of America and the Canadian Labour Congress, where he was involved in the creation of several projects dedicated to fighting for the rights of migrant agricultural workers in Canada. He recently was a community legal worker at Parkdale Community Legal Services, where he continued advocacy work with precariously employed workers across the gta. Besides his political work, he completed a graduate degree at the Ontario Institute for Studies in Education – University of Toronto (Sociology and Equity Studies), where his research focuses on race and migration studies.

Wayne Reeves tried to fit as many beer references as possible into H_7O: *Toronto's Water from Lake Iroquois to Lost Rivers to Low-flow Toilets*, which he co-edited with Christina Palassio for Coach House in 2008. Some claim too much of his spare time is spent beer hunting and beer judging.

Wayne Roberts is manager of the Toronto Food Policy Council, the most senior body of its type in the world. He's a veteran labour and green activist who's written several books, most recently *The No-Nonsense Guide to World Food*. He lives with his wife and younger daughter in the Toronto Beaches; his older daughter is finishing her doctorate in political economy at Princeton.

Cecilia Rocha is associate professor in the School of Nutrition, and director of the Centre for Studies in Food Security at Ryerson University.

Damian Rogers was born and raised in suburban Detroit. She now lives in Toronto, where she works as a writer and poetry pusher. Her first book of poems, *Paper Radio*, was published by ECW Press in fall 2009. She loves food.

Erik Rutherford is a Toronto-based writer and the creator and editor of Ryeberg Curated Video (ryeberg.com).

Airin Stephens is a high school teacher at George Harvey Collegiate Institute and a member of the school's Green Team. She also works with Learning for a Sustainable Future on sustainability education resources for classroom teachers. Airin uses food as a way to engage with her students' personal histories and to connect to the wider community.

Bronwyn Underhill's experiences in food-related issues include working as a labourer-teacher with Frontier College on fruit farms in the Niagara region and vegetable farms in the Simcoe region and volunteering with Not Far from the Tree and at the Stop Community Food Centre's breakfast drop-in. When not scouring Niagara for fruits and veggies, she works as a health promoter at Fairview Community Health and happily munches on seasonal produce.

RM Vaughan is a Toronto-based writer and video artist. Please visit www.rmvaughan.ca.

Stéphanie Verge has worked as a cocktail waitress, translator, bookstore clerk, bar manager, fact-checker, researcher and freelance writer. She is an associate editor at *Toronto Life* and has been writing regularly for the magazine since 2005. She once dabbled in veganism, but just couldn't give up the cheese.

Gary Wilkins graduated from York University in Toronto and is a member of the Canadian Institute of Planners and a registered professional planner. Since 1995 he has held the position of Humber Watershed Specialist at Toronto and Region Conservation. His primary responsibilities involve the establishment of partnerships at the local level to achieve healthy communities through leading-edge watershed management activities.

Mary F. Williamson is an enthusiastic collector of cookbooks of the eighteenth to mid-twentieth centuries. She writes about cookery, cookbooks and traditional foods in Canada.

Jessica Duffin Wolfe is the reviews editor of *Spacing* magazine and a doctoral student in literature at the University of Toronto. She writes regularly on documentary film for *POV* magazine and has taught several courses in print history at the Ontario College of Art & Design. Her short film *Berlin* opened the Rooftop Film Festival in Manhattan in 2008.

Katie Wolk has lived in Toronto for twenty-seven years and has witnessed the dwindling of neighbourhood farms in the GTA. She is a social justice and environmental advocate working in various capacities with local organizations.

Christina Palassio is the managing editor of Coach House Books. She co-edited *The State of the Arts: Living with Culture in Toronto*, *GreenTOpia: Towards a Sustainable Toronto* and *H₂O: Toronto's Water from Lake Iroquois to Lost Rivers to Low-flow Toilets*. She has also written for the *Globe and Mail*, the *Montreal Gazette* and *Matrix* magazine.

Alana Wilcox is the Senior Editor at Coach House Books and one of the founding editors of the uTOpia series, which includes *uTOpia: Towards a New Toronto*, *The State of the Arts: Living with Culture in Toronto* and *GreenTOpia: Towards a Sustainable Toronto*.

Image credits

p. 15 City of Toronto Archives, Fonds 1231, Item 0096

p. 17 City of Toronto Archives, Fonds 1244, Item 2557

pp. 33, 35 Photos by Steven Biggs

pp. 39, 41, 42, 43 Photos by Bronwyn Underhill

p. 47 Photos by Darren O'Donnell

p. 59 City of Toronto Archives. Fonds 200, Series 372, Subseries 41, Item 28.

p. 60 City of Toronto Archives. Fonds 200, Series 372, Subseries 41, Item 37.

p. 63 City of Toronto Archives. Fonds 1244, Item 1989.

p. 64 City of Toronto Archives. Fonds 200, Series 372, Subseries 41, Item 33.

p. 66 from J. Timperlake's *Illustrated Toronto Past and Present* (Toronto: Peter A. Gross, 1877).

p. 67 Courtesy of the Toronto Public Library

p. 68 from Henry Morgan's *Types of Canadian Women* (Toronto: Wm. Briggs, 1903).

p. 98 Advertisement from the *Evening Telegram*, Feb. 2, 1900.

p. 99 Advertisement from the *Evening Telegram*, Feb. 24, 1900.

p. 99 Advertisement from the *Evening Telegram*, March 8, 1900.

p. 100 Advertisement from the *Evening Telegram*, Feb. 24, 1900.

p. 100 Advertisement from the *Evening Telegram*, March 20, 1900.

pp. 102–105 Photos by Liz Clayton

pp. 129, 130, 132 Photos courtesy of the Toronto and Region Conservation Authority

pp. 136, 137, 138 Photos by Norm Betts, courtesy of the Royal York Hotel

pp. 140, 142, 146, 147 Greenhouse drawings from the United States Patent Office.

p. 141 Map from the Insurance Plan of the City of Toronto, 1892; Toronto Public Library

p. 143 Map from the Insurance Plan of the City of Toronto, 1914–1917; City of Toronto Archives

p. 144 Map and table by Mark Fram

p. 157 Illustration by Evan Munday

p. 163 City of Toronto Archives, Fonds 1244, Item 338B

p. 164 City of Toronto Archives, Series 372, Subseries 1, Item 224

p. 168 Photo by Anna Prior

p. 171 Photo by Greg Edwards

p. 173 Photo, top, by Stop staff

p. 173 Bottom five photos by Anna Prior

pp. 176–177 Four advertisements, courtesy of the Toronto Reference Library

pp. 181–183 Photos courtesy of dialogue38 and Eric Lau Photography

pp. 185–188 Illustrations by Dawn Boyd

p. 199 Watercolour by Richard Baigent. Toronto Reference Library, Baldwin Room, T 10850.

p. 200 top, Photo by Octavius Thompson. Toronto Reference Library, Baldwin Room, T 10891.

p. 200 bottom, City of Toronto Archives, Fonds 200, Series 1054, Item 93.

p. 201 Photo by Jack Mitchell. City of Toronto Archives, Series 497, Subseries 5, File 4.

p. 202 Photo by Wayne Reeves

p. 206 Courtesy of Black Oak Brewing Company

p. 207 Photos by Wayne Reeves

p. 209 left, Postcard courtesy of Great Lakes Brewery

p. 209, right, Photo by Wayne Reeves

pp. 227, 231, 232 Photos by Alyssa Katherine Faoro

pp. 241–244 Photos by Chiara Smith

p. 246 Map by Chris Hardwicke

p. 247 City of Toronto Archives, Fonds 1231, Item 0612

p. 248 City of Toronto Archives, Fonds 1478, Item 0021

p. 249 left, City of Toronto Archives, Fonds 1244, Item 0299

p. 248 right, City of Toronto Archives, Series 0372, Subseries 0001, Item 0175

p. 250 Images by Chris Hardwicke

p. 272 Photo by Bert Archer

pp. 279, 281, 282 Photos by James Ramsay Photography Inc.

p. 290 Image by Brendan Cormier

Cover art and title-page foods by Keith Jones

Typeset in Utopia and Formata
Printed and bound at the Coach House on bpNichol Lane, 2009

Edited by Christina Palassio and Alana Wilcox
Designed by Alana Wilcox
Cover art by Keith Jones

Coach House Books
80 bpNichol Lane
Toronto ON M5S 3J4

416 979 2217
800 367 6360

mail@chbooks.com
www.chbooks.com